Fortress Ploesti

The Campaign to
Destroy Hitler's Oil

Other books by Jay A. Stout

Hornets Over Kuwait (1997)
The First Hellcat Ace (2001)

Fortress Ploesti

The Campaign to
Destroy Hitler's Oil

CASEMATE
Havertown, PA

Published by
CASEMATE
2114 Darby Road, Havertown, PA
Phone: 610-853-9131

Typeset and design by
Savas Publishing & Consulting Group

ISBN 1-932033-18-1

First edition, first printing

Cataloging-in-Publication data is available
from the Library of Congress

Printed in the United States of America

My mother Violet and my father Alfred
made me into the person who could write this book.

My sisters Polly and Joan
never killed me when they likely had good reason.

I love them all beyond measure.

This book is dedicated to the mothers, fathers, sisters, brothers, sons,
and daughters of all the warriors.

I promise that you also are loved beyond measure.

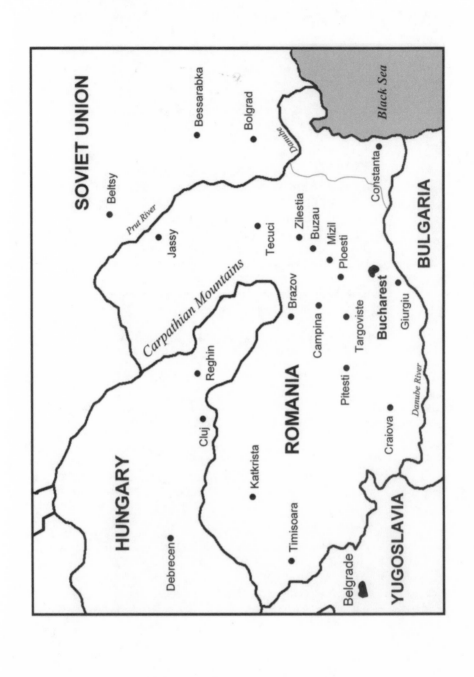

Contents

Contents (continued)

Contents (continued)

Maps and Illustrations

Foreword

PLOESTI.[*]

Among those familiar with the name, it typically evokes images of the grim heroics that characterized the near-ruinous low-level attack of August 1, 1943. And while that mission was a watershed event in the history of aerial warfare—and will be covered in detail within these pages—it is only part of the story. The greater campaign that ultimately turned the great petroleum complex into little more than twisted metal and ash really got underway during the following year, 1944. It was an effort that comprised 5,446 bomber sorties and 3,498 protective fighter sorties, spread over twenty-four missions and several months.[1] This relentless campaign makes up a far-reaching story that is unlike any other of World War II.

Like all stories, it is one made up of people and circumstances. And in order for it to be understood, these people—the warriors who destroyed Ploesti—and their circumstances, must be put into perspective.

* * *

---

[*] Ploesti is pronounced "Ploi-yesht."

The American men who fought in the skies of World War II didn't step out of a Norman Rockwell painting, wiping a milk mustache with one hand and clutching a baseball glove with the other. Like all of us, they were real people, from a real time. They experienced the same joys and the same heartaches as we do. They came from happy homes, and they came from broken homes; many of the men came from single-parent families—in which death and divorce took their toll. They came from farms and from cities. They were regular people—no more intelligent, brave, or good than their counterparts from any other generation.

What set them apart, and ultimately left a unique mark on their lives, came about because of timing and history. For the most part, they were born in the years between 1915 and 1925, grew up during a staggering economic depression, and came of age just in time to participate—to fight—in the defining event of the Twentieth Century. World War II, truly a global clash of unprecedented proportions, was characterized by a struggle in the skies of such colossal magnitude that it is unlikely that it can ever be repeated.

No nation possessed enough extraordinary men ready to fight in this struggle for the skies; they had to be trained. No nation came close to producing as many of these men as did the United States. Our nation's fliers, in greater numbers than any other nation, fought for, died for, and ultimately won supremacy in the air over every theater of the war.

When they finally came home, their souls and sense of self forever seared by the branding iron of war, they went back to the cities and the farms. Putting the war behind them as best they could, they went on with their lives. They became doctors and construction workers. Some became accountants. Others became senators, or engineers. One became The President of the United States. In short, when they came back from the skies of World War II, they, along with their earth-bound brother warriors, led the nation to become the most powerful and respected on the globe.

The vast majority of them were unheralded. They returned to the States, a job well done, and got on with their lives. They were role models for those of us from that post-war bulge in the nation's population that became the Baby Boom Generation. They were our fathers and our uncles, and grandfathers to some of us. They were the cranky guy who lived in the house at the corner and yelled at us for driving through the neighborhood too fast. These men who had survived the bloody skies were all around us.

They were all around us because their numbers were astounding. In 1940, with the war in Europe already underway, and a conflict with Japan nearing a certainty, there were approximately 6,000 pilots in service with both the Army Air Forces and the Navy combined.[2] By war's end in 1945, nearly a *quarter of a million* pilots had been trained![3] This meant, in rough terms, that in 1945 only one in forty pilots had been in military service before the war. And that included only the pilots. The Army Air Forces grew from a small force of 25,000 total officer and enlisted personnel, to a gargantuan organization of nearly two-and-a-half million.[4] To be sure, growth across all of the services was staggering. America's armed forces were truly composed of citizen-soldiers.

How were such incredible numbers of men given such specialized skills in time to make a difference in the war? It wasn't easy. While war in Europe was brewing, the government recognized the need for an established pool of pilots with basic skills. One response was the establishment in 1939 of the Civilian Pilot Training Program (CTPT) through which college men received flight instruction at minimal cost and very little obligation. Thousands of young men took advantage of this program and it paid dividends early in the war—at the beginning of 1942 there were 10,000 CTPT graduates flying with the services.[5]

Incredibly, in this time before the silicon chip, hundreds of thousands of young men were screened and recruited as potential airmen. There was no lack of qualified candidates, but almost from the beginning there was a backlog in getting them to training. There were hundreds of processing centers, training facilities, and airfields to be prepared. In the end it worked, although most of the men would snort at the suggestion that it was an efficient process. Still, most of them pointed out that with the nation's entire focus directed toward winning the war, it worked. "You've got to remember that virtually none of us had done this before," one of them said. "Nobody. Not the clerks, not the instructors, not the cooks. Nobody! We all just did the best we could."[6] And they did pretty well. Young men who were only a year or two removed from pushing and shoving in the high school lunch line, were sharpened into the most formidable aerial force in the world.

It wasn't just the men in the armed forces who were doing their best. American industry produced aircraft and aviation equipment at an astonishing rate. The pace of expansion was extraordinary—like nothing seen before or since. In 1940 the Army Air Corps and the Navy accepted roughly three thousand aircraft. During 1944, the last full year of the war, the combined acceptance was 77,126—a twenty-five-fold increase. All told, from 1941 until the end of the war, the United States produced 297,318 aircraft of all types for delivery to its own air arms and those of its allies.[7]

Let's put these enormous numbers in perspective: The current on-hand strength of fixed wing aircraft of the American military services today is approximately 10,000. Some of these airframes are more than forty years old. In *one month* during the war, March 1944, the United States produced more than *nine thousand new aircraft*.[8] One pilot put patriotism aside. "We didn't win the war because we were smarter, or better trained, or more determined. And not because our airplanes were particularly better than theirs either," he said. "We just overwhelmed them with numbers."[9]

He certainly had a point. Aircraft production by the United States alone exceeded the aircraft production of Germany, Japan, and Italy combined (178,785), by better than a 5:3 margin.[10] America's incredible industrial base, its pool of relatively educated and skilled workers, and its natural resources, in combination with its geographic isolation, were probably the most important contributing factors to its victory in World War II.

The sheer size of the effort came with its own set of problems, not least of which was the leadership of the huge numbers of new soldiers and sailors and airmen. Leadership is not learned in a year or two. Some men are born to it, others gain their experience on the job, and still others never learn it. Because the men were so young—training could begin as early as seventeen years of age—the leaders who were screened from their ranks were by necessity, also young. A twenty-two-year-old squadron leader was not unheard of. This "barely man" could daily be charged with making life-and-death decisions for more than two hundred men. The job wasn't easy. The young men he was leading were not careerists, and the temporary transition to military strictures and discipline was often a difficult one.

These were young men with young libidos thrown into a world of chaos, a world where death was very real. In a time before "stress" became a catchword they sought ways to escape from the stresses of the war. Many times these involved alcohol and women. For the most part their play, though often wild, was innocent. Nonetheless, to think they always behaved at their Sunday-school best is wrong. Several of the men described incidents that today would have landed them directly in jail. Believe it or not, our fathers and grandfathers had urges and passions, and they didn't always act with discretion. They behaved like young men have always behaved.

In the end they came home—our fathers and uncles and the cranky guy down on the corner. And though war is never a good thing, there was a positive side to what these men underwent. Aside from the emotional tempering that many of the men experienced, they were exposed to much more of life—and death—than they would have ever encountered otherwise. They were given a technical education that would have been beyond the reach of many of them before the war. The discipline that was instilled and demanded of them during their wartime service also stood them in good stead in the years following the conflict. And it should be remembered that before the war many of them had never ventured out of their home state—let alone the continent. Nevertheless, their military service took them across the world and exposed them to peoples and cultures they had never heard of. And perhaps most important, the GI Bill, provided by a grateful nation to her victorious veterans, provided educational opportunities that returned benefits to the country which defy measure. "I was from the farm," one pilot said, "and would have stayed on the farm. Because of the war and what I learned, I ended up with a career and a life that would have been beyond my wildest dreams."[11]

The war changed the demographics of the nation. Like many of their service brethren who had never left their home states before the war, a great number of the aircrews never returned to their home states after the war. Exposed to other climates and lifestyles, and training, experience, and confidence gained at the expense of a war, they settled elsewhere. California, Texas, and Florida, which during the war served as bases for a great many war activities, saw a huge postwar influx of veterans. This inflow of educated veterans changed the complexions of these states forever.

These men then, wiser, and tempered by the fires of war, went on to lead our nation to preeminence. And now, nearly sixty years since the end of the war, they are "going West" in ever increasing numbers. Each day the obituaries carry an unremarkable paragraph or two about these very remarkable men. The time isn't too far away when these heroes will be gone. Our nation will be poorer for it.

*   *   *

These were the men who destroyed the vast oil refining complexes at Ploesti. The role that the campaign played in the defeat of Nazi Germany is impossible to quantify, but it can hardly be overstated. Hitler's armies were dependant on modern, mechanized equipment; their strategies and tactics demanded it. But tanks and aircraft are useless without fuel to operate them. And useless is what the German tanks and aircraft became at the end of the war. Thousands of vehicles sat immobile as German soldiers abandoned them and withdrew further into their Reich on foot and by horse. And thousands of aircraft sat unmoving, unable to protect their retreat.

Acknowledgments

I didn't want to write this book.

Eric Hammel, my editor and an award-winning writer and publisher, asked me to do it. I resisted because I thought Ploesti had already been done to death. But the more I picked at it, the more I realized there was a tremendous story waiting to be told. No one had ever covered the campaign from start to finish. What I started (almost petulantly) evolved into a passion that ultimately produced what you have in your hands. It reads as well as it does because Eric's fantastic editing righted my written wrongs, and saved me from potential embarrassment. That process was painful and nearly caused me to not like him any more. But only nearly. Thank you very much, Eric.

Lyle McCarty was a navigator assigned to the 459th Bomb Group. He served too late to see service over Ploesti, but fought the Germans in raging battles over other targets later in the war. As a unit historian he was a tireless correspondent and provided a copy of *The Air Battle of Ploesti*, the single most important resource I used. McCarty's book *Coffee Tower* was also an important asset and one of the best unit histories I have seen.

I relied a great deal on the works of many other authors. The most exciting account of the TIDALWAVE mission I encountered is *Ploesti: The Great Ground-Air Battle of August 1, 1943,* by James Dugan and Carroll Stewart. I must also commend Robert Sternfels, the pilot of *The Sandman*, who has done much to clear up many of the questions and misconceptions surrounding the famous low-level raid, with his book *Burning Hitler's Black Gold!*

Small details and anecdotes are what make the bigger story more readable and interesting. I received help in this regard from many people: Vesko Stoyanov, a tremendous friend of America and son of Bulgarian fighter pilot Stoyan Stoyanov, helped me with the details of his father's service against the American bomber streams; author Denes Bernad provided photos and information about the Romanian Air Force; Mustang ace Bob Goebel granted me use of his notes; Harold Wicklund, Halpro veteran and lead navigator of the TIDALWAVE mission, took time to answer some very important questions; Dick Kahler graciously shared his research on the P-38 low-level raid. His own efforts ultimately led to the location of Carl Hoenshell's remains in 1998; Bud Markel of the 484th Bomb Group provided good information regarding that unit's actions; Norval Seeley's experiences as a bombardier with the 97th Bomb Group gave me a feel for what day-to-day life was like; Corneliu Nastase sent information from his native Romania; Bill Mason facilitated my correspondence with his father, Ben Mason—one of the survivors of the P-38 raid who is still alive; Paul Daugherty, Al Blue, Martin Cope, Tom Oliver, Craig Linn, and Verne Cole offered research assistance. Of course, the veterans whose names and stories are detailed within these pages were the most important contributors. My thanks and the thanks of our nation go to them.

Good photographs are essential to this type of story. I had none when I began, but received help from all quarters. Please note the names of the contributors below each photograph. Their generosity has improved this book a great deal.

David Farnsworth of Casemate Publishers and Book Distributors recognized the value of this story and gave the book a good home. I wish him continued success.

I am retired from the Marine Corps. During my time as a Marine I served as a fighter pilot for nearly twenty years. I tried as hard as I could to be the very best fighter pilot ever to take to the skies in defense of his country. I owe a great debt to the Marine Corps. The Corps made me an officer—a leader of Marines. And there is no greater privilege. The young men with whom I had the pleasure of serving made me look better than I ever deserved. They did it with spirit, with class, and with a generosity that was equaled only by my own family. Too, the men who mentored and schooled me during my career were the very best. The care they took teaching me how to lead, how to fight, and how to fly was so special and effective not because they were technically the best to ever wear a uniform, but because they cared so dearly about their service and their country—and the legacy they left behind. Their gift is a debt I'll never be able to repay. I can only hope that the skills, the values, and the guts I tried to imbue in those who followed me also contribute to the future heritage and success of the Marine Corps.

I'll always be a proud Marine.

My wife, Monica, is looking at my back this very moment. She's had to put up with a good deal of the back of me during the last couple of years. I love her for it. And the graciousness and good sense of my two beautiful daughters is a treasure that I hold dear. They've given me a sense of security and well being that has made the book easier to write. Thank you Kristen and Katherine.

Chapter 1

Oil

SS-OBERSTURMBANNFÜHRER Joachim Peiper was damned if he did, and damned if he didn't. It was December 20, 1944, and the highly decorated veteran of some of Nazi Germany's greatest battles was at the cusp of the Ardennes Offensive, more popularly known as the Battle of the Bulge.

The handpicked officer's own Kampfgruppe Peiper was stalled near the tiny Belgian town of Stoumont. After leading his panzers on a four-day assault that had sent American soldiers reeling in disarray, he had pulled up short of his immediate objective—desperately low on fuel. Without it, his King Tiger and Panther tanks, arguably the best armored vehicles in the world, were immobile. If he advanced and engaged the disorganized Americans, his tanks might stall—a death sentence for armor. On the other hand, if he stopped his attack to prepare a defense, the new stocks of fuel he so desperately needed might never arrive, and the advantages he had gained over several days of bloody combat would be thrown away. Peiper's decision was made more difficult with the certain knowledge that the Americans would soon regroup and return to face him in force.

With his armored units starved for fuel, Peiper decided to err on the side of caution. He stopped. Ultimately, the massive German offensive was beaten back. Unable to adequately fuel its war machine for much of the war, Nazi Germany, too, was finally defeated only a few months later.

*   *   *

Even before Adolf Hitler began gobbling up territory and nations in pieces and wholesale—beginning in 1936 with the reoccupation of the demilitarized zone of the Rhineland, followed by Austria and the Sudeten areas in 1938—he knew he could not hope to wage his war without a ready and reliable source of crude oil. Fielding the modern, mechanized forces that he was developing would require petroleum resources beyond those available in Germany. During 1939, the Nazi nation accounted for only two-tenths of one percent of the world's total production of crude oil.[1]

Conversely, Germany's future enemies had ample stocks. The Soviet Union, an exporter of oil to Germany until the Nazi invasion of June 1941, had more reserves than it could exploit. The United States, too, was blessed with enormous oil fields and a petroleum industry and infrastructure second to none. Indeed, on the eve of World War II, the United States was responsible for the production of 60 percent of the global output.[2] Even tiny Britain had petroleum assets in the Middle East and Far East that dwarfed Germany's supplies.

Hitler, then, would have to exercise the ingenuity of the German people, and his own greed, to get the oil he needed. To this end existing fields in Germany and Austria were exploited to the fullest. More important, Germany set about developing the largest synthetic fuel industry in the world.

German industrial giant IG Farben had for some time possessed patents on a process for developing high-quality gasoline from low-grade lignite coal—a grade of coal available to Germany. The process, while not as cheap as refining crude oil, was economically viable. Further, the industrial expertise within the country was sufficient to develop it.

Wasting no time, Hitler gave support to the German firm as early as 1933, the year he achieved power. By 1936 the development of a full-blown synthetic fuel industry was well underway. When Germany invaded Poland on September 1, 1939, there were no fewer than thirteen synthetic fuel plants in operation, and more were under construction. A year later, these plants were producing 72,000 tons of fuel per day, or nearly half of Hitler's requirements.[3]

But the synthetic fuel plants could not meet all of Germany's needs. Not soon enough, anyway. To make up the shortfall, Hitler was forced to look beyond Germany's borders to Hungary and Romania.

Both nations had significant oil fields and refineries, but Romania's were by far the most extensive and best developed. Located thirty-five miles north of the capital city of Bucharest, the city of Ploesti was the center of Romania's petroleum industry. Sitting at the foot of the Sub Carpathian Mountains—also known as the Transylvanian Alps—the site was first settled in the 1500s as a military encampment. Unknown to those first inhabitants, the thick, soft, sandstone formations, or flysch, that made up the local geology were heavy with crude oil. This came into play in 1856 when Ploesti became the site of one of the world's first oil refineries.

Development came quickly. Foreign interests, aware of the enormous profit potential promised by the huge oil fields, invested heavily. This foreign investment was possible largely because Romania possessed neither the financial nor technical means to exploit the resource. The region grew in such importance that it was already of strategic consequence by World War I. It was taken by the Germans during 1916, and subsequently returned—albeit wrecked—to Romania at the cessation of hostilities. By the time post-war reconstruction of the infrastructure was complete, foreign firms controlled the majority of petroleum production and processing in Romania. A quick review of the major operations illustrates this point: The Astra Romana company was a joint English and Dutch concern; as was the Unirea operation; the Steaua Romana refinery was jointly held by the English, the French, and the Romanians; the Sirius Concordia refinery was operated by joint French, Belgian, and Romanian concerns; and Standard Oil of New Jersey owned the huge Romano Americana complex. Only the Credit Minier operation was wholly Romanian.

This heavy foreign participation in the construction and operation of the Ploesti petroleum infrastructure would pay untold dividends during the future war in a way that was unanticipated. Information provided by engineers and workers who had worked in Romania would prove to be invaluable in making targeting decisions for the great air raids of 1943 and 1944.

By the late 1930s Ploesti was surrounded by thirteen major refineries, many smaller complexes, and the infrastructure to support all of them.

Nearly all of it was still owned and operated by the largest oil companies in the world.

Ploesti's position as the largest petroleum complex on the continent was unchallenged. For that reason, Romania and the plum that was Ploesti were too much for Hitler to resist.

*   *   *

Romania's history, like the histories of many of the nations of central Europe, is a tangle of back-and-forth settlement and conquest dating from prehistory. The Romans displaced the Dacians around 100 A.D. and in turn were pushed out by various warrior tribes from the east. Goths, Huns, and Tatars, among others, left their imprint on the plains and forests and mountains that eventually became Romania.

Precisely because it was so often invaded, the modern concept of the nation of Romania was a long time coming. In fact, it wasn't until 1861, near the end of a long and brutal Ottoman rule, that the principalities of Walachia and Moldavia joined to form the nation of Romania. After complete independence was gained from the Ottoman Empire in 1879, the nation was governed by a succession of wealthy rulers, mostly on the backs of rural peasants, into the next century.

The start of World War I found Romania looking on in angst but uncommitted to either side. Uncertain which way the tide would turn, and capable of fielding only a second-rate army, it wasn't until the Allies promised to reward Romania with territory from the Austro-Hungarian Empire that the nation's rulers entered the war against Germany and the Central Powers on August 29, 1916.

It was a disaster. Unable to match the experience and fire power of Austrian and German forces, the Romanians fell into retreat within weeks, and by December 6 had lost their capital, Bucharest, to the Germans. Romanian wheat and oil would service the Central Powers until the end of the war. Worse, the Central Powers dismembered and divided chunks of the country amongst themselves.

Happily for Romania, though, the Allies won the war—and kept their promises. Not only did the hapless nation regain all its lost territory, it was additionally rewarded with sections of Hungary, including Transylvania, Bukovina, and Banat. After the last treaties were signed Romania was one-third larger than it had been at the start of hostilities.

After bumping along through the 1920s, Romania's poor peasants were hit hard by the worldwide depression of the 1930s. A fascist counter-government movement, the Iron Guard, rose to prominence and played to popular sentiment by blaming the country's woes on Jews and Communists, among others. The Iron Guard grew in popularity until 1938, when King Carol II, fearful of the movement's very real threat to his parliamentary-style government, crushed it and established himself as dictator.

By this time Nazi Germany had begun to destabilize Europe. For its part Romania, significantly increased in size since its participation in World War I, wanted no part of any change in the status quo. It looked to powerful France—a sponsor of the treaty by which Romania had gained so much of its territory—as a guarantor of that status quo. Still, Germany was a rich and powerful nation, and Romania sought to improve its own condition by entering into economic agreements with the Nazis during 1939. Through these agreements, Germany was able to exert a considerable influence on the Romanian economy.

The fall of France in 1940 marked a turning point for Romania. Not militarily strong, and allied with no one worthwhile, the country was beset by demands for territory. The Soviet Union demanded Bessarabia and Bucovina, Hungary wanted parts of Transylvania returned, and Bulgaria demanded Dobruja in the south. These demands, especially those of the Soviet Union, put not only Romania but also Hitler in a very difficult fix. Hitler wanted nothing to do with ceding chunks of Romania to Stalin, but he had a war to tend to in the West and could ill afford to upset the Soviet leader at that moment. The demands by Hungary and Bulgaria further complicated the mess. The Nazi leader took the easy way out. At Hitler's insistence, King Carol II acquiesced to these demands and the lands were ceded, in return for which Hitler guaranteed the sovereignty of the remainder of Romania. German troops and aircraft began arriving in July.

The Romanian populace was outraged. Carol appointed General Ion Antonescu as prime minister then abdicated to his son Michael on September 6, 1940. Antonescu was a fascist who had been a major participant in the seamier side of Romanian politics for several years. The new King Michael, only nineteen years old, was little more than a figurehead for Antonescu's dirty political machinations. For the next four years, aside from a quickly quashed re-emergence of the Iron Guard, there was no serious resistance to the growing German economic and military presence in Romania. In fact, under Antonescu's leadership, Romania grew to become one of Germany's staunchest allies.

Hitler had gained Ploesti without firing a shot.

Chapter 2

BEGINNINGS

HITLER WAS not alone in recognizing the importance of Ploesti to Germany's ability to conduct his war. With its huge reserves and tremendous refining capacity, the significance of the region was obvious to all. British war planners earmarked the complex as one that demanded attention early on. Prime Minister Winston Churchill himself aptly labeled Ploesti as the "taproot of German might."

In fact, the British defensive actions in Greece and on the island of Crete were undertaken in part with an eye toward preserving them as bases from which to launch bomber offenses against Ploesti. Hitler, just as determined to prevent this, prevailed in both campaigns, and any immediate British plans for an aerial assault against the Romanian oil fields were stymied.

The Soviets recognized Ploesti's importance as well. Notwithstanding the huge American strikes later in the war, the Red Air Force was the first to bomb the refineries. Within a month of being betrayed and invaded by the Nazis, the Soviet Union sent aircraft against Ploesti—on July 13, 1941. The hope was that the Luftwaffe would be forced to shift fighter units from the front to Romania to defend the oil fields. As it turned out, considering its size, the small force of six bombers sent against the Astra Romana, Orion, and Unirea refineries on the southern outskirts of the city, caused significant damage. More than 9,000 tons of oil were set ablaze and a number of storage tanks and railway tanker cars were also destroyed. Nevertheless, the Red flyers paid a high price for their success; four of the six bombers fell to German fighters. Further, the strike caused no displacement of German fighter units from the front.[1]

The Soviets continued to attack oil targets within Romania. Constanta, the Black Sea coastal port, refined, stored, and shipped petroleum products and was served by a network of pipelines. Largely for this reason the city was hit by more than fifty Soviet air raids. These raids continued until late 1941 when the German capture of Soviet air bases in the Crimea put a virtual stop to them.

The Soviet attacks were undertaken with no strategic objective and were small and scattered in nature. They proved little more than nuisance raids. More than two years would pass before anyone devised a strategic campaign with the ultimate goal of destroying the refineries at Ploesti.

*   *   *

The United States was on the defensive early in 1942. In the Pacific, stunned American forces were retreating from the all-consuming Japanese hydra. At the same time American forces in Europe were still virtually nonexistent. On the home front American citizens had only just started to divert their energy from panic to productivity. It was a dark time; morale was poor.

It was during this period—March 1942—that Col. Harry A. Halverson was called to Washington to be given command of the B-24-equipped 98th Heavy Bombardment Group, then located at Barksdale Field in Shreveport, Louisiana. Halverson was an opinionated but highly professional officer with a distinguished record and ties to some of the most influential officers in the Army Air Forces. He had helped to crew the *Question Mark*, a Fokker C-2 that set an airborne endurance record of more than six days, from January 1 to January 7, 1929. The crew had been led by Maj. Carl A. "Tooey" Spaatz, who later headed the United States Strategic Air Forces in Europe. Also on board had been Capt. Ira C. Eaker, who later headed the Eighth Air Force based out of Great Britain. Alongside Halverson, and like Halverson a first lieutenant, Pete Quesada would later make his mark as the pioneering leader of the IX Tactical Air Command, so crucial to providing ground support to advancing Allied forces in Europe.

Halverson was ordered to use the 98th Bomb Group to prepare a force for a secret campaign overseas with an emphasis on long-range operations. It was the assumption of many that those secret operations were to be conducted against Japan from bases in China. No one was to place any obstacles in Halverson's path.

With this mandate Colonel Halverson set about taking the best of what was available in the 98th—it had yet to receive its full complement of aircraft or personnel—and preparing for his mission. Halverson's actions angered a number of senior officers, because his "cream-skimming" was upsetting training and deployment plans within the U.S.-based Third Air Force. Nevertheless, the colonel's orders were ironclad, so he pressed on, accountable only to Washington. His mission was officially named Halverson Project 63, but this was variously shortened to the Halverson Project, or Halverson Detachment, or most commonly, simply as Halpro.

Conditions were such that only twenty-three of the thirty-six crews of the 98th were, in Halverson's view, suitable for his mission. He dedicated the bulk of the 98th's resources to training these crews, the idea being that he would rather take a smaller, more effective element into combat than a larger one that was not as finely honed. Training began during March and continued into April. At the end of the first week of April, elements of the 98th were moved to Fort Myers, Florida, and based out of what was eventually called Page Field—a primitive and as-yet-unfinished installation. Halpro would be based there until late May.

Though Halverson and his manner of doing business were not looked upon too keenly by other senior officers of the Third Air Force, he was nonetheless well respected by the officers under him. He was a fine officer and leader who not only worked hard but played hard as well. He further endeared himself to his younger officers when he was able to get the majority of them, who were only second lieutenants, promoted to the rank of first lieutenant only a few months after they had been commissioned into the service. During peacetime, the same progression in rank would have taken years.

Ed Cave, one of those lieutenants, remembered that he "liked Colonel Halverson quite a bit, though some people didn't. I know that he was real good friends with General [Henry] Arnold. I thought he was a real nice man."[2]

*   *   *

The B-24 heavy bombers Halverson was to take with him were B-24Ds, the first model produced that would see combat in significant numbers. These had been delivered from California to Mobile, Alabama, and were picked up by Halpro crews on April 28, 1942. These twenty-three aircraft were taken to Fort Myers on May 1, and then flown up to Wright Field in Dayton, Ohio, to be modified. In Ohio the unreliable, ventral, ball turrets were removed, and the resultant holes were skinned over with aluminum. Also, two 400-gallon auxiliary fuel tanks were installed in the forward bomb bay, one on each side. Perhaps to make up for the loss of the ball turret, two fixed .50-caliber machine guns were mounted in the lower portion of the glazed nose. These were actuated by means of a button on the pilot's control yoke. Otherwise the aircraft were equipped with the standard waist, upper-turret, and tail guns.[3]

After training through most of May 1942, it was time to leave, ready or not. Each airplane carried its own crew and two ground crewmen. The latter were to fulfill the duties of the normal complement of seven or eight ground crewmen per plane until the support echelon arrived from the States. The bombers were further loaded with all sorts of spare parts, clothing, food, and sundry gear and equipment. There was no extra room in any of the aircraft, and each was overloaded by several tons. Because of the vagaries associated with their route and mission, each first pilot was designated as a finance agent and was issued five thousand dollars in one- and five-dollar denominations. This money was to cover the pay of the crews until a more conventional arrangement could be set up.

From Florida, starting on various dates from mid May 1942, the twenty-three Halpro B-24Ds began to hopscotch individually across the Caribbean, through South America, across the Atlantic, over western and northern Africa to Egypt. The movement alone was a challenge the likes of which Halverson and his men had never encountered before. Flying long over-water routes into exotic but primitive "postcard" destinations taxed the piloting, navigation, and maintenance skills of detachment personnel more than anything they had ever attempted. The weather at those tropical latitudes could be particularly violent, not to mention that the B-24 was a new aircraft, still experiencing significant teething problems. "We had such a load that we had to land in daylight and take off at night," Ed Cave recalled. The cool nights increased the take-off performance of the bombers and made it possible—heavily loaded as they were—to get airborne.

On the trans-Atlantic trip from Natal, Brazil, to the Gold Coast of Africa, Cave hauled his ship airborne at 2100, directly into a line of thunderstorms. After he had climbed through the violent weather he found himself above an expanse of tabletop-smooth clouds that reached to the horizon. "At around three or four in the morning my navigator, Harold Wicklund, called over the intercom to say that he had some bad news and some good news. The bad news was that we were past the point of no return. The good news was that he thought he knew where we were. By ten that morning, he had us right on the nose of Accra on the west coast of Africa!"

That no aircraft were lost along the way was a testament to the skill of the young crews, and perhaps their luck. The trail they helped blaze was at that time in its infancy, however it was the primary route by which bombers would move into the Mediterranean Theater—and beyond—and would be subsequently transited by thousands of other crews and aircraft. The number of wrecks that ultimately marked the route was grim evidence of its inherent dangers.

Officially, no one except the detachment's leadership and each aircraft's navigator knew the final destination. These men were sworn to secrecy. Nevertheless, one pilot recalled that on the first leg of the trip—from Fort Myers to Puerto Rico—his navigator broke the news that they were to fly to a base in China. From there, they were to fly three missions to Tokyo, and then return to the States. The objective seemed similar to Doolittle's famous morale-building mission, though it would take place at least a few months later.

By the time the crews reached Khartoum, the Halpro mission had been overcome by events. The Japanese had captured the Chinese bases that were to have been used to launch attacks against Japan. On May 27, 1942, the detachment moved to the RAF base at Fayid, near the Suez Canal, rather than proceed on to China.

As events were developing, the Halpro crews and aircraft were needed in North Africa anyway. Despite increasing American aid, General Irwin Rommel's Panzer Group Afrika was still thrashing the British Eighth Army, and in fact, when the detachment reached the continent he was engaged in the battle that would drive the British out of Libya. Before June was out, the great Commonwealth bastion at Tobruk was in German hands. This being the case, the Halpro mission was ordered to prepare for operations out of North Africa.

*   *   *

First Lieutenant Harold A. Wicklund had been Ed Cave's "good news, bad news" navigator during the trip from Fort Myers. He performed double duty as the bombardier aboard their ship, *Hellsapoppin'*, during the final preparations for combat operations. "We flew mainly practice bombing missions on a large target drawn on the sand out in the desert. We dropped 500-pound bombs—my first ever." Through luck, Wicklund narrowly avoided serious injury or even death on one of these missions. "While landing on the sand runway at Fayid the nose wheel collapsed and the navigation compartment filled with sand. Normally, I remained in that compartment putting my maps and navigation equipment into my kit, but on this mission I chose to watch the landing from behind the pilots. I don't know why I chose to do so, but I do know that it saved me from suffocation or serious injury."[4]

While the crews of the Halverson Project were trying to catch up on training, the decision to strike Ploesti was made. It was hoped that, even though the strike might not be composed of a large number of aircraft, it might be effective enough to stem some of the fuel bound for Rommel. Further, it would demonstrate the long reach of America's newest strategic bomber, and perhaps force the enemy to divert more resources to air defense. Also, a successful long-range strike would serve to boost morale on the home front; after all, it would be the first American strike against continental Europe. Finally, it would underline America's declaration of war against Romania—which had taken place only a few days earlier, on June 5, 1942.

In point of fact, America's declaration of war against Romania was undertaken in part to legitimize the pending air raid. Romania had declared war against the United States soon after the United States and Germany had exchanged declarations, but for a number of reasons the United States had yet to reciprocate. The mission against Ploesti provided the needed impetus.

The young participants first learned of the impending mission on June 10, 1942, when thirteen crews were selected and announced. The briefing took place on Thursday, June 11, and was given in part by the executive officer, Col. George F. McGuire. Takeoff would be later that same night, and the bombers would proceed individually to the target, as the crews were not trained for night formation flying. The plan called for the aircraft to fly a route from Egypt, around Turkey, across the Black Sea into Romania and on to Ploesti. If the route was correctly flown,

Halverson's bombers would arrive over the target at sunrise. After they released their bombs, the aircraft were to be turned southeast, around Turkey and into Iraq, where they were to land at the RAF's Habbinya airfield in Baghdad. An alternate plan, involving recovery at a Soviet airfield in Tblisi, was also discussed. However, formal permission from the Soviets had yet to be received. Syria was also a potential recovery point.[5]

The briefing, which was attended by RAF representatives, showed the route bypassing neutral Turkey. This was done to appease the British, who had warned their American allies against traversing the non-belligerent nation. Officially neutral, Turkey was leaning closer to the Axis at this time in the war and there was no predicting what its reaction to American bombers overhead might be. In the event, the British advice was ignored.

Ed Cave remembered: "After the first briefing Colonel Halverson brought us all together in another room after the British had left. He had a map with a red line that ran straight across Turkey. Evidently the navigators had already known about it, but, anyway, he said that we weren't going to mess with going around Turkey, we were going to fly right over it." In the end, Halverson's decision to ignore the British was appropriate; greater fuel consumption caused by the longer route would have jeopardized the mission.

Halpro was only about twenty days removed from Fort Myers, Florida, when the first of the thirteen operational B-24s, heavy with fuel and bombs, struggled airborne into the dark at about 2230 on June 11, 1942. It was followed at short intervals by the remainder of the aircraft assigned to the mission. Ed Cave, piloting *Blue Goose,* had a fire in his number-two engine soon after takeoff. He quickly extinguished it, got the engine running again, and proceeded with the mission.

Within a few hours all the bombers had made their way north across the Mediterranean and over neutral Turkey. Searchlights reached up to locate the trespassing aircraft but were unsuccessful. No antiaircraft fire or fighters were encountered over the neutral nation.

Once across Turkey and over the Black Sea, the aircraft climbed to altitude—up to 30,000 feet in some cases. The higher altitudes made them less vulnerable to fighters and antiaircraft fire. "Damned cold" was how one crewman characterized the often debilitating, high-altitude temperatures. This bitter cold, along with the lack of oxygen available at higher altitudes, would be every bomber crewman's nemesis over Europe until the end of the war.

The individual aircraft encountered sporadic and mostly ineffective antiaircraft fire at the Romanian coast. It was here that one of the thirteen aircraft, suffering from frozen fuel lines, cut its mission short and dumped its bombs on the port city of Constanta. The remainder of the aircraft pressed toward Ploesti.

The B-24s arrived over south-central Romania just at dawn. Several crews reported an undercast that forced them to drop their bombs using simple dead reckoning. Others indicated that they could see the ground and that there was enough daylight to use their bombsights. Several navigators reported being confused by changes in the landscape caused by the overflowing Danube River. Regardless, these problems were their biggest challenges as the enemy offered little resistance; only a few crews reported sporadic antiaircraft fire and encounters with enemy aircraft. At least two aircraft were hit, and two crew members sustained light injuries.

Lieutenant Ed Cave descended his ship through the clouds so that his navigator and bombardier, Lieutenant Harold Wicklund, could drop their load of bombs visually. "It was no use dropping the bombs through those clouds, so we descended down from about 24,000 feet to 8,400 feet." During this time, the anxiety level increased as the number-two engine caught fire again. Cave quickly blew the fire extinguisher and feathered the engine. "We were all set up when Wick made me go around and set up for another run—he had found something else that looked better. I was getting kind of upset and reminded him that we had just lost an engine, and that if he didn't drop the bombs I was going to go ahead and salvo the whole rack. Anyway, we made another run and dropped our bombs. I think we were the only ones who even hit the refineries."

*   *   *

Romanian records reveal that the strike was ineffective. The scattered nature of the attack confused the Romanians, but it diluted the effectiveness of the attack. And because the Americans had no effective means of bombing accurately in darkness or through the weather, they inflicted no real damage.

Reports of the American bombers had started to reach various Romanian headquarters just before 0400 on June 12. The raiders appeared to be striking at numerous targets throughout the central and southern portions of the country. This was true, but it wasn't by design. It was simply what happened when the ill-equipped bomber crews individually reached what they believed to be their target.

The Romanian reports were confused. Strikes were identified over Bucharest. Ploesti was alerted. There were reports of parachutes. In Constanta, two bombs fell between the slaughterhouses and the docks and others fell into the sea. Another string of bombs fell into a forest preserve. German Freya radar got into the game only after the initial alerts. Whether this advanced technology was any help is unclear. Back at Ploesti, six bombs fell into the town and killed three people and injured three more. Six bombs fell on Berceni, causing no damage. Another bomber was spotted as it attacked the villages of Prundu and Comana, where no damage was sustained. A German barracks was hit at Buzau, though most probably by Soviet aircraft. Another attack by Soviet aircraft at Buzau destroyed 150 meters of railroad track.[6]

These pitiful results were hardly what the raid's planners had hoped for. Rather than inflicting a sharp, telling blow on the refineries at Ploesti, the American force groped blindly about the country, randomly dropping bombs on no worthwhile target. It was an embarrassing beginning to an effort that would ultimately be characterized by a precision and weight that was irresistible.

* * *

Cave and Wicklund didn't encounter enemy fighters during the mission, but that wasn't the case for at least two of the bombers.

Romanian Air Force Adjutant Pilot Vasile Pascu of Fighting Squadron 59 was standing alert at the airfield at Tirgusor during the night of the attack. He had spent most of the evening at his aircraft—a Romanian-built IAR 80 single-engine fighter. He became aware that something unusual was underway at about 0345. "I slept until 0300, when I started the engine to get it warm. Shortly, I noticed the searchlights of the antiaircraft artillery sweeping the sky at 4,000 meters' height." Soon thereafter Pascu heard the rumble of a B-24 approaching the airfield. Without orders he roared into the night sky and raced after the big bomber. His departure had been so hasty that he got airborne without his headset or parachute.

"The enemy plane started pitching to the left and right, and the crew opened fire with its onboard [machine guns]." The Romanian chased the B-24 to the Ploesti area where it was engaged by what Pascu described as "intense fire" from antiaircraft batteries. After dropping its bombs the big aircraft descended into some clouds, where Pascu lost sight of it. Guessing that the bomber was headed for the Danube delta, the Romanian pilot raced south toward Braila-Galati to attempt an intercept. "I was flying at 3,900 meters altitude. Before Urziceni, through a break in the clouds, at 100 meters in front of me, the plane appeared. Suddenly I hit its inner left engine and the fire started. As I was very close to the plane and its oil tanks ruptured, the oil spread in the air, covering my windscreen and cutting my visibility."

At this point the Romanian pilot watched the American bomber draw away—seemingly on fire and mortally hit. At the same time he began a descent because his own engine had begun to misfire. Shortly he coaxed the engine back to health and started to climb again. He spotted another B-24 over Buzau and noted to himself that the American operation must have been more complex than he realized. He had no idea that the separate flights he was encountering were simply the result of a haphazard plan, primitive navigation, and happenstance.

This second bomber was coming from the direction of Zilestia, where the Luftwaffe operated from a sizable airdrome. "I attacked below from a very good position, but my ammunition finished." With no other good options Pascu broke off the engagement and returned to the area where he had attacked the first bomber. He claimed that he spotted flaming wreckage spread over a large area. After flying over it several times he landed at the airfield at Mizil, refueled and rearmed, and returned to Tirgusor. "I made a round tour over the airdrome, rocking the wings—the sign of victory."[7]

Pascu's initiative, aggressiveness, and piloting skills were laudable. Launching into the dark and pressing an attack against a huge and well-armed bomber was not a task for a novice or one faint of heart. Nevertheless his victory claim is not borne out by the records. Neither is the claim made by a German pilot who also managed to find one of the thirteen American bombers. Romanian forces directed to locate the wreckage of the supposedly downed bombers came up empty-handed. That there was confusion about whether the bombers went down or not is understandable. The darkness of the early morning combined with clouds and the excitement of combat would no doubt have made it difficult to determine with total accuracy the fate of the engaged bombers. To the enemy pilots' credit, at least two of the thirteen raiders did sustain damage, and two crewmen were lightly injured. But none of the attackers were brought down by enemy fire.

* * *

The mission deteriorated even further as the American aircraft started out of Romania. Despite the planning that had preceded the attack, it became apparent to some of the crews that they didn't have enough fuel to get to Iraq. Harold Wicklund recalled what happened aboard the *Blue Goose* with Ed Cave: "After leaving the target, we set a course across the Black Sea, due east to Tblisi—in Russia. Once settled on course, Ed asked me for the estimated time of arrival. I transmitted this information back to him over the interphone, and he responded that he didn't believe we had enough fuel to get to Tblisi."

Following a hurried discussion during which the crew also discussed diverting into Syria, Cave made the decision to make for Ankara, Turkey. He changed the aircraft's heading from east to south and kept a sharp lookout for fighters, as it was now bright daylight. Extra ammunition went overboard and fuel was transferred and balanced for the trip into Ankara. Once they were safely on the ground, they planned to rely on the American embassy to clear their return to Egypt.

Cave and his copilot, 1st Lt. Eugene Ziesel, sighted the Turkish airfield at Ankara just before noon on June 12. Cave had the landing gear lowered and checked earlier than usual, as there wasn't enough fuel remaining to attempt to go around if they weren't down and locked. "As we got closer I could see two B-24s already parked on the ramp, and a group of Turks working on the end of the runway. I knew I had to cut it close, because the runway was only 3,000 feet long. When we hit down, I told Ziesel that I had it under control—but I didn't. My legs were jumping on the brakes and another engine quit, which pulled us off the runway and we sank down to the hubs of our wheels. We didn't do any other damage, but we were stuck. I had a gut feeling there was something wrong, because none of the fellows from the other B-24s came out to give us some jazz about not being able to land an airplane."

As it turned out, four B-24s diverted into Ankara, where they were joined by an Me-109 fighter. The enemy pilot had given chase but had outrun his fuel and, instead of downing his quarry, followed it into Turkey. It must have been embarrassing in the extreme.

*   *   *

Predictably, the Turkish authorities took a dim view of the violation of their sovereignty, interned all the crewmen, and confiscated their B-24s. "We were told beforehand that if we went into Turkey, we'd be on our way out within twelve hours," Cave recalls. "Well, it was more like seven months and twelve hours."

The bomber crews waited on diplomatic efforts for several months in an abandoned schoolhouse just outside of Ankara. When the weather grew colder they were moved into a filthy hotel just off of Ataturk Boulevard in Ankara. There, the airmen languished in a sort of netherworld of semi-captivity. While not strictly prisoners of war, the crews had their movements restricted and were locked down each night. They were allowed to exercise and attend some embassy-sponsored functions, and were in fact featured in the September 14, 1942 issue of *Life*. Occasionally they were escorted to movie theaters where they were sometimes able to slip away from their guards and patronize local drinking establishments.

After a time the Turks became anxious to operate the B-24s. During October they made arrangements for some of the crewmen to fly two of the bombers to the base at Eskisehir. Ed Cave was one of the pilots, and he flew *Little Eva* to the Turkish installation. Here, through the autumn and into winter, he and other crewmen made a great show over providing just the barest bits of instruction to Turkish crews. Living conditions were not the best, and Cave developed a debilitating case of jaundice. It was while he was hospitalized that one of the crews, led by his co-pilot, Eugene Ziesel, managed to steal one of the B-24s and fly it with a partial crew to British-held Cyprus. By the rules of diplomacy the bomber had to be returned, but the crew was not.

Several months into their internment—exhausted and increasingly unfit—Cave and Harold Wicklund, along with another officer, were advised of an opportunity to escape. In mid-January they climbed down a rope from their second-floor bathroom window and into a foot of snow. Over the next few days they traveled warily northward until reaching the safety of the British consulate at Mersin, near the Syrian border. There, the British arranged passage for the three Americans to Palestine aboard the *Inviken*, a Norwegian ship loaded with aluminum ore.

Their first attempt at boarding the ship was thwarted by a suspicious customs official. The Norwegian captain was not so easily put off, though. He complained to the local constabulary that three of his seamen had jumped ship and gotten drunk in town, and that he wanted them back immediately. Cave recalls: "So they poured a little cognac on us and got some on our breath, and we acted like we were about half shot. They took us back into town, and there was Captain Olson, standing under the streetlight. We didn't know him and he didn't know us. We walked up and he started giving us the devil about why we didn't get back on the ship and all that." A short time later the three men were safely aboard the *Inviken*. After reaching port at Haifa, Palestine, a diplomatic escort took them to Egypt where they rejoined American forces.

Cave was sent home because of his illness, but Wicklund was back flying combat within a very short time. He would see Ploesti again.

*   *   *

The crews on the June 12 raid that did not divert into Turkey did have enough fuel to make it to either Syria, or Habbinya, in Iraq. After a short time they brought their aircraft back to Egypt and continued operations against the Axis. The B-24s that landed in Turkey were kept by the Turkish government, and along with aircraft that diverted into the country during subsequent years, were pressed into Turkish military service.

*   *   *

It takes a dedicated optimist some careful study and a good bit of salesmanship to portray the Halpro mission in a positive fashion. The damage caused was so minimal that it does not merit mention. Although no aircraft were shot down, the four B-24s that landed in Turkey were confiscated and their crews were interned for more than six months—a loss rate of more than thirty percent. And because the damage inflicted at Ploesti was virtually nonexistent, there wasn't even much propaganda value to be had. It was the first strike on continental Europe by United

States forces, but it was some time before even the barest details were made known to the American public.

For all that, the mission did demonstrate the long reach of the B-24 and the will of the Americans to use it. This was a lesson that was not lost on the Germans. And because it wasn't lost on the Germans, the Americans were going to suffer horribly for it in the future.

Chapter 3

LIBERATOR

THE CONSOLIDATED B-24 Liberator is associated with the air campaign against Ploesti more than any other aircraft type; it flew more than two-thirds of the missions. B-17s flew missions against Ploesti, British Halifaxes and Wellingtons made night raids, and P-38s were used as dive-bombers on one occasion. But their contributions to the overall campaign were secondary compared to those of the B-24.

It wasn't a pretty airplane. Nor was it particularly reliable or strong. The evidence shows this. But many of the thousands of men who flew the B-24 into combat argue quite vociferously otherwise. That they do so is understandable: Men form incredible bonds to the machines in which they ride to victory. But it should be remembered that these same vocal champions of the B-24 are not the same men who died in it. And many thousands did die in it.

The B-24 came about as the result of an Army Air Corps requirement issued in early 1939 for an improved bomber to augment the Boeing B-17 four-engine heavy bomber that was already in production. Earlier, in 1938, Consolidated Aircraft Corporation had been approached to build the B-17 under license but turned down the opportunity as they felt they could build something better. In response to the Air Corps requirement of 1939, they came forward with a four-engine design that was striking for its many unusual features. First, it was designed with a tricycle landing gear that was unorthodox for a heavy bomber. Further, its shoulder-mounted wings, though unusually narrow, incorporated an advanced laminar flow design—the Davis wing—that provided improved performance at higher altitudes. Its deep, slab-sided fuselage no doubt created more drag than a smaller design would have, but it gave the airplane a greater bomb-carrying capacity than the B-17 and provided room for a bomb-door actuation rack and rollers. It was marginally bigger than the B-17, with a wingspan of 110 feet, a length of 67 feet, and a gross weight that eventually reached more than 60,000 pounds.

A contract was signed for a single prototype on March 30, 1939, and amazingly, the first flight of the new XB-24 took place only nine months later, on December 29. This aircraft was followed in 1940 by seven pre-production machines that incorporated various changes and improvements. With Europe already at war, and an unprecedented need for aircraft of all types by America and her allies, there was little doubt that the army would accept the new design. A production order was placed for thirty-six aircraft, twenty-seven of which would be built as B-24Cs with turbo-supercharged Pratt & Whitney R-1830 engines producing 1,200 horsepower each. This order was the first in a number of orders that would bring production of the B-24 to more than 18,000 machines—the most produced American aircraft ever. It would also become the most produced four-engine design in history.

The Consolidated Aircraft Corporation did not build these aircraft alone; it didn't have the means. The great American auto manufacturer Ford Motor Company, along with aircraft makers Douglas and North American also produced large numbers of B-24s. At the peak of production during 1944, one B-24 was produced every 100 minutes.

The B-24, nicknamed the "Liberator," met its performance targets and outpaced the B-17 in terms of range, airspeed (just barely), and bomb load. But except for its range and carrying capacity, the performance margins the B-24 held over the B-17 were insignificant. In fact, the B-17 had a higher service ceiling than the Liberator.

While it met its design requirements, the B-24 was more difficult to fly and operate than the B-17. It was an inelegant airplane that demanded a strong and competent pilot. It was said that one didn't so much land the B-24 as much as got it headed towards the earth and then did his best to minimize the effects of the impact. That being said, it was no comfort to the pilots then that the nose wheel assembly was weak and collapsed too often, sometimes with disastrous results.

A more critical shortcoming was that formation flying in the B-24, particularly in the earlier models with geared controls, was very difficult. It was slow to respond to flight control and power inputs, and the strength demanded just to move the yoke required that the pilot and copilot fly in turns so as not to become too exhausted. In a wartime survey one co-pilot suggested that, "Men who are picked to fly B-24s should be picked for their physical abilities; there should be no pilots under 160 pounds because the physical strain of formation flying is too much."

This difficulty was no small matter as tight formations were necessary in order to concentrate the defensive gunfire of all the aircraft of the formation against attacking enemy fighters. Stragglers outside of the formation were easy marks. A bomber that fell out of formation while under attack by fighters had little chance of survival.

The B-24's fuel system was a constant headache throughout its service. It was complicated beyond reason and confounded easy operation. There were eighteen self-sealing fuel tanks—nine in each wing—and the aircraft was capable of accommodating two more tanks in the forward bomb bay for extended-range missions. The enlisted flight engineers were required to work continuously to ensure a steady and balanced flow of fuel to the four engines. Fuel was transferred from the tanks on one wing to the tanks on the other through rubber U-hoses that had to be manually decoupled and reattached by the engineer or some other trained member of the crew. Mishandling could cause air blocks or fuel starvation, both of which would cause failure of one or more engines. Worse, the rubber fuel lines were routed through the bomb bay, where damage from flak—*Flieger Abwher Kannon*—was a danger. Fuel fires in the bomb bay denied the crew their primary means of escape in the event they needed to bail out. There are many accounts of crew members tumbling from a stricken bomber, their clothes and parachutes afire.

The fuel gauges were simple vertical glass tubes routed directly from the tanks and mounted just behind the pilot. This glass could shatter, which posed a tremendous fire hazard. Further, the system was notorious for leaking. Quite often the fuel lines leaked so badly that pools of aviation gasoline formed throughout the aircraft. This gasoline was hugely volatile, and more than one ship was lost through accidental ignition of leaking fuel. Improvements were made to the system as the design matured, but it remained a frustrating, overly complicated affair that continued to cost lives.

*   *   *

The hydraulic system wasn't much better. Complicated and difficult to maintain, it operated the landing gear, flaps, brakes, bomb-bay doors, and tailskid. Like the fuel system, it often leaked, and like aviation gasoline, the hydraulic fluid was inflammable.

As large as the fuselage on the B-24 was, it was a difficult aircraft to move around in. Movement from the flight deck to the rest of the aircraft required crew members to crawl along a narrow, tenuously braced catwalk that ran through the middle of the bomb bay. Doing so required some dexterity, particularly with full flight gear and—at altitude—an oxygen bottle. It wasn't easy to do, particularly for a big man.

The wing, aerodynamically advanced as it was, was a double-edged sword. Its advanced design provided outstanding performance and a significant saving in size and weight. But the saving in size and weight made for a wing that was structurally not as tough or resilient as that of the B-17. Thumbing through photo archives, one is struck by images of B-24s plummeting earthward with one or both wings folded, missing, or aflame.

The Liberator often seemed to have a devious or mean streak—ready to punish the unwary. Robert Carlin of the 456th Bomb Group recounted how, after exiting the target area, one of the group's bombardiers took a stack of magazines and his chest parachute down to the nose wheel well to relax. With his parachute set up as his pillow, he settled down on top of the wheel doors for the trip home. Unfortunately, the doors were only held in place by light springs. The rest of the formation watched in horror as the unfortunate man fell spread-eagle amid a cloud of fluttering magazines.

It is important to point out that other strategic bombers also had problems. The B-29, used to such devastating effect against mainland Japan, was so beset with problems that its early operations nearly met with failure. And a significant part of the B-24's misfortune was that it was constantly compared to its fairly reliable brother-in-arms, the B-17. But the B-17 had its own set of faults, as did the large British and Soviet bombers. For their part, the Germans and Japanese, daunted by the challenge of designing and producing such complex aircraft, among other reasons, never even bothered to produce strategic bombers.

It wasn't that many of the problems with the B-24 couldn't be fixed. A large percentage of them were. But to make really significant changes required production to cease for a time until tooling and procedural changes could be made on the assembly line. The army couldn't afford these work stoppages and opted to accept aircraft with shortcomings rather than take the time to fix the problems. The result was that major changes had to wait until production of new models began.

So, with all these problems, was the B-24 a success? The answer has to be a resounding "Yes!" Despite all its faults, the B-24 was more than capable of filling the role for which it was designed. Throughout its service it carried tons of bombs at high altitude over a great distance, and then discharged them with precision on top of the enemy. It did this effectively from 1942 until the end of hostilities in 1945.

One component to its success was its extremely long range—a range that was unparalleled until the introduction of the much larger and more advanced B-29 late in the war. As an aside, this range was invaluable in fulfilling a role that most are not familiar with. The Liberator was the only aircraft with enough range to close the previously unpatrolled gap in the Atlantic between bases in England and North America. Previously, this expanse had been exploited by German U-boats to savage Allied convoys, and to rearm, resupply, and recharge unmolested from the air. With the introduction of British and American-flown B-24s equipped for hunting submarines, the Germans no longer had a safe haven and the demise of Hitler's submarine wolf packs was hastened.

Aside from its range and bomb-carrying capacity, the B-24 was reasonably fast for its size and type. This helped to ease the stress and fatigue on its crews and gave planners some flexibility when planning missions. It also made it possible for escort fighters to protect the B-24, although they still had to develop specialized tactics for doing so.

While a fighter escort was always preferred, the B-24 carried a fairly robust defensive armament. The exact mountings varied from model to model, but it typically carried two .50-caliber machine guns in the nose; two in the top fuselage turret; two in the retractable ventral fuselage, or ball turret; two in the tail turret; and one each at the two waist positions. This total of twelve machine guns often was more than enough to make enemy fighter pilots hesitate or break off their attacks early. When massed together with other bombers in formation, the defensive fire could be absolutely withering.

The guns themselves were typically Browning M-2s that fired approximately 800 rounds per minute, about 14 rounds per second. The .50-caliber (half-inch) was a fairly heavy round and had an effective range of about six hundred yards. When fired, it gave off a reassuringly deep-throated rumble. A volley of rounds slamming into a fighter-sized target was devastating. Overall the gun was much loved by the crewmen who manned it and very highly regarded by the pilots who flew against it.

Very important, indeed of prime importance, was the fact that the B-24 could be mass-produced. To win the war the Allies needed bombers quickly, and as many as could be produced. Yes, it was a complex machine, and yes, its construction consumed a tremendous amount of resources, but the fact remained that it filled the bill. At one time five separate plants were producing the Consolidated design and rushing deliveries to the Army, Navy, and Marine Corps, as well as several different nations. Foreign users included Great Britain, Canada, Australia and South Africa. It was the most-produced American aircraft in history.

The most important key to the B-24's success was the huge number of highly trained and dedicated men who flew and maintained it. A typical crew might consist of a pilot, co-pilot, bombardier, navigator, flight engineer, radio operator, turret gunner, ball gunner, two waist gunners, and a tail gunner—anywhere from eight to twelve men. The numbers could go up or down depending on how many, and what type, of crewmen were available. Sometimes crew members were able to fulfill more than one task; for instance a flight engineer might also pull duty as the turret gunner. Conversely, a fully manned crew might be augmented by the addition of a specialist such as a photographer or meteorologist.

The miracle of these bomber crews was their ability to not only work within their own crews but to perform as they were trained (and as demanded by the exigencies of combat) as a member of *any* crew. That the Army Air Forces was able to train so many men so thoroughly was a credit to the service. That the nation was able to provide so many good men to the Air Forces was a credit to the people.

These men performed brilliantly and gave willingly of themselves to their brother airmen in the midst of a maelstrom of horror. Much more was about to be asked of them in the skies over Romania.

Chapter 4

PREPARATIONS

THE CASABLANCA Conference of January 1943 brought President Roosevelt, Prime Minister Churchill, and other representatives of the Allied powers together for a council to set future strategy for the war. The Allies' determination to accept nothing less than unconditional surrender from Germany and Japan was perhaps the most important decision to come out of this council. Also agreed to, was the concept of the Combined Bomber Offensive to be launched against Germany, primarily by the United States and Great Britain. It was to be a carefully planned and coordinated effort with distinct, clearly defined objectives. An important parallel decision to come out of the bomber offensive discussion was an agreement that the Romanian oil industry at Ploesti had to be destroyed, the sooner the better.

Planning for a decisive strike against Ploesti got underway almost immediately. The objective was to demolish the refineries so grievously as to effectively take them out of the war. As the region was supplying from 30 to 50 percent of Germany's needs, it was assumed that its destruction would yield telling effects almost immediately. These effects were expected to manifest themselves most convincingly on the Eastern Front, where the beleaguered Soviets were engaging the bulk of the German military. In a way, the destruction of Ploesti was seen as a small concession to Stalin, who was adamant that the Allies open a second front to relieve pressure on his forces. In 1943 the Allies were not capable of engaging the Germans with a second front on continental Europe. An air offensive, along with continued massive contributions of material and equipment through the Lend Lease program was the best they could do.

As it was, the United States in January 1943 was really in no position to mount a huge bomber offensive. It would be many more months before large numbers of bombers would arrive in Europe and the Mediterranean from factories in the United States; and it would be more than a year before the Eighth Air Force in England would be able to begin staging strikes of one thousand aircraft or more.

At this time, early in 1943, the western Allies were working to push German and Italian forces out of North Africa. American ground forces had landed in French Morocco and Algeria late in 1942 and were finally engaged directly with German ground forces—nearly a year after the United States declared war against the Axis. Although the Allies had a preponderance of men and material in the campaign, victory was not a foregone conclusion.

The Ninth and Twelfth Air Forces were providing air support to the Allies in North Africa during this period. The Ninth had been formed out of the Middle East Air Force in November 1942, and was under the command of Maj. Gen. Lewis H. Brereton who had been in command of the Far East Air Force at the outbreak of war on December 7, 1941. Why his forces were left on the ground to be demolished by the Japanese a day after the attack on Pearl Harbor is a question that has vexed historians, and in fact frustrated General "Hap" Arnold, the commander of the Army Air Forces. Nevertheless, the disaster hadn't hurt Brereton's career. He left the Philippines before the Japanese completed their invasion, and subsequently took command in the emergent China-Burma-India Theater. He was transferred to North Africa during June 1942.

When Arnold, as a result of the conference at Casablanca, assigned the Ploesti mission to the Ninth Air Force, Brereton made certain that planners and operators had full access to every resource. He delegated responsibility for operational planning, necessary preparations, and overall conduct of the mission to Brig. Gen. Uzal G. Ent, the IX Bomber Command commander.

The planning for the mission itself was assigned to Col. Jacob "Jake" E. Smart, a staff advisor to General Arnold. Arnold, who was familiar with Smart's expertise and ability, personally made this assignment. Smart was a competent, professional, obviously respected officer, and a bomber pilot by trade. His shortcoming was that he had no combat experience, or first-hand familiarity with operations out of North Africa or into Europe. He did his best to ameliorate this lack of experience by selecting a staff of experts. This staff included higher ranking aircrew with combat experience from Europe; an intelligence expert; RAF bomber crews with experience in North Africa; and, notably, an engineer from the British Army who had managed the Astra Romana Refinery at Ploesti for eight years. Why Smart did not include any American B-24 aircrew from the units in North Africa is unexplained. These were the officers who would actually fly the mission, yet they were absent from the planning.

The development and preparations were extensive. The most unusual aspect of the mission was that it was to be flown at low-level. And the final run from the IP, or Initial Point, into the target was to be flown at "minimum altitude." This meant the heavy, awkward bombers would fly over the target at less than two hundred feet.

A low-level ingress had merits. The primary purpose of maintaining low altitude was to evade radar detection. Radar cannot see below the curvature of the earth, and physics preclude radar detection of earth-hugging aircraft from beyond about thirty miles. Further, radar is not capable of seeing through mountains or hills. The route into Ploesti was planned with an eye toward using terrain features to mask the formation from German radar. If the American bombers could get close to Ploesti without being detected, then enemy defenses would have little warning and the mission should sustain minimal casualties.

Another advantage inherent in a low-level attack was the increased accuracy it promised. A high-altitude attack at that time was by definition an area attack. Any pretense at precision was purely for propaganda purposes. Experience had shown that the spread of bombs from a formation of high-altitude bombers could range over an area of thousands of feet—indeed, sometimes more than a mile. The difficulties in bombing from high-altitude at that time were many. First, the actual target had to be found and identified. Overcast weather often precluded this. If the weather was not a factor, finding the target among the confusing mosaic that was Europe's farms, villages, and cities was still not a foregone conclusion. Next, the formation had to be steered over the target as compactly as possible. This required a great deal of time and maneuvering space—and skill. Additionally the bombing equipment, with its associated bombsight, computing devices, and autopilot, had to be calibrated and working properly. And maneuvering to avoid enemy flak and fighters was precluded in the final moments of the bombing run. This was so that the formation would be at the exactly prescribed point in time and space when the bombs were released. Finally, there was no guarantee that strong winds aloft would not play havoc with the bombs as they dropped several miles from the bomb bays of the aircraft to their targets. In short, successful high-altitude bombing required some amount of luck, a great amount of skill, an equally large dose of courage, and—in order to ensure adequate coverage—a large number of bombers.

Jake Smart could only count on about two hundred bombers being available for the mission. Studies had already shown him that he would need more than one thousand bombers to get the required results from a high-altitude attack. Drawing on intensive studies completed by various experts, it was determined that the destruction of just forty-one key elements of seven different refineries in the Ploesti complex would reduce Germany's entire refining capacity by up to 30 percent. Further, and perhaps more importantly, it would reduce its capacity to produce high-octane aviation fuel by up to 95 percent. These forty-one key elements included cracking towers, steam plants, important pipelines, and various other special components.[1]

To achieve the bombing accuracy and coverage that the destruction of these key components demanded, Colonel Smart decided, probably correctly, that the aircraft would have to attack from low altitude. With accurate navigation, acquiring the large, vertically prominent refineries at low altitude was almost assured. Further, the high-altitude bombsight and other associated equipment would not be required. It would be removed and replaced by an elementary, mechanical bombsight. Finally, when the bombs were released over or near the target from a very low altitude, simple physics precluded them from falling anywhere else. From two hundred feet or less, there just was not enough time for any of the bugaboos associated with high-altitude bombing to have any effect on the bombs. In other words, from low-level it would be difficult to miss the targets.

A low-level profile provided some defensive advantages as well. Enemy fighters would be unable to mount attacks from below the heavily laden bombers. In effect, a low-level formation denied approximately 50 percent of the approaches normally available for aerial attack. Additionally, because of the low-altitude ingress, the limited amount of time the bombers would be within the range of enemy antiaircraft positions would theoretically give gunners less time to prepare, aim, and fire their weapons.

But there were also disadvantages associated with coming in at low-level. Accurate navigation was difficult. At very low-level the landscape moves past an airplane very quickly. Instead of having a "God's-eye" view of the terrain as presented by a high-altitude approach, the view from low level is almost the same as it is from the ground. This provides little opportunity to fix a position by comparing a landmark to others nearby, and then comparing that observation to a navigational chart. Thus, navigating at high speed and low-level on this mission would demand exquisite timing, airspeed, and heading control, as well as a keen eye and top-notch chart interpretation.

Another disadvantage was the fatigue associated with flying so close to the ground. After more than seven hours of formation flying, the pilots would have to drop their formation right down to the deck. Here, they would not only have to constantly wrestle against the prop wash from preceding aircraft, but they would also have to maneuver without running into the ground or other obstacles such as trees or telephone poles. Although avoidance of the ground is somewhat instinctual, it was tiring, and aircraft and crews were routinely lost to collisions with terrain. Additionally, if an aircraft suffered damage or sustained a malfunction at low-level there would be no cushion of altitude to use while dealing with the emergency.

Probably the biggest drawback, and the one which would ultimately take the most lives, was the fact that the aircraft at low altitude would be within the envelope of virtually every antiaircraft weapon in the enemy's arsenal. These included not just the large-caliber, relatively slow-firing flak cannon, but the smaller, fast-firing machine cannon. If the antiaircraft crews were forewarned and prepared, the huge American bombers would be easy targets—regardless of how quickly they traversed the enemy gunners' fields of fire.

Smart's staff began its work in March 1943. Somewhere along the way, American codename convention stuck the operation with the name of SOAPSUDS. This name did not sit well with Britain's Prime Minister Churchill—of all people. He thought that it trivialized a mission that might very well claim a large number of American lives. His staff prevailed on their American counterparts and the more appropriate code name of TIDALWAVE was assigned.

The basic plan had been approved by General Arnold by May 1943, and was far enough along to be presented to Roosevelt and Churchill at the TRIDENT conference in Washington. Here it also received approval, but not without some reservations from the staff of the theater commander, Lt. Gen. Eisenhower. Both Lt. Gen. Carl A. Spaatz and RAF Air Chief Marshal Arthur Tedder questioned whether one mission could achieve the required results. They also warned of tremendous losses. Nevertheless, Colonel Smart's plan to execute the attack from low-level was endorsed. To achieve the degree of destruction desired, with the available resources, there simply was no other option.

Those resources would be the B-24s of five different bomb groups. B-24 groups were selected because there was no other type that could make the 1,200-mile trip to Ploesti, and back. The five groups were: the 44th, with 36 aircraft, commanded by Col. Leon W. Johnson; the 93d, with 36 aircraft, commanded by Lt. Col. Addison E. Baker; the 98th, with 46 aircraft, commanded by Col. John R. Kane; the 376th, with 30 aircraft, commanded by Col. Keith K. Compton; and the 389th, with 30 aircraft, commanded by Col. Jack W. Wood. Of the five bomb groups, only the 376th and the 98th belonged to the Ninth Air Force. They had been working out of airfields in Palestine and the Nile delta. The veteran 44th and the 93d groups were assigned to the Eighth Air Force—headquartered and based in England—and had been sent south for the mission. The 389th had only recently formed in the States, but upon arrival in England, was also sent to North Africa. It had not seen combat.

By the middle of May 1943, the German and Italian forces in North Africa had capitulated, and Sicily had become the next logical stepping stone to Italy and the European continent. In late June, the five bomb groups were assembled at airfields in Libya, near Benghazi. From here they supported the Allied invasion of Sicily.

*   *   *

The support for the invasion of Sicily lasted until mid-July. It was by then time to train for the mission to Ploesti. If anything can be said about the low-level strike, it is that there was a great deal of preparation. This preparation included validation of the low-level concept by conducting real strikes at minimum altitude against enemy targets during the invasion of Sicily. These actually were quite effective, and bolstered confidence among the planners that the Ploesti mission might work as hoped.

By this time, the TIDALWAVE mission had been set for August 1, 1943. Two weeks prior, the five bomb groups suspended combat operations and practiced flying low-level attacks against dummy targets in the desert. An engineering unit had assembled crude, scale replicas of the various refineries south of Benghazi. Constructed of metal, wood, and fuel drums, this ersatz Ploesti proved to be a valuable training aid. Much to the frustration of its builders, parts of it were constantly picked over and dismantled by scavenging nomads.

To further assist the aircrews in identifying their assigned targets, a smaller, highly detailed, scale model of Ploesti and its various plants and refineries was constructed by experts in Britain, and then flown down to Benghazi. Moreover, oblique sketches of the targets were prepared so that the aircrews would know exactly how their target would appear to them when they were on their final attack heading. The planners even went to the extreme of preparing a motion picture of simulated attacks against the scale model—from various headings—to further prepare the crews.

Low-level flight was something new to most of the crews. Previously, low, fast flying was the domain of showoffs and ill-disciplined pilots. It was dangerous, and because it was dangerous, pilots caught "buzzing" the ground were often grounded—or worse. But the sense of speed caused by the blur of the ground rushing past was absolutely exhilarating, and the temptation was hard to resist. It was one of the few regimes of flight where the ungainly B-24 felt fast and exciting.

Now the crews weren't just being allowed to fly low, they were being *ordered* to do so! As they put more and more practice flights under their belts, their confidence grew. Results of their runs against the dummy targets were encouraging, and confidence among some of the more senior officers began to grow. General Brereton, in particular, had been an early skeptic, but he became especially caught up in favor of the operation. He reportedly would brook no resistance to the plan and threatened to relieve any of his commanders who gave anything less than their full support.

On the other hand, Brereton's IX Bomber Command commander, Brig. Gen. Ent, did not hesitate to discuss his misgivings with Brereton. Indeed, he nearly lost his command when he drew up a dissenting petition that he intended to have the five bomb group commanders sign.[2]

Nevertheless, when it became clear that Brereton would not change his mind regarding the low-level aspect, Ent threw his support behind the mission as he realized that his continued opposition would do more harm than good.

There were other dissenters too. Lieutenant Colonel John R. "Killer" Kane, commanding officer of the 98th Bomb Group, intensely disliked the plan. He thought that it was too dangerous and that, it had been invented by "some idiot armchair warrior in Washington."[3] He had been flying combat operations in North Africa for a while and feared that this low-level mission would destroy his veteran bomb group. His dissatisfaction with the plan was well known and did not abate over time.

These dissenters weren't alone; criticism of the plan was widespread among the more senior aircrew. One of the chief concerns was the extreme range of the strike. The route was planned from Benghazi, Libya, across the Mediterranean to the island of Corfu, positioned just off the west coast of Greece, thence across parts of Albania, Yugoslavia, Bulgaria, and finally into Romania. Return was to be by the same route. On a map, discounting the distance traveled while circling to join the formation, and perhaps to rendezvous after the attack, the round trip was approximately 2,400 miles—depending on the actual target being struck. Except for the Halpro mission of the previous year, a mission of this length was unprecedented. That being said, even some of the Halpro mission aircraft had run short of fuel. And unlike the Halpro mission, this one would be huge, and would be flown in formation. Formation flying required the pilots to constantly jockey their throttles—a practice that significantly increased fuel consumption and contributed to engine wear.

To their credit, the planners did in fact launch a test sortie over a route that demonstrated the aircraft could complete a mission of 2,400 miles. Nevertheless, critics pointed out that the sortie was not flown under the same conditions that would be encountered on the actual mission.

Another concern associated with the mission length was whether or not the B-24s would be mechanically up to the task. Even if the aircraft could carry enough fuel, there were worries that the engines would suffer from oil starvation. The harsh desert environment generated a powdery abrasive dust that permeated everything—engines, armaments, windscreens, etc. Such was the abrasive quality of this dust that oil consumption was higher than normal, and engine changes were performed at intervals of fifty to sixty flight hours, rather than the two hundred flight hour intervals that were more common in other environments.

It wasn't just machinery that suffered; the dust made life miserable for the men who operated and maintained the equipment. It got into clothes and bedding and food. Some men never got used to its gritty presence between their teeth. The powdery stuff found its way into every crevice on a man's body—turning ordinary sweat into a muddy glaze, and the misery was compounded by a miserly water ration. What a man didn't drink was what he used to shave and keep himself clean.

Miserable or not, the men kept doggedly to their task. But, though the practice missions seemed to be going well, there were those who pointed out the obvious: The flat deserts of Libya were nothing like the hilly, forested country that the massed formation would encounter along much of its route. There was little the planners could do about this.

Perhaps the biggest criticism was that Colonel Smart's staff and those senior officers who supported the plan seemed to be overly reliant on their confidence that the enemy would be surprised by the attack. Even in the highly unlikely event that the huge formation wasn't spotted and tracked in one fashion or another during the estimated seven-hour trip to the targets, certainly there were spies among the Arabs, or the Allies, or perhaps even among the Americans themselves. These spies could have divulged very harmful information. There also can be little doubt that the Germans had noticed that virtually every American B-24 in the theater had ceased combat operations. This fact must have been a tip-off that something special was afoot. And it is probably certain that the unusual low-level practice missions did not go unnoticed.

* * *

Regardless of all complaints, the mission was going to use Colonel Smart's low-level plan—ambitious as it was. It called for the aircraft from the five bomb groups to rendezvous over the Benghazi airfield complex and proceed northbound in the following order: The 376th was to lead the formation with Brereton in the lead aircraft piloted by Col. Keith K. Compton, the group commander. Second in the formation was to be the 93d led by Lt. Col. Colonel Addison E. Baker. The 93d was to be followed by Col. John R. "Killer" Kane, leading the 98th. It was decided that General Ent would fly aboard Kane's B-24, *Hail Columbia.* The middle of the formation was an unusual position for a senior officer, but it would give him a unique vantage point from which to watch the progress of the mission. Ent and Kane were to be followed by the 44th, led by Col. Leon W. Johnson. The 389th, led by Col. Jack W. Wood, was to bring up the tail of the column.

Target assignments were variously made among the different bomb groups. Compton's 376th was assigned in its entirety to destroy the easternmost target, the giant Romana Americana complex (which planners had designated White I). The 93d was to break into two separate elements in order to attack the Concordia Vega (White II), Standard Petrol Block, and Unirea Speranta refineries (combined as White III). The 98th, with the most aircraft, was designated to strike the Astra Romana and Unirea Orion refineries (combined as White IV). Destruction of the Colombia Acquilla refinery (White V) was assigned to the part of the 44th led by Colonel Johnson. Lieutenant Colonel James Posey, with the other portion of the 44th, was to separate from the main formation after the initial point to hit the Romanian Creditul Minier operation at Brazi (designated Blue, it was geographically separate from the roster of White targets). Finally, the 389th, which would also separate from the main formation, was to hit the Steaua Romana refinery at Campina (Red).[4]

The nature of the defenses around Ploesti was largely an unknown. A decision that some claim was a serious mistake, was that no reconnaissance flights were made over the target. The senior planners were worried that an overflight of Ploesti would tip their hand, and were thus willing to accept the risks associated with inadequate intelligence of the enemy's air defenses. What was known was that the Halpro mission of a year earlier had not encountered an effective defensive effort. Existing intelligence described both heavy and light antiaircraft guns, explosive-laden barrage balloons, and fighter aircraft, but their numbers, locations, and the training and motivation of their crews were unknown. It was conjectured that the main defensive array would be oriented eastward—in preparation against attacks by the Soviets.

With this in mind, the senior brass received unsettling news on July 27, 1943—only five days before the attack was scheduled. A defecting Romanian pilot described in-depth defensive measures in place around Ploesti. And rather than questionably motivated Romanians, he reported, a large proportion of the guns were manned by top-notch German crews. The plan was not changed despite this new information.

*   *   *

Following the final practice mission, General Brereton gave a pep talk to express his utmost confidence in his men, their equipment, and their ability to destroy Ploesti. Aware of the historic significance of the undertaking he declared "we should consider ourselves lucky to be on this mission." His men took some heart from the speech, but the uplifting effect seemed transitory, for the prevailing mood quickly turned to dark apprehension. Rumors of expected losses of 50 percent or more made the rounds. Colonel Kane perhaps contributed to the agitated frame of mind of his men when he declared that if the targets were destroyed, the mission would be a success—*even if no one survived*. Kane himself noted the apprehension, the frenzy of letter writing, the absence of the customary banter and chatter among the men. He also took some time for personal reflection—gazing at the stars while contemplating the upcoming mission.

Staff Sergeant John Blundell was a combat photographer assigned to Kane's 98th. He, too, was grimly contemplating the next day's mission when he was summoned to meet with the commanding officer:

> We had been told that some of us would not make it back, so we all were instructed to write a letter home and place it on our bed along with anything we wanted to send back home. Those who did not return from the mission would have their letters, along with anything else, picked up and sent back to whomever they had indicated. Writing those letters was a pretty hard and somber thing to do. We all felt that we would be the one to come back. After all, we had been issued a survival pack consisting of food rations, a location map printed on silk, some of their [Romanian] money, plus a twenty dollar gold coin. Somehow this gave us additional security that we would be the ones to make it back.

About ten o'clock that night, Col. John R. Kane sent for Blundell to come to his tent. He went over and found Kane sitting outside in his jeep. The two men talked for a short time about the stars and how bright they were. Then Kane said to Blundell, "Sergeant, you are not going on this mission in the morning."

Unsure of what Kane meant, Blundell answered, "Oh, yes sir. I am flying with Colonel Bleyer's crew."

"No, you are not. I have changed that order," replied the colonel. "You are to stay here and process the film that comes back."

"But, sir, I have men who are trained to do that," said Blundell

"This mission is too important for anything to go wrong back here," answered Kane. "I can replace you easier on this mission than I can here at headquarters. So you will stay here and await the film that returns from the mission."

"Yes, sir," replied the sergeant, who walked back through camp to his tent keenly disappointed by what had just transpired. By this time it was late, remembered Blundell, "but I could tell that most of my friends were still up, so I stopped by to see them. When they found out that I was not going on the mission a couple of them gave their letters to me to hold in case they did not return."

Everyone going on the mission was on a high key. The excitement of the mission, the letter writing, telling their friends good-bye—all of this made for an emotional evening. There would not be much sleep that night for anyone.

"Neither of the two men who gave me their letters that night returned from the mission," remembered Blundell. "It was difficult collecting their personal belongings and sending them back, but I also wrote a letter to go along with theirs."[5]

There were others who were not as unsettled. Technical Sergeant Earl Zimmerman was a nineteen-year-old radio operator with the 389th Bomb Group. Raised in Chicago, he had enlisted in June 1942 and now, barely a year later, he was already a veteran. He had survived a mid-air collision and crash over England several months earlier in a mission that killed the crew's navigator. It took place just as the 389th was starting to practice their low-level work in preparation for the big mission; at the time, they had no idea what they were practicing for. And just a couple of weeks earlier, on July 16, Zimmerman's airplane had been badly shot up by fighters over Bari, Italy. With wounded on board, no instruments, no hydraulics, and a load of bombs that couldn't be jettisoned, the crew only barely made it back to Libya on three engines. Just before touching down, they lost two more. Still, they survived.

Zimmerman was no stranger to tough missions. He recalled the night before Ploesti: "I can't remember having any special thoughts about the mission. It was like a 'follow-the-leader' type of thing—if the old man was going, he must have thought that he was coming back."[6]

*　*　*

The last two meals served to the crews were intended to boost morale. They did not. Saturday evening supper was a steak dinner specially flown in from Ninth Air Force headquarters in Cairo. Such fare was unprecedented. A breakfast of real eggs on the morning of the mission was equally unheard of. Instead of lifting spirits, the meals had the opposite effect. Many of the men felt as if they were living their last day on death row.

*   *   *

The leadership of the mission underwent a serious revamping on the day before it was to be flown. At the eleventh hour General Arnold forbade General Brereton and Colonel Smart from participating. Despite his enthusiasm for, and patronage of the effort, Brereton would be too valuable to the enemy if shot down and captured. Likewise, Smart was privy to too many secrets—information linked to the atomic bomb among them.

Instead, the mission would be commanded by General Ent from aboard Colonel Compton's B-24, *Teggie Ann*. Although he was well liked, the choice of Ent has been criticized because of his lack of experience. He was not a B-24 pilot, nor even a rated heavy bomber pilot; he was a *balloon* pilot. Nevertheless, he was still the commander of IX Bomber Command, and the ranking officer behind Brereton.

Chapter 5

EN ROUTE

FEW OF the 1,700 men who would crew the big bombers to Ploesti the following morning would get a good night's sleep. They were awakened by 0400 and fed a hurried breakfast. The bulk of them were airborne by 0730. It was Sunday, August 1, 1943. It was the day that would become known to history as Black Sunday.

Prior to the first aircraft getting airborne, things seemed promising. The mission planning had called for 154 aircraft to achieve the desired results. Aircraft availability was such that the number was exceeded by more than twenty. Each airplane was carrying more than two tons of bombs, a full load of machine gun ammunition, and as much gas as could be put aboard, including extra fuel tanks installed in the forward bomb bay.

Though it was massive beyond what the Americans had ever before attempted, the launch started reasonably well—particularly since each group was taking off from its own separate field. Soon, however, the mission was dealt a literal, smoking black mark. The *Kickapoo,* a ship from the 98th with a substitute crew from the 93d, lost its number-four engine shortly after takeoff. Pilot Robert Nespor and his crew wrestled the outrageously heavy aircraft back toward the runway. In the dust and confusion, and while trying to avoid hitting aircraft that were both airborne and on the ground, Nespor struck a concrete pole as he landed.

The aircraft was consumed by fire. Miraculously, two of the crew survived.

Aside from some delays caused by dust clouds stirred aloft by all the activity, the rest of the formation got airborne and made its way across the short strip of desert and out over the Mediterranean. In a letter he wrote soon after the mission, 1st Lt. John McCormick, pilot of the 389th Group's *Vagabond King*, described the beautiful blue sea, the magnificent formation of stolid bombers, and his feeling that at that moment it was difficult to think that things could become dangerous.[1]

But simply *being aboard* a B-24 could be dangerous. As the formation approached the end of the long over-water leg of the mission near the island of Corfu one of the bombers in the lead formation suddenly spun out of control and fell into the sea. The plane was the 376th Bomb Group's *Wongo Wongo*. It was a burning, black pyre on the water.

There was no clue as to why the *Wongo Wongo* fell into the sea. Various theories have been put forth, to include a fuel imbalance in the wings, an autopilot malfunction, or a failure of one or more engines. Occurring at the formation's altitude of about 4,000 feet, any one of these problems could have made the aircraft impossible to recover. It didn't matter. The remaining B-24s droned on in radio silence, seemingly unperturbed by the smoking wreck on the water that only a moment before had been part of their formation.

The pilot of *Desert Lilly*, also from the 376th, broke formation and procedures when he descended to circle what was left of *Wongo Wongo*. To what purpose he left the rest of the bombers is debated. There almost certainly were no survivors, and had there been he was in no position to render assistance. The crews carried no life rafts inside the bombers, and the closest landfall was in enemy hands. As it turned out *Desert Lilly* was unable to catch up to the rest of the formation and was left behind—a mission abort caused by poor judgment.

*   *   *

In books and other accounts written after the mission, it has been stated, and virtually accepted, that *Wongo Wongo* was carrying the lead navigator, and that the deputy lead navigator was aboard *Desert Lilly*. Thus, the implication is that the formation was left on its own without the lead or deputy navigator. Worse, some accounts hold that Colonel

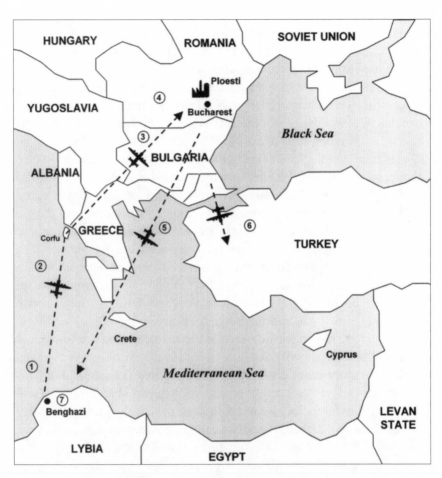

(1) Just after dawn, five bomb groups (44th, 93rd, 98th, 376th and 389th) get airborne from their bases in and around Benghazi, set formation, and head north across the Mediterranean;

(2) Prior to reaching the turn point at Corfu Island, for unknown reasons *Wongo Wongo* crashes into the sea. Contrary to published reports, this aircraft did *not have* the lead navigator aboard;

(3) Colonel John R. "Killer" Kane, at the head of the 98th Bomb Group, loses touch with the two lead groups (376th and 93rd). The 44th and 389th Bomb Groups are trapped behind him;

(4) The five bomb groups are heavily engaged in and around Ploesti by defending German and Romanian aircraft and gun batteries. Tremendous damage is inflicted on the refinery complexes;

(5) By afternoon, those aircraft still able to fly take various routes to Benghazi. They are engaged by fighters based in Romania, Bulgaria, and Greece;

(6) Many aircraft, short on fuel, damaged, or both, recover or crash in neutral Turkey;

(7) The last B-24 recovers at Benghazi after nightfall.

Compton, the pilot of the lead aircraft, *Teggie Ann,* on which General Ent was located, was positioned in the middle of the lead portion of the formation—protected by surrounding aircraft.

Colonel Compton refuted all of this in an interview conducted during 2000—fifty-seven years later—by Robert Sternfels who piloted the famous *The Sandman* on the TIDALWAVE mission. During the interview Compton said that from the very beginning of the mission, *Teggie Ann*, was the lead aircraft. Further, he reiterated that he was the commander of the 376th Bomb Group and was designated as the primary mission leader with the assigned responsibility of leading the entire formation of five bomb groups to the target. At no time was *Wongo Wongo* leading the formation, nor was *Desert Lilly* the second aircraft in the formation. Moreover, neither the lead navigator nor deputy lead navigator was aboard either ship. Colonel Compton identified Capt. Harold Wicklund—of the earlier Halpro mission—as the mission lead navigator aboard *Teggie Ann* with himself and General Ent.[2] Captain Wicklund verified this information to the author.[3]

Relative to the suggestion that he hid his aircraft in the formation, Colonel Compton strongly disagreed again, saying that he was perplexed at how the story was ever started. He stated that the information was "entirely incorrect," and that he did not try to protect himself or General Ent within the formation. He reemphasized his desire and responsibility to lead—and that the mission orders called for him to lead. Moreover, he said that General Ent would have never allowed himself to be given any special protection—particularly by hiding the airplane within the formation and "using other aircraft as a screen."[4]

*   *   *

After turning northeast at Corfu, Compton led the formation across Greece, Albania, Yugoslavia, and into Bulgaria. By this time, the enemy knew that a large American formation was airborne. German listening stations had intercepted and decoded information that the B-24s were airborne and en route. That information was refined further when the formation was spotted by German radar stations in Sicily and along the Adriatic coast. Reports from ground observers along the route strengthened the radar reports. Defenses were put on alert throughout the Mediterranean and southern Europe.

The Bulgarians, allied with Nazi Germany and warned by radar positioned in Sofia, attempted to intercept the B-24s. Six obsolete Czech-built Avia B-534 biplanes were launched from Vrazhdebna Airdrome near Sofia. Four more B-534s were sent airborne from a nearby airfield, Bozhurishte. Also scrambled for the intercept from the airfield at Karlovo were ten modern German-built, Bulgarian-piloted Me-109s.

The intercept was unsuccessful. The pilots of two B-534s did spot the column of heavy bombers as it headed north, but they were unable to chase it down. The remaining B-534s never made contact, and neither did the Me-109s. The Americans saw the B-534 biplanes and guessed that they were trainer aircraft.

By this time the American bomber formation was definitely not a secret. It is most likely that its target was no longer a secret either.

*   *   *

The five bomb groups, rather than flying as one unbroken column, slowly began to spread out. Distance built between the two leading groups and the others. This was not planned. Colonel Compton, who was leading the formation, set the power and airspeed in his airplane and expected the rest of the formation to stay with him. His experience led him to fly at higher airspeeds and power settings in order to take advantage of the attributes of the Davis Wing. These higher airspeeds caused the aircraft to fly in a level or even slightly nose-down attitude, rather than a slightly nose-up attitude. The higher power settings did increase fuel consumption but they also resulted in higher airspeeds that in turn netted greater range, or miles-per-gallon.

Colonel Kane was not a proponent of Compton's method, and in discussions before the mission had argued stubbornly against it. As it turned out, Kane, at the head of the 98th—the third group in the column—predictably used lower power settings and failed to keep up with Compton. He believed he was preserving the engines of his group's aircraft, as well as precious fuel. Regardless, he fell back—and he trapped the other two bomb groups—the 44th and the 389th—behind him. The separation grew worse as the formation approached the cloud-shrouded Balkan Mountains just before the Bulgarian border with Romania.

*   *   *

Previous histories have attributed much of the separation to the different techniques that the two separate formations used when penetrating the clouds over the Balkan Mountains. It has been written that Compton climbed the 376th and the 98th to 16,000 feet in order to clear the clouds. In so doing, he supposedly picked up a brisk tailwind and stretched the distance between the first two groups and the rest of the formation. In fact, Compton and others who were in the formation dispute this. In his interview with Sternfels, Compton asserted that he climbed no higher than 9,000 feet in order to conserve fuel. He then took the formation through the clouds as best he could.[5]

Kane later wrote that he climbed to 11,000 feet and also wound his way through the clouds.[6] If a tailwind existed, it is most likely that Kane's higher formation would have gotten a better push. In light of this information it is most likely that the separation within the overall formation was caused by the strong-willed Kane, who insisted on flying slower than Compton. Conjecture aside, it was Kane's responsibility to keep his place in the formation. He failed to do so.

*   *   *

Once across the Balkan Mountains and into the clear, Compton descended his formation. Knowing that Kane had dropped behind, he slowed and made a series of small turns in order to give the trailing groups an opportunity to close the distance. It didn't work. Kane had fallen too far behind. Compton's gunners reported to him that the trailing groups were not in sight.

Inasmuch as his weaving threatened to throw the lead formation into disarray, Compton gave up on rejoining the two halves and set to the task at hand. Across the Danube River and into Romania, he was now only 500 feet above the terrain. He pushed the throttles forward and increased his airspeed to 190 miles per hour.

Chapter 6

CHAOS

ASIDE FROM every other task involved in leading the mission against Ploesti, Colonel Compton actually had to *get* to Ploesti. To do this accurately was no small undertaking. Normally he would entrust this task entirely to his navigator, in this case Harold Wicklund. But because this mission was so important—and the low-level navigation so difficult—he also carried his own set of charts and other visual aids.

At a low level, one village, road intersection, or hilltop looks much like another. For this reason the heading and airspeed of the aircraft must be very carefully monitored against a predetermined time. Wind can also push an airplane off course, and corrections must be made to counter it.

Wicklund's problem had been made even more difficult by the series of small turns that Compton made after crossing over the Balkan Mountains. These turns, combined with the changes in airspeed that the formation had undergone, presented quite a navigational challenge.

Wicklund's working conditions were not particularly conducive to precision work. Inside the small glass nose of the bomber, he was shoehorned in with the lead bombardier Maj. Lynn Hester, two .50-caliber machine guns, ammunition cans, and flak vests, helmets, parachutes, and briefcases. He hardly had room to move. Working with his charts and instruments on a small plotting table proved particularly troublesome. Further, at low altitude on an August day with the sun high overhead, the glass compartment was more like a greenhouse than a crew station.

After crossing the Danube, the planned route called for the formation to continue on an easterly heading using the towns of Pitesti, Targovisti, and Floresti as navigational checkpoints. Throughout the flight Compton used charts and pictures to navigate, as well as information from Wicklund. His co-pilot, Capt. Ralph Thompson was at the controls for much of the time.

The formation continued to race at very low-level across the countryside. Gunners and pilots, bombardiers and navigators alike, returned the arm-swinging waves of people on the ground, who almost certainly had no idea what the formation was, or its purpose. Pilots and co-pilots maintained position as best they could against the propeller-churned air that was made even more unstable by naturally occurring wind and turbulence. Compton alternately studied his charts and the landscape as the miles raced underneath his aircraft—deeper and deeper into enemy territory.

Earlier, Wicklund had passed Compton an ETA for Floresti, the final checkpoint—or Initial Point—prior to the last turn directly toward the targets at Ploesti. Just as the clock ticked to Wicklund's ETA, Compton spotted a town that seemed to match descriptions of Floresti. With no time to deliberate, he made his decision and turned the formation to the final attack heading.[1]

It was a huge mistake.

Compton had turned too early—at Targovisti instead of Floresti. The formation was headed directly for Bucharest.

*   *   *

Various accounts and histories give conflicting reports of what actually happened. There are reports that other aircrew in the formation recognized the error immediately and called out over the radio to Compton. This is probably true, for Compton later said that since strict radio silence was to be observed, he was monitoring only his airplane's intercom and would not have heard any radio calls. But there was no dissent from anyone on his crew—including General Ent and Harold Wicklund—when he made the turn.

In the years since there has been much debate and some finger pointing about the reasons for the early turn at Targovisti. Some point to the loss of *Wongo Wongo* and *Desert Lilly* early in the mission. Both Compton and Wicklund refute this. In fact, Wicklund personally took

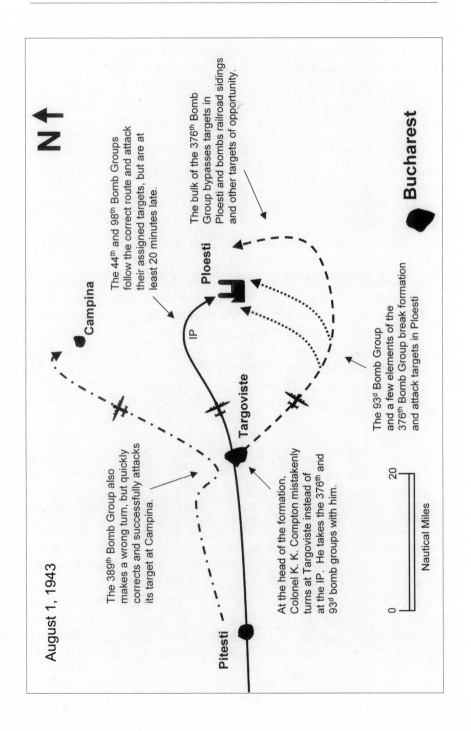

August 1, 1943

N↑

The 44th and 98th Bomb Groups follow the correct route and attack their assigned targets, but are at least 20 minutes late.

The bulk of the 376th Bomb Group bypasses targets in Ploesti and bombs railroad sidings and other targets of opportunity.

Campina

Ploesti

The 389th Bomb Group also makes a wrong turn, but quickly corrects and successfully attacks its target at Campina.

IP

Targoviste

The 93d Bomb Group and a few elements of the 376th Bomb Group break formation and attack targets in Ploesti

At the head of the formation, Colonel K. K. Compton mistakenly turns at Targoviste instead of at the IP. He takes the 376th and 93d bomb groups with him.

Pitesti

Bucharest

0   20

Nautical Miles

responsibility for the incorrect ETA, saying that he simply made a mistake. For his part, Compton insisted that as the mission leader he bore the responsibility.[2]

*   *   *

Compton pushed on. Intent on setting the formation up on the exact attack heading, it was several minutes before he realized his mistake. By this time the outskirts of Bucharest, the Romanian capital, were visible—as were the limp profiles of the many barrage balloons tethered above the city.

Compton turned to General Ent and told him that they had turned too early. There was no way to maneuver the huge formation back onto the correct heading in order to hit the assigned targets. He asked Ent for approval to order the aircraft in the formation to hit targets of opportunity. General Ent gave his consent, and Compton came up on the radio for the first time. It was his voice that gave the order to attack targets of opportunity.[3] Then, prior to reaching Bucharest, Compton turned north to Ploesti. Halfway back in the formation, Lt. Col. Addison Baker, at the head of the 93d, had already turned his group north.

*   *   *

Prior to the IP the bombers had flown normal route formations in boxes of six aircraft each, with three aircraft in a V formation to the front and three aircraft slightly offset to one side and behind in a similar grouping. But as they made the turn from the IP to the target they adjusted to a configuration that was broader than it was deep, with the trailing group moving forward and to one side. Only some twenty feet separated the wing tips of one bomber from the next. Approaching the targets, the boxes joined with other boxes to form a broader front. These formations were followed by other similar formations that gave the impression of waves of attacking bombers. The nature of these attacks made it difficult for individual airplanes to maneuver to avoid enemy fire or other airplanes, but ensured that the pattern of their bombs on the target would be effective.

*   *   *

By now the defenses in and around Ploesti had been alerted. Between German radio and radar contact, sightings over Bulgaria, and the spectacle created by the heavy bomber formation motoring from the Danube at extremely low altitude, the defenders of Ploesti knew that an attack was coming. And the possibility of an alert via German intelligence channels cannot be discounted.

The air defenses in place around Ploesti were among the very heaviest in the world. Under the stewardship of Luftwaffe Colonel Alfred Gerstenberg, the Germans and Romanians together had assembled nearly three hundred heavy and medium antiaircraft guns and thousands of smaller weapons. Augmenting these guns were more than one hundred carefully positioned barrage balloons. Aside from the deterrent effect created by the balloons themselves, they were made more deadly by small bombs suspended from them by cables. These cables were designed to ensnare an airplane so that the tethered bombs would detonate upon making contact.

Just as fearsome as the guns and balloons were the fighter aircraft stationed in defense of the refineries. Based at several airfields in and around Ploesti and Bucharest were more than two hundred Romanian and German fighters. German types included the latest models of the Me-109, as well as the Me-110. The Romanian units were also equipped with Me-109s, as well as indigenous IAR 80 single-engine fighters that, while not as capable as the Me-109s, were still dangerous foes.

In addition to these defenses, the enemy had taken passive protective measures. Smoke-making equipment had been installed to preclude attacking aircraft from pinpointing targets within the refinery area. This measure was designed to foil attacks from high altitude, in particular. And steps had been taken to alter the visual appearance of the refineries with paint and other camouflage in order to confuse the pilots of attacking aircraft.

The incoming Americans had no idea that the enemy defenses were as strong as they were. The intelligence annex for the mission confessed that there had "been no recent reports to determine the antiaircraft defenses of the target." It went on to declare that reliable sources indicated that there were fewer than one hundred heavy and medium antiaircraft guns in the entire target area. It also estimated that there were fewer than one hundred barrage balloons of "ordinary German type." As to fighter defenses, the intelligence annex allowed that there were six airfields in the area for defense of the refineries, and that both German and Romanian aircraft operated from those fields. It promised information on fighter strength prior to the mission.[4]

The intelligence annex made it a point to mention that neither the fighter or antiaircraft gun crews had been in action for more than a year, and that a "resultant decline in efficiency is to be expected." It went on to estimate that the defenses had been arrayed so as to protect against attacks from the east and northeast—presumably against raids by the Soviets. And the annex declared that no information had ever been received that the enemy had made provisions for a defense against a low-level daylight attack from the west. Perhaps the most misleading information was a statement that declared that the briefed course to the target had been devised to avoid all antiaircraft defenses en route, and similarly, the return course was not routed across defended areas.

In hindsight it is easy to see that launching an aerial reconnaissance sortie prior to the mission might have been a prudent move.

*   *   *

Immediately upon approaching the outskirts of Ploesti, the American bombers began coming under heavy fire. Lieutenant Colonel Baker and his co-pilot, Maj. John Jerstad—who had completed his combat tour and volunteered for the mission anyway, pressed doggedly north in *Hell's Wench*. They were breaking their formation away from Compton and Ent in an attempt to hit something worthwhile. As the attack developed, the target that Baker pointed his formation at was the Columbia Acquilla Refinery, originally assigned to a portion of the 44th.

Fire from antiaircraft guns of all calibers was intense and deadly. The shells of the larger guns were fused to detonate at point-blank range, while the smaller guns made up for their lack of size by putting up a curtain of fire. It seemed to come from everywhere; guns in open fields were even camouflaged as haystacks.

Early in the bomb run, unable to maneuver for fear of colliding with other aircraft in the formation, Baker and Jerstad severed a balloon cable. Next, the nose section took a direct hit, and the aircraft started to burn. Baker's *Hell's Wench* wasn't the only aircraft that took fire. Every bomber in the group was hit. Streams of flame trailed from stricken aircraft, while terrified aircrew jumped for their lives—their parachutes often not blossoming before they hit the earth. No one was immune to the wicked fire. Men were hit and fell at their stations, then were hit again and again. Aircraft were literally knocked into the ground and consumed within huge clouds of dust and smoke and fire.

The Americans gave it back. Their .50-caliber machine guns were devastating at close range. The dust and sparks kicked up by the heavy half-inch slugs sent frantic antiaircraft gun crews scurrying for cover. Stricken enemy gunners slumped at the stations where they were killed, and then were hurriedly pushed out of the way by replacements.

Baker and Jerstad knew that *Hell's Wench* had been mortally hit, but rather than putting their bomber down in the flat fields outside the complex, the two elected to continue to lead the formation. Unable to stay airborne with a full payload, Baker jettisoned his bombs and continued toward the target—miraculously maneuvering through, below, and among the refinery infrastructure. His bomb group—what was left of it—followed him through it all.

Finally, Baker and Jerstad cleared the refinery. The bombs of the 93d turned it into a flame and smoke choked inferno. *Hell's Wench* was also a mass of flames, yet it continued to take enemy fire. After absorbing one last heavy antiaircraft round, Baker tried to climb the aircraft high enough to allow his men to bail out. Some tried and tumbled to their deaths. Finally, the shot-up ship would hold together no longer. It fell off on a wing and plummeted to the ground, killing the remainder of the crew. For their courage far beyond the call of duty, both Addison Baker and John Jerstad were posthumously awarded the Medal of Honor.

Others also made the ultimate sacrifice—and their courage cannot be in doubt. One bomber, its wings sheared off, skidded down a Ploesti street and plowed into a women's prison, where it exploded and set the building afire. Another hit a barrage balloon and exploded. Still another mortally hit B-24 lurched into a climb while two crewmen bailed out. Suddenly the ship fell to the ground in a slow motion, blinding explosion. The two crewmen, suspended underneath their parachutes, fell flailing into the flames.

*   *   *

Ion Popa was a Romanian gun commander on that day. He and his crew had been bored and frustrated with the incessant drills and alarms they had endured during the previous week. But now it was for real.

At the first alarm they had readied themselves and pointed their guns skyward—ready for the big bombers. They were shocked then, when the great winged giants came in just above their heads. Popa's incredulity was stretched further when he saw red sand from the Libyan desert whipping out of the bomb bays of the American ships and onto his native Romania.

The bombs inside the B-24 bomb bays were easily visible as the Romanian crews opened fire at point-blank range. At a distance of less than two hundred feet—nearly face-to-face—Popa and his men engaged in a deadly shooting match with the American gunners. It seemed to him that the bombers were almost living beasts with real skin that ripped when torn by their shells.[5]

Popa prayed to God for safety from the terrifying ships. Terror and horror ran both ways at Ploesti on that day.

*   *   *

While Addison Baker was leading the main element of the 93rd against the Colombia Acquilla Refinery, the remainder of his bomb group—led by Maj. George Brown and Maj. Ramsey Potts—paralleled his course as they attacked the Astra Romano Refinery, originally assigned to the 98th Bomb Group. The men of this group also braved horrendous fire to drop their bombs on target. And at terrible cost. Only fifteen of the 93d Bomb Group's original thirty-nine B-24s actually cleared the target area.

*   *   *

In the meantime, Colonel Compton and the aircraft of the 376th Bomb Group had dispersed to hit targets of opportunity. Only one small group, led by Maj. Norman Appold, managed to carry off a concentrated attack against a worthwhile target. Appold's flight of only five aircraft hit the Concordia Vega complex so hard that an estimated 40 percent of the refinery was destroyed.

Ion Rotaru, a worker at the Vega complex, saw the bombers coming in over the River Teleajen. A group of ships separated and headed straight for the refinery. At barely one hundred feet above the ground, every detail of the B-24s was visible to Rotaru. He was spellbound by the sight of antiaircraft fire punching sprays of fuel out of the flying ships and the subsequent spectacular fires that literally burned them, one by one, out of the sky.[6]

*   *   *

The 376th, because most of its crews hit targets outside of the complex or simply jettisoned their bombs and did not become subject to the worst of the enemy fire, lost only two aircraft.

*   *   *

The bombs being carried on the mission were a combination of 500- and 1000-pound high explosive bombs and smaller incendiary devices. The high explosive bombs were intended to destroy large structures by brute, inflammable concussion. The incendiary sticks were last-minute additions. The crews were supposed to fling them out of the roaring bombers by hand. They were intended to ignite fuel and oil spilled free by the larger bombs. The majority of the bombs, by weight, were the larger 500- and 1000-pound bombs.

These large bombs were variously fused. Some were fused to detonate instantaneously on impact, while others were designed to detonate at intervals of 45 seconds to several hours after being released. The intent of the delayed fuses was to make fire fighting and bomb disposal difficult for the enemy; it being particularly unnerving to operate with the knowledge that an unseen bomb might explode at any moment.

*   *   *

The trailing formation of three groups led by Colonel Kane arrived at the scene just as the first formation was reforming for the perilous return trip. Unlike Compton, Kane had flown to the correct initial point at Floresti, and in so doing had made up a bit of time while Compton's formation was flailing about on the outskirts of Bucharest.

Kane's run-in to the target from Floresti with his 98th Bomb Group measured about fifteen miles on a southeasterly heading. Just a few hundred yards to the southwest, Col. Leon Johnson had pulled his 44th Bomb Group alongside Kane's 98th. Between them, paralleling their course was a railroad on which the Germans operated a flak train. This flak train was equipped with antiaircraft cannon of heavy and light calibers. It was designed to be a sort of mobile, or roving, antiaircraft battery that could be quickly dispatched to "hot spots." Putting its guns into battery required little preparation when compared to a gun unit that had to be towed from place to place by truck or horse.

The flak train at Ploesti made Kane's and Johnson's attack hellish. Because its crew had received enough warning, the German train had a good head of steam when the American aircraft arrived, and it did its best to run with the two bomb groups. The gunners aboard the train let loose with everything they had—hardly needing to aim. The American bombers were so big, so close, and so low that they were difficult to miss. Even worse for the Americans was that the speed of the train made the relative speed of the bombers appear preposterously slow. The duel with the train was a slow motion nightmare.

It *was* a duel because the gunners aboard the big bombers fought back with their .50-caliber machine guns. So close was the train that the gunners aboard the bombers were able to pour their own withering fire back into the guns mounted on each one of the railroad cars. Finally, between Kane's and Johnson's gunners riddling the track-mounted monster from either side, the locomotive's boiler was blown, and the Train from Hell was left behind.

* * *

The deadly crossfire of .50-caliber slugs that the B-24s used with such effectiveness against the enemy probably took a toll on friendly crews and aircraft as well. Though the gunners had been trained against it, it can be argued that in the heat of battle with aircraft just barely under control and fired on from all directions, that there undoubtedly were streams of slugs put into accompanying bombers. Under such conditions—outside the realm of sanity—it would be a miracle if there had been no damage caused by friendly fire.

* * *

Kane could see that his assigned target, the Astra Romana complex, was already belching smoke and flame, and he realized that for whatever reason it had been hit by aircraft from either the 376th or 93d. Regardless, he knew that it would be impossible to keep his formation together if he switched to a different target and he decided to add his group's bombs to the burning maelstrom.

First Lieutenant Robert Sternfels was the pilot of *The Sandman*, an aircraft in Kane's 98th. Farther back in the formation, he and co-pilot 1st Lt. Barney Jackson were doing their best to keep their bomber upright.

The prop wash from preceding aircraft was so violent that they had to move their control yokes from stop to stop just to maintain control. More than once Sternfels looked down to see the bottom of his control yoke and the placard that read: THIS CONTROL WHEEL IS UPSIDE DOWN.[7]

Dead ahead he spotted a silvery balloon cable silhouetted against the black smoke pouring out of the stricken refinery. Unable to maneuver for fear of running into other aircraft in the formation, Sternfels could do little more than kick his aircraft's rudders to keep the cable from slicing into the nose of *The Sandman*. The propeller on his number-three engine caught and severed the cable. Portions of the steel strand wrapped itself around the propeller hub, while another long section broke loose and sliced through the thin-skinned fuselage. Fortunately no one was hurt.

Sternfels watched the ships at the head of the formation disappear into the mass of black smoke and bright orange flames that marked the refinery complex. It was horrific to behold; the big bombers were slugging their way through the defensive fire, dodging falling wingmen, and steering clear of burning wrecks, only to throw themselves headlong into a towering, burning hell. One pilot's memory was forever scarred by the sight of bodies blasted through the air by the explosion of their own bomber.

The black-and-orange horror boiled hundreds of feet above them like an all-consuming specter. Sternfels could only gape wild-eyed while he fought to keep his bomber on course. Within seconds it was his turn to penetrate the fearsome cloud. He and Jackson pulled back on *The Sandman's* controls to clear the wall around the complex, and at the same time hoped that they would miss obscured towers and aircraft. Once in the blackness, they winced against the flashes of exploding bombs. The bombs dropped by preceding B-24s were armed with delayed fuses and were only just now detonating. This was one of the greatest tragedies associated with the mission—B-24s were lost to the detonating bombs of earlier aircraft.

In the thick of the smoke, Sternfels' bombardier, 1st Lt. David Palaschek, released the bombs. The entire crew knew when the bombs were away, because the ship seemed to leap—as it was suddenly lightened. *The Sandman* broke into the clear seconds later and Sternfels started a climbing turn to join on Colonel Kane's ship, *Hail Columbia*. As he did so, *The Sandman* was caught on film by an automatic camera installed aboard 1st Lt. Donald Johnson's airplane, *Sneezy*. The resultant image is one of the most enduring and evocative of the entire conflict.[8] It shows *The Sandman* racing away from the burning wreck that was the Astra Romana refinery. The viewer is left on his own to reckon how the aircraft made its way through the fiery maelstrom.

* * *

Ion Nan was a worker at the Astra Romana refinery that day. He remembered that the big B-24s had a star with five corners, and mistakenly wondered how the Russians could have the technology to build such aircraft? He climbed in a fellow engineer's motorcycle sidecar and together they raced out of the complex to escape the bombing. In the Prahova River they spotted a wounded American airman who was stuck in his parachute and near drowning. They pulled him out of the river and took him to a local hospital so that he could be treated for his burns. Nan was touched when the American tried to thank him by giving the Romanian his fountain pen. He told the battered flyer to keep the pen; he would need it to write letters to his family.[9]

* * *

While Kane's 98th was running toward its target, Johnson's 44th was also brutalized as it raced into the defenses protecting the Columbia Acquilla refinery. The running horror that the crew aboard *Sad Sack II* experienced illustrates the savagery that was typical of the run into the target. Piloted by 1st Lt. Henry Lasco and 1st Lt. Joseph Kill, *Sad Sack II* was inbound at only fifty feet with the rest of the formation when one of the waist gunners was struck in the thigh. He made a move to bail out, but reconsidered when he realized the nearby treetops were level with his position.

Soon after, just before bomb release, the tail gunner was shot dead. Only a moment later—inside the blackness and fire overhead the target—the bombs were dropped and the navigator was struck by a large caliber round that tore away his chest. Also by now, the number-two engine had been shot out and feathered.

Bursting clear of the conflagration, Lasco and Kill manhandled the bomber toward a formation of six ships ahead of them. Once again under intense fire, the top turret gunner and the radio operator were hit. While trying to bring their badly vibrating ship into the protective formation of the other bombers, *Sad Sack II* was attacked from the rear by a pack of

Me-109s. The gunners aboard the stricken ship scored some hits, but they took a beating as well. One of the legs of the other waist gunner—who had not been wounded up to this point—was nearly torn off by an enemy shell.

Sad Sack II was a flying wreck. Both Lasco and Kill knew that there was no way it would make the trip back to Benghazi. It was increasingly difficult to control, ammunition on board was on fire and cooking off, and it was holed in dozens of places. Worse, most of the crew was wounded or dead. The two pilots looked for a place to put the big bomber down.

It was then that an Me-109 circled around and attacked from the forward quarter. Lasco's face and jaw were shot through and he fell over his control wheel. While the gunners battled against enemy fighters who would give no quarter, Kill flew the airplane into a cornfield. The mortally damaged bomber crumpled into pieces and caught fire as it crashed to a halt.

Kill, who had been relatively unharmed to this point, sustained two broken legs. In shock and suffering from wounds, the crewmen who were still alive managed to pull each other from what was left of their bomber. As they stumbled around the wreck, injured and badly burned, the crewmen were variously beaten, stoned, and robbed by Romanian peasants. Finally, cooler heads prevailed among the local populace and the Americans were rounded up and eventually given medical treatment.[10]

Colonel Johnson lost nine of the sixteen bombers he led over the Colombia Acquilla complex.

* * *

The enemy fighters had finally thrown themselves into the fray in significant numbers. Romanian and German units had been on alert for several hours while the inbound B-24 formation was tracked. As the list of potential targets was narrowed by the big bombers' progress, the levels of alert were intensified. When Colonel Compton dropped the lead formation down the northern side of the mountains lining the border between Bulgaria and Romania, German radar units in Bulgaria lost their track. Their counterparts, watching from near Bucharest and Ploesti, were unable to pick up Compton's formation. The big bombers were too low and still too distant. It was during this time that the nervous air defense officers in Bucharest and Ploesti gave their fighter echelons permission to launch.

The Romanian units—equipped mostly with IAR 80s—took off from their bases at Pepira and Taxeroul and immediately stationed themselves overhead Bucharest. The exact target was still unknown but they were anxious to defend their own capital. The Germans—equipped with Me-109s and Me-110s—climbed out of their bases at Mizil and Zilistea and put themselves into position to defend the oil complex at Ploesti. The Romanians and Germans were each protecting their own priorities.

All of the defending fighters went high. Smart's planners had been right: The German radar that guarded Ploesti was unable to pick up the low-level bombers. And the Axis fighters sent aloft to protect Ploesti and Bucharest were looking for the Americans at altitude; for who had ever heard of a low-level attack by heavy bombers? American strategists had been unbending in their commitment to high-altitude, precision bombing.

Ground observers frantically called the fighter controllers to warn of the low-level attack. The fighter controllers in turn tried to get through the chaos on the airwaves to their fighter leaders. They had little success. High above a cloud layer the pilots of more than fifty German Me-109s were a frustrated lot. Despite all the radio traffic, despite the fact that the Americans were obviously in and around Ploesti, they couldn't find them. The Romanian IAR 80 pilots were having better success; by now they had dropped down on Lieutenant Colonel Baker's formation as it turned north away from Bucharest toward Ploesti.

Finally, the German fighter formation dropped down below the clouds and spotted the explosions that were beginning to wrack the refineries. It was then that someone cried out that the bombers were down "deep." And against all odds, they were indeed. The Axis fighters screamed down to catch the first Americans coming off of the target.

The Germans actually got the worst of the first pass. Two of the Me-109s were cut down by the fusillade of .50-caliber fire put up by the retreating bombers. But the fight didn't stay one-sided for long. As the integrity of the American defensive formations began to break up under continued ground and aerial fire, the fighters switched tactics and teamed up in smaller packs to hunt down and kill straggling B-24s. The Me-109s concentrated on cripples and aircraft outside of protective formations, and soon began to score. By now the delineation of effort by the different types and services had muddied, and fighters of all types were swarming the bombers like sharks after bloody prey. Romanian fighters mixed with their German counterparts in a deadly free-for-all.[11]

By this time the Germans and Romanians had ordered every flyable aircraft into the air, in part because they were unsure about American intentions toward their airdromes. As German and Romanian aircraft of all types flushed from their various bases the scene took on the look of an African stampede. Huge, elephantine B-24s madly stormed out of the target area, pursued by the lion-like fighters. The other types—transports, trainers, and spotter aircraft—wildly flung themselves clear of the path, hoping to avoid the wicked crossfire that flew between the bombers and fighters.

*   *   *

Leading the other portion of Colonel Johnson's 44th Bomb Group was Lt. Col. James Posey. Posey was tasked with hitting the Creditul Minier Refinery in Brazi, just south of Ploesti. This was Blue Target. The refinery was particularly important because of its capacity to produce high-octane aircraft gasoline. To take it out, Posey was actually assigned a larger share of the 44th than Johnson; he had twenty-one bombers.

Unlike Kane and Johnson, Posey's ingress to the target didn't take him within range of the dreaded flak train; his route was further to the southwest. Also, unlike the other two leaders, Posey didn't have to hit a target that had already been stirred up. The Creditul Minier refinery was unmolested and only the comparatively wispy veil from smoke pots hung over the complex. His attack was one that would actually resemble the plan that Colonel Smart and his staff had developed.

Although Posey didn't have to treat with the deadly flak train, he and his formation still came under fire from defensive positions. In his own ship, *V for Victory,* one of the waist gunners was killed on the run to the target. Other bombers were also hit.

With a precision that mirrored their practice strikes at Benghazi, the pilots of the 44th aligned their bombers on their assigned targets. The practices and drills and study were paying off. Lifting up to clear parts of the complex, the crews made final adjustments before dropping their 1,000-pound bombs dead on target. Once clear, they pushed back down to the deck and raced for home. Posey's wave lost none of its twenty-one bombers on the run to the target. Only two were lost on the dash for home—these to a combination of fighters and ground fire.

Posey's attack gave a glimpse of what might have been. Making the run to their assigned target—one that hadn't been previously hit—his crews struck the complex so accurately that it was taken completely out of the war. It gave some amount of credibility to Smart's plan.

*   *   *

The last bomb group in the second formation was the 389th. It wasn't going to Ploesti. Instead, the twenty-nine aircraft of the 389th led by Col. Jack Wood were under orders to strike Red Target—the Steaua Romana refinery at Campina, eighteen miles northwest of Ploesti. Among some of the crews of the 389th there was hope that this complex—located away from the main concentration of refineries—would be less fiercely defended than the others.

Wood, like Compton nearly a half-hour previously, was deceived by the town of Targoviste. Confused by various landscape features, and a cloud layer that covered the tops of prominent hills, he turned too early and headed southeast toward Bucharest. The rest of his bomb group obediently followed. Several crewmen in the formation recognized the error yet did not break the strict radio silence that their leaders had mandated.

It wasn't until Wood's group had covered several miles that he realized his mistake. Without hesitating he lifted his aircraft and turned northeast to clear the ridge that separated him from the valley that contained his route to Campina. Again, his well-disciplined warriors followed without a word. Once clear of the ridge Wood turned back to the southeast and settled his thundering formation only a few feet above the valley floor. The refinery was dead ahead.

Like Posey's attack a few minutes earlier on the Creditul Minier refinery, Wood's strike on the Steaua Romana complex was taking place according to plan. The axis of attack was what the men had practiced in Libya, and moreover their target had not been struck by any of the earlier errant groups. All of this made it easier for the crews to find and concentrate on their specific aiming points.

Unlike their practice flights, though, the air around them was ripped with antiaircraft fire. Wood's ship, piloted by Capt. Kenneth Caldwell, bore past and over the blazing enemy guns. His own gunners replied in kind. At only thirty feet above the ground, Wood's bombardier, John Fino, put a single delayed-fuse bomb into a boiler house, and then dropped the rest into secondary targets. The boiler house, which was volatile in its own right, exploded almost immediately just from the kinetic impact of the bomb. The bomb itself would not explode for nearly another full hour.

* * *

Here, as at the other targets, secondary damage caused by the bombers was extensive. The massive oil storage tanks that made up such a significant part of the various complexes were not specifically targeted, as their destruction would only deny the enemy the oil stored within—just a few days' worth of production. Those portions of the plants that actually refined the fuel were much more important.

Nevertheless, many of the storage tanks were destroyed. They proved to be surprisingly thin-skinned, and therefore susceptible to armor-piercing and incendiary rounds from the bombers' .50-caliber guns. Once afire, the tanks often exploded, literally blowing their tops into the paths of trailing bombers. This flying debris was as deadly to the aircraft as the aimed fire of the enemy gunners.

* * *

Following Wood was a B-24 piloted by 1st Lt. Lloyd Hughes. In the run just prior to the target, Hughes's ship was hit and began to spew a huge quantity of fuel from one of its bomb bay tanks. Penned in the middle of the group, Hughes opted to press on with his bomb run rather than try to slide clear and risk collision with the other aircraft in the formation. Facing a huge wall of fire created by proceeding bombers, Hughes drove steadfastly on, no doubt aware that his aircraft would soon become a flaming torch.

Hughes flew into the inferno, saw to business, and after his bombs were released steered clear of the rest of the group. His B-24 was a mass of high-octane flames. Still under control he winged the burning bomber into a dry riverbed intent on giving his crew a chance to escape. Just prior to touchdown the right wingtip struck the ground and sent his B-24 cartwheeling. Miraculously, two men survived the explosion to become prisoners of the Romanians.

For his heroics, Hughes was posthumously awarded the Medal of Honor.

*   *   *

Hughes's wasn't the only heroism on display from the 389th that day. Each crew rode the hail of fire into the inferno that the refinery had become. And nearly every ship had the wounds to show for it—engines shot out and great holes and rips throughout. The damage wasn't confined to the bombers, though; many men were also shot up, bleeding and dying inside the lumbering aircraft. One wounded co-pilot flew his airplane alone—after the pilot's head was torn away by an enemy shell.

*   *   *

The 389th's Earl Zimmerman, the young radioman who the night before felt he'd seen his share of tough missions, now had another one to tuck under his belt. On the run to the target—with no duties as the radioman—he was assigned to the bomb bay. The doors had a tendency to creep closed; if this occurred, a design interlock prevented the bombs from dropping. Keeping one eye on the doors, Zimmerman blazed away at whatever targets he could see with an old Springfield bolt-action rifle. He had no intention of sitting on his hands while it seemed that the rest of the world was shooting at him.[12]

Zimmerman's crew was part of the last three-ship element to cross the Steaua Romana complex that day. The bombardier, TSgt Grover Edmiston, salvoed their bombs directly into the assigned target. Shattered by the impact alone, the building was turned to rubble when the delayed-fused bombs exploded forty-five seconds later.

Coming off the target Zimmerman was horrified when he caught sight of Lieutenant Hughes's ship exploding in the riverbed. A few minutes later, Zimmerman's pilot and copilot—1st Lt. Harold James and 1st Lt Robert Schwellinger—joined on the only other bomber they could catch, *Hitler's Hearse*. Its pilot, Capt. Robert Mooney, was dead. The bombardier, Rockly Triantafullu, sent a message by Aldis lamp from the waist gunner's window: "Pilot dead, wounded on board, request heading for Turkey." Zimmerman signaled back the requested information, and both ships set course for Turkey.

*   *   *

In all, six of Colonel Wood's bombers failed to return. But the destruction they had dealt was devastating. The Steaua Romana refinery was not returned to operation until after the war. Again, like Posey's attack on the Creditul Minier complex, the validity of Colonel Smart's plan was vindicated, at least in part.

Chapter 7

EGRESS

THE 389TH'S *Vagabond King* piloted by John McCormick was the last B-24 across a target at Ploesti on August 1, 1943.[1] After dropping his load on Red Target, McCormick joined the rest of the retreating bombers in their pell-mell rush to get out of Europe. It was not an orderly withdrawal. Damage and fuel leaks caused many ships to fall behind, whereas others simply became lost in the smoke and fire and confusion that bedeviled them on the way into and out of the target. Enemy fighters and antiaircraft batteries continued to dog and break up formations of the lumbering American ships.

In the end, B-24s from various groups bunched together to afford each other mutual protection and support for the long return trip. That trip was at least 1,200 miles and for many crews the biggest question was whether or not their aircraft had the fuel or stamina to make it. Many of the ships had burned more fuel than planned during their low-level dash into and out of the target. Others had lost fuel because of holed gas tanks.

Fuel concerns aside, the bombers that had lost one or more engines were in an even more desperate gamble—their fate hung on the reliability of the remaining powerplants. It wasn't a good bet; if one engine was gone, the others had to work harder to make up for the loss. Because they were working harder the remaining engines consumed more fuel and oil, and were subject to greater wear and tear—and subsequently were more likely to fail themselves. It was a snowball effect that would be exacerbated by the climb across the mountains of Bulgaria, Yugoslavia and Greece. Once across the mountains, there were hundreds of miles of featureless water to navigate to safety.

*   *   *

And there were more fighters. Aside from the German and Romanian aircraft that were still harrying them as they fled the target area, the B-24s would have to face a gauntlet of defenses that had been readied for their return trip. First in line were the Bulgarian forces that had been frustrated by their lack of success at intercepting the bombers during the northbound leg of their mission. They did not want to be embarrassed again.

This time the Bulgarians put more than fifty Avia biplanes into the air. Augmenting them was a much smaller number of Me-109s. The mountains around the Bulgarian capital of Sofia were obscured in part by a shroud of cumulus clouds and towering thunder heads. This cover provided some protection for the Americans against the enemy biplane fighters that struggled to make contact. But, the Avias were ultimately able to fly themselves into a position from where they could make a high-side attack.

Down they came, technological vestiges of the last war, firing their light machine guns against the great ships. It was an incongruous picture; the braced biplanes rat-a-tat-tatted at the Davis-winged, four-engine giants with little effect. Predictably, though they scored many hits, the Avias caused little injury. Their guns just didn't carry enough punch. Conversely, the heavier guns of the B-24s caused quite a bit of damage to the attacking Bulgarians, several of whom did not return to their bases.

Once through with their firing pass, the first formation of Avias was finished. The dated fighters simply did not possess the performance to set up for another attack. But a second group of biplanes had worked itself into position for a pass at the bombers. Again, the Avias scored some hits with their light machine guns but failed to inflict any mortal damage. Like the first group of Avias, the second was unable to get into position to mount another attack.[2]

The Bulgarians weren't done though. From overhead Sofia in his Me-109, Lt. Stoyan Stoyanov spotted the formation of American bombers. He had been sent to Germany during the late 1930s and had impressed his German instructors with his instinctual flying skills. Now, in 1943, he was one of the most experienced pilots in the Bulgarian military, but still he had yet to see combat.

Stoyanov was struck by the cumbersome appearance of the B-24s. "Like big, fat birds," he remembered them. His first instinct was to let them pass unmolested, as they did not appear inclined to attack Sofia. But after a moment's hesitation he decided to press an attack, as there was no guarantee in his mind that they wouldn't turn toward the city and dump any unexpended bombs.

With his wingman in tow, Stoyanov increased his airspeed and overtook the American bombers from behind. As he closed the distance he was surprised to see that they were large, four-engine aircraft, rather than the two-engine types he had expected. He noted that the bombers tightened their formation as they caught sight of him and his wingman. This being his first combat encounter, Stoyanov hesitated as he took in the awesome sight of eighteen heavy bombers in close battle formation. As he came within range, the gunners on board the American planes took him under fire. Deadly tracer rounds narrowly missed his fighter, and Stoyanov slid to one side, out of range, and started a climb.

"I felt my heart starting to beat strongly; some cold sweat has appeared on my face. My wish to attack was now becoming less eager. I felt that I had not sufficient strength inside me." He was like a lion that had cornered a herd of angry, wounded elephants—unsure of exactly what he had gotten into. He wanted to turn away, but his honor wouldn't let him.

Finally, steeling himself for what he knew his duty demanded, Stoyanov pushed ahead of the B-24s, then swung sharply around into a head-on attack. The clouds were thickening and his window of opportunity was shrinking rapidly. It wouldn't be long before the American formation would be able to hide in the safety of the darkening weather.

Stoyanov singled out the lead B-24 and simultaneously opened fire with his 20mm cannon and 7.62mm machine guns. "I press triggers and watch how my gunshots are making fire traces and sink in the glass nose of the heavy bomber." But the B-24 was not accepting the attack passively. "I throw fire balls to the nose of the big plane, which is approaching me, and the same fire balls immediately come back on me. Some of them pass very close to my plane but still do not touch it." The Bulgarian pilot broke off his attack at the last possible moment and passed just over the top of the B-24—stitching it from front to rear as he did so.

Anxious to clear out of the American formation as quickly as possible, Stoyanov knifed over onto his side, then dropped down into a vertical dive. Looking back he saw his target plummeting toward earth. Unnerved by the attack he leveled off, then climbed into the safety of some nearby clouds, where he was able to catch his breath.[3]

The ship he had hit was *The Witch*, from Kane's 98th piloted by Julian Darlington. Miraculously, Darlington was able to maintain enough control to minimize the crash. None of his crew was killed, including three men who had bailed out on the way down.

The crew of *Prince Charming* was not so fortunate. Also part of the 98th, it was caught up in the same attack. Piloted by James Gunn, *Prince Charming* was brought down by another Me-109 piloted by Peter Bochev. The big bomber went down in flames and surrendered only one survivor—the tail gunner.[4] It was the second and last bomber lost that day to the neophyte Bulgarian fighter crews.

*   *   *

But the Bulgarians' German allies weren't finished yet. Controllers in Greece had been monitoring the progress of the American bombers for several hours. Now, as a sizable formation of B-24s made its way across the mountains towards the Ionian Sea, a flight of ten Me-109s was readied for intercept. With typical German precision the fighters were launched from the aerodrome at Kalamaki so as to make contact at the point that would allow them the maximum time in combat.

The German fighter leader, Lieutenant Burk, brought his fighters to the pre-plotted position and intercepted the American bombers just as planned. This was the same formation that had been hit by the Bulgarian Avias and Me-109s—a mixed bag from several different bomb groups. Rather than attack immediately, Burk paralleled the bombers' course until he had time to look the Americans over. They were a sorry-looking bunch. Holed and ragged, some with engines out, they were limping along, clinging together for mutual support.

Satisfied with what he saw, Burk dove out of the sun ahead of four other fighters. The Americans were ready. They opened fire and drew first blood, shredding one of the Me-109s and forcing its pilot to bail out.

Nevertheless, one of the B-24s was also hit and slowly fell out of formation toward the sea. It was not seen again.

The Germans mounted a second attack. This time they targeted the ship piloted by Ned McCarty. His airplane, damaged earlier by the Bulgarian Avias, now received mortal hits from the deadlier German machines. It, too, fell out of formation. Though parachutes were seen, no survivors from McCarty's ship were ever recovered.

After this second attack, Burk turned his fighters loose to attack as opportunities presented themselves. German aircraft flung themselves at the big bombers from all directions. Another ship caught fire and went down into the water. This time there were no parachutes. The Americans exploded one more Me-109 before the Germans mortally wounded another bomber. The ship piloted by Reginald Carpenter was unable to stay airborne on two engines and after a time executed a controlled ditching. Though one man was seriously injured, eight of the ten-man crew managed to escape the broken ship and were picked up by an Air-Sea Rescue craft more than a day later.

Finally, after knocking four of the American ships out of the sky, the Germans broke off the attack and headed for their home, low on fuel. The engagement had cost them only two fighters. Meanwhile, what was left of the American formation hunkered down for the last leg home; it seemed to them that the mission would never end.[5]

*   *   *

It was the longest bombing mission undertaken to date. Eight or more hours after launching, most of the B-24s were still airborne—a crippled string of flying hulks that ranged from the Balkans, across the eastern Mediterranean, and even into Turkey. And even after being aloft for so long, most of the bombers were still several hours or more from landing. Or crash-landing.

Most of the bombers had sustained some sort of damage; and many of the crews on those same ships were nursing wounded. John McCormick, piloting *Vagabond King,* had a wounded radioman onboard. Coming out of Ploesti, he teamed up with several other damaged bombers—wingmen of opportunity—and helped escort them to Turkey. Once into neutral territory he angled away from the other B-24s, changed course to the southeast, and made for Cyprus alone. There the British maintained airfields that could handle his stricken heavy bomber.

Having survived the nightmare at Ploesti, McCormick nearly lost his plane and crew to fuel-transfer problems while scraping over the mountains of Turkey. All four engines stopped suddenly, then started again, then stopped once more. *Vagabond King* was nothing more than a winged, whistling box. Worse, McCormick had nowhere to set it down. Fortunately, David Shattles, McCormick's crew chief, was able to work some magic with the B-24's complex system of fuel valves. With little time to spare, the four engines rattled back to life and the *Vagabond King* just narrowly escaped crashing into the mountains.[6]

Not all the retreating bombers that took that route would be so fortunate. The crews of eight bombers were either killed or interned in Turkey. Ironically some of them were intercepted and forced to land by Turkish airmen in American-built P-40s.

At least a hundred similar stories were unfolding at the same time. Most of the crews struck out for Benghazi—their starting point. For every one of them, fuel was a worry. Most of them throttled back their engines to a point where the aircraft was just barely hanging in the air. To lighten their weight and save fuel, many crews threw out everything that wasn't necessary to keep the bombers flying. First to go were the guns. Many of the men were terrified of parting with their only means of defense. The weapons had stood them in good stead in the target area and beyond; if they were dumped overboard the aircraft would be defenseless. Nevertheless, the guns and their associated hardware were heavy—nearly a hundred pounds apiece. As the chances of being jumped by enemy fighters diminished with every mile, most of the heavy weapons literally went out the window. Along with the guns went just about anything that wasn't fastened down—ammo, oxygen bottles, etc. And fire axes were wielded against much of what was fastened down; if it didn't keep the bomber airborne, it came apart and went over the side.

*   *   *

McCormick, in *Vagabond King,* finally cleared Turkey's southern coast. After briefly considering putting the bomber down on one of the beaches, McCormick continued for Cyprus, nearly a hundred miles further south. He wasn't certain that there was enough fuel aboard to make it. Worse, his navigator was working with an old schoolbook map. The crews hadn't been issued aeronautical charts for that part of the Mediterranean. And it was getting dark.

McCormick could hear other aircraft—all in some measure of distress—making calls over the radio. After making a wrong turn toward what he thought was the island but what turned out to be a mirage of clouds and shadows, he began to despair of finding any land at all. Then, as it grew darker, he spotted the airport beacon at Nicosia. After exchanging signals with the control tower he brought his bomber into the unfamiliar field and safely set it down on the upward-sloping runway. The quiet that followed the shutdown of the bomber's engines once it cleared the landing path was eerie. Their roar had been a constant reassuring companion. Now, after bearing the big bomber aloft for more than fourteen hours they were disquietingly silent.[7]

Killer Kane followed McCormick. With one engine feathered and his plane shot up, Kane misjudged the approach and smashed his aircraft into the dirt before he even made the runway. No one was injured and a different runway was put into service. More bombers were able to follow the first two aircraft into the airfield.

*   *   *

Within a couple of hours Kane and his men were guests of the RAF at one of the island's finer dining establishments. For the crew, the incongruity between the dining club and the conflagration at Ploesti was surreal; their clothes and skin still stank of the battle, and their combat-shocked demeanor and weariness contrasted sharply with the soft furnishings of their surroundings. Dead-tired and no doubt suffering from some degree of shock, some of them fell asleep where they sat.

*   *   *

Other bombers made their way to Sicily and Malta. A number of them went down in the water, where some crews were saved and others were not. The first ship back to the Benghazi complex was Colonel Compton's *Teggie Anne,* with General Ent aboard. Following the egress from Ploesti, Ent had dispatched a radio message indicating that the mission had been a success, but the command echelon back in Libya—Brereton and his staff, along with Colonel Smart and others—had nothing else to go on. The RAF was reporting a huge number of distress calls from B-24s over the Mediterranean, so it was obvious that the mission had been a rough one.

Both Compton and Ent were subdued. Separated as they were from the rest of the formation they were as yet unsure as to exactly how the mission had unfolded. They did know that it hadn't gone according to plan and that losses had been extraordinary. Reactions from other crews were varied. Some tumbled out of their ships, furious at their leaders for what had happened. Others were in tears. The wounded were stoic, exhausted, or unconscious. The dead could show no emotion as they were pulled out of the bombers—sometimes in pieces.

The last bomber reached Benghazi sixteen hours after taking off. The *Liberty Lad*—with two engines out on one wing, no hydraulics, no brakes and no instrument lighting—touched down in the darkness and coasted for a mile before coming to a stop. The hulking, broken beast that was *Liberty Lad* was the perfect metaphor to mark the end of what was truly a watermark in the history of military aviation. The longest, bloodiest, most heroic bombing mission in history was over.

Chapter 8

ASSESSMENTS

ANY DISCUSSION about the August 1, 1943, low-level bombing raid against Ploesti eventually necks down to one obvious question: was it worth it?

The question will never be answered to the satisfaction of everyone. Within a few weeks of the attack it was estimated that approximately 40 percent of the refining capacity at Ploesti had been taken out of service. This level of effectiveness was particularly impressive despite the fact that two of the targeted complexes—the Romana Americana and the Unirea—were not even hit. Nevertheless, by the time a consensus had been reached as to the amount of damage caused—only a matter of weeks after the attack—Ploesti was producing more fuel than it had before the strike.

How could this be? First, the Romanians and Germans went to work with a brilliance and energy that underscored the Axis's priority on petroleum production. Throughout Hitler's Reich, first priority for parts and expertise was given to the effort. Pipes and lines from damaged components were rerouted to operational sections until repairs could be completed. Older, idled equipment was either brought back into service or cannibalized. Existing reserves were tapped to ensure that flow was uninterrupted, and production at undamaged portions of the complex was simply speeded up. And the Germans had thousands of slave laborers at hand to remove debris and perform other menial but essential chores.

Perhaps most important to the recovery effort was Gerstenberg's matrix of pipelines that interconnected much of the complex. This made the rerouting of petroleum from one plant to another markedly less chaotic than it would otherwise have been. This system of pipes, above ground though it was, was perhaps more susceptible to damage, but it was eminently more repairable than an underground system would have been.

Rather than bombing the Ploesti operation to a standstill, the net effect of the raid—after a period of only a few short weeks—was an increase in fuel production for Hitler's war machine. But it did come at a price. The repairs put into place were a patchwork of ad hoc fixes that met the needs of the moment but were not as reliable and efficient as the original equipment. Not only that, but because the Creditul Minier refinery had been completely taken out of the war, and other refineries had been severely damaged, the remaining equipment was worked that much harder. This increased use caused more breakdowns and resulted in less efficiency. Although it was producing, much of the vast complex at Ploesti was hard-used and aging—and needful of an overhaul.

What had it cost the Americans?

Arguably, the price was too high. Figures vary, but it is commonly accepted that 54 of the 177 bombers that took off from the Benghazi bases never reached a friendly airfield. It has been estimated that just over 40 aircraft were lost to enemy fighters and antiaircraft fire. Turkey interned 7 more aircraft, and several more were lost to accidents.

These tallies are only part of the cost. Many of the B-24s that returned were absolute wrecks and never flew again; their only use was as spare parts bins. These wrecks were cannibalized to cobble together Frankensteinian machines that could soldier on. In effect, the mechanics at Benghazi were recycling battle-worn bombers.

The human losses were the most telling. The mission claimed the lives of 310 American airmen. The enemy captured an additional 108 crewmen, and Turkey interned 78. Thus, nearly 500 trained crewmen were lost on the mission. This number doesn't include those wounded who did not return to service, for onboard the aircraft that managed to return to safety were 54 men who had been hit. And among those crewmen taken captive, most sustained wounds—some severe.

Winston Churchill (above) recognized early in the war the importance of Ploesti and called the Romanian complex "The taproot of German might." At his behest, American planners changed the codename of the bloody low-level attack of August 1, 1943, from SOAPSUDS to TIDALWAVE. Churchill believed the former name trivialized a mission sure to claim the lives of many men, and one that might ultimately change the course of the war. He was right. *National Archives*

(Left) The fortunes of Adolf Hitler's war machine soared when he brought Romania— and Ploesti— into the Axis fold in 1940. A loyal ally until late in the war, Romania turned over much of the oil complex's output to the Third Reich. Hitler would not have been able to accomplish what he did militarily without his precious Romanian oil. *LC*

The B-24D was the first variant of the Liberator to see combat in numbers. This aircraft, photographed over Greece in March 1943, was the type that made up the TIDALWAVE force. *John Blundell*

Colonel John R. Kane (standing, right) was the commanding officer of the 98th Bombardment Group. He was awarded the Medal of Honor for his role in TIDALWAVE. *John Blundell*

Above: Aircraft maintenance at the Benghazi airfields was a primitive affair. This B-24 is undergoing engine work. Note the high-explosive bombs and fins waiting to be assembled in the foreground. *Earl Zimmerman*

Below: Someone, somewhere, was missing their bathtub. One can only guess at how this unusual arrangement came to be. The airfields at Benghazi were not a normal, or comfortable place. Note the scattered nature of the men's tents in the background. This arrangement made them more difficult to attack from the air. *John Blundell*

Above: Eddie Rickenbacker—America's leading ace during World War I—addresses airmen before the TIDALWAVE mission. *John Blundell*

Below: B-24Ds en route to Ploesti on August 1, 1943. *John Blundell*

Stoyan Stoyanov finished the war as one of Bulgaria's leading aces. He successfully engaged American bombers on several occasions. He is perched (above) on a Bulgarian Me-109G. At right is another image of a smiling Stoyan. *Vesko Stoyanov*

The Romanians often worked in bare feet during temperate weather. *Denes Bernad*

Ray Weir, aboard the *Tupelo Lass* of the 93d Bombardment Group, took this photo on the run into Ploesti. The smoke plume likely marks the wreck of another B-24D. Note the scratches, bugs, and dirt on the windscreen. *Art Ferwerda*

A bomb bay camera captured this remarkable image of a B-24D racing low over Ploesti. *Reuben Weltha*

B-24Ds can be seen flying over the refineries in the break between the smoke. *Reuben Weltha*

Above: This image illustrates how low the bombers flew over the target. *Reuben Weltha*.

Below: Technical Sergeant Earl Zimmerman fired a .303 Springfield rifle from the bomb bay of his ship during the TIDALWAVE mission. He and the rest of the crew were interned when diverted to Ankara, Turkey. Zimmerman is standing third from the left at an embassy-sponsored event in Turkey. He was repatriated in 1944. *Earl Zimmerman*

One of the most famous images of World War II shows *The Sandman*, piloted by Robert Sternfels, as it emerges from a pall of smoke during the TIDALWAVE mission. Another view of *The Sandman* as Robert Sternfels brings it clear of the target. *John Blundell*

This was one of many ships that returned from the TIDALWAVE mission with extraordinary damage. *John Blundell*

The gunner who manned this top turret did not survive the TIDALWAVE mission.
John Blundell

This B-24 was downed over Romania on April 5, 1944. This date marked the first mission of the 1944 campaign that ultimately turned Ploesti into rubble. *Dénes Bernád*

This is a target photo of the April 24, 1944 mission against the Ploesti marshaling yards. *Reuben Weltha*

William Harvey (standing, second from right) was part of the B-24 crew of *Maiden U.S.A.* The crew's first mission was to Ploesti on April 5, 1944. They completed ten more missions in twenty days, including two more to Ploesti, before being downed by fighters over Varese, Italy, on April 25, 1944. Harvey was one of the four crewmen who survived. Back row, from left: H. M. Dressler, POW, W. H. Sullivan, KIA, W. J. Kelly, KIA, W. H. Harvey, WIA/POW, F. G. Miliauskas, KIA. First row, from left: C. L. Davidson, KIA, V. L. Coil, KIA, J. H. Mays, WIA/POW, A. Raffoni, KIA, V. P. Hanson, POW. *William Harvey*

Lieutenant Colonel Ben Mason, 82nd Fighter Group, seated (above) in *Billy Boy,* his P-38 named after his son, and atop the same plane (below). Mason dropped a 1,000-lb. bomb into the Americana Romana refinery during the low-level raid of June 10, 1944, and then shot down an Me-110. *Ben Mason*

Above: Small caliber antiaircraft guns such as these scored against the low-flying P-38s. *Dénes Bernád*. *Below*: Carl Hoenshell was credited with four aerial victories during the P-38 low-level raid of June 10, 1944. He was killed on that mission when his P-38 was shot down by a flight of Me-109s. *Liz Wilson*

Above: The Romanian IAR 80 and IAR 81 fighters were mistaken by American airmen for the German FW 190—an aircraft very similar in appearance. *Dénes Bernád*

Below: Airmen of the 463d Bombardment Group relax after a mission. This scene was repeated by thousands of men throughout the Fifteenth Air Force after every big mission. *James Patton*

The higher echelons at Benghazi and Washington weren't quite sure how to react to the mission. Losses had been extraordinary, yet prior to the mission it was accepted that the loss rate could have been much worse. Projected losses on paper were one thing, while missing faces and empty aircraft hardstands were quite another. Though the damage to Ploesti was not as extensive as had been hoped, there was no denying that real and telling injury had been done to the complex.

What couldn't be denied was the heroism and valor of the men who flew the mission. And it wasn't. Five Medals of Honor were awarded—more than for any other single air action in history. One went to Killer Kane for his decision to continue leading the 98th through the hell thrown up by the flak train and into the inferno that was the Astra Romana refinery. Colonel Leon Johnson received another for taking his 44th Bomb Group alongside Kane's 98th, and into the fire that leapt from the Columbia Acquilla complex. Two more went posthumously to Addison Baker and John Jerstad who—in the same airplane—changed course at the last instant and led the 93d to the Astra Romana refinery despite being mortally hit. The final medal went posthumously to Lloyd Hughes, who courageously kept his flaming aircraft on course until he was through the target.

A large number of Distinguished Service Crosses and Silver Stars were also awarded. And in an unprecedented move that acknowledged the horrific nature of the strike, every man on the mission was awarded the Distinguished Flying Cross. This was remarkable; most wartime fliers never received the coveted award. The next most awarded medal was the Purple Heart—for injuries sustained in combat.

*   *   *

What made this mission so horrible was its low-level execution, and the simple associated physics. As mentioned before—and as borne out on the actual raid—the bombers were within the lethal range of everything from sticks and stones to heavy antiaircraft artillery. Once an airplane was mortally hit, there was little that the crew could do to survive. A few men managed to bail out and survive at the extremely low altitudes that were flown, but really there was little choice but to ride the aircraft into the ground—hopefully under control—and pray that it didn't explode into flames. Too often the bombers did catch fire. The Germans and Romanians noted that many of the corpses they pulled from the wrecks were too badly burned to identify. In simple terms, the crews on this mission just didn't have the cushion of miles of altitude below them that was typical of normal heavy-bomber missions, and that could give them time and space to evacuate their stricken aircraft.

*   *   *

Inevitably there was finger pointing. Many men were incredulous that their leaders had sent them into such a firestorm of defenses. There was also murmuring about the fact that the commanders of every group took their men into the teeth of the defenses while the overall commander, General Ent on board Colonel Compton's ship with the 376th, steered clear of the worst fire. Kane was taken to task for causing the huge gap that essentially divided the mission into two separate forces. Compton was especially angry about this. During the return leg to Benghazi he brought the subject up with Ent. When he asked if Ent would bring charges against Kane for not complying with the mission orders, Ent replied that he would not. He pointed out to Compton that Kane was not alone in bearing fault for what had gone wrong; their own premature turn at Targoviste had sent the mission awry and scattered many of the leading elements of the strike.

Brereton, the commander of the Ninth Air Force, took official notice of the mistakes made. He criticized Ent, among others, but no official reprimands were given. In a post-mission report one of the points he made was: "The decision of the commander to execute an attack from the south after his formation had been lost and missed its IP was unsound. It resulted in wrong targets being bombed, destroyed coordination, and sacrificed the benefits of thorough briefing and training of the crews. Each individual crew had been assigned an individual target and trained to recognize it from models and photographs based on an approach from the northwest." But he softened his criticism when he went on to say: "Although tactical errors and erroneous decisions are pointed out above, no blame is attached to any commander or leader participating in the mission for decisions which were made on the spot under the stress of combat. On the other hand, the IX Bomber Command is deserving of the highest praise for its excellent staff procedure and leadership displayed in the planning, training, and execution of this most difficult mission." In the end, both Ent and Compton received the Distinguished Service Cross for their roles in the mission.

Despite the enormous losses, the mission was played out in both America and Europe as a heroic success. A press release from the very day of the raid declared, "It is reasonable to suppose that the gallant action of the Ninth Air Force only a few hours ago has materially affected the course of the war. If indeed the Ploesti plants have been completely crippled, then the Axis may have been deprived of the margin of aviation and other motor fuels it requires to continue effective resistance, certainly in Italy and very possibly in Russia." In a later congratulatory letter from King George VI of Great Britain to President Roosevelt the King sent his heartfelt sentiments: "The gallantry with which the crews pressed home their attacks at a very low level was beyond praise, and their devotion to duty in spite of heavy losses has stirred the hearts of all who fight with us in the cause of freedom."

There was no arguing with the photographs released to the press. The stirring images of the big bombers hurtling through the smoke and fire gushing out of the complex made a significant impact on the psyche of the people at home. This was obviously not a typical, sterile, high-altitude bombing run over a barely discernible target. The men at Ploesti had looked death in the face. For their part, the Germans and Romanians were very nearly stunned by the bravery and precision exhibited by the American flyers. In particular, the Romanians were impressed that there were so few civilian casualties—highly unusual relative to the bombing campaigns underway throughout the rest of Europe.

Later studies would show that airplane for airplane, the attackers on this particular raid caused more damage than any other subsequent raid against Ploesti. In the face of the losses, however—despite the damage done—no commander would ever again attack Ploesti from low altitude with heavy bombers.

Chapter 9

Strategy

THE NINTH Air Force never again launched a significant heavy-bomber raid. On the day following the low-level Ploesti raid, General Brereton wasn't able to muster even fifty serviceable bombers. Those groups that had been borrowed from the Eighth Air Force in England—the 44th, the 93d, and 389th—were soon returned, and never flew in the Mediterranean Theater again. The remnants left behind flew their last bombing mission on September 20, 1943, against targets in Italy. They were then either moved with the Ninth Air Force headquarters to England, or folded into the Fifteenth Air Force at new bases in Italy during the next few months.

The next phase of the Ploesti campaign would be a while coming. At this point in the war, the United States was pouring out thousands of aircraft and training the men to fly them, but the thousand-plane raids that marked American ascendancy in the sky over Europe were still many months away. And though the number of bombers in theater available to assault Nazi-occupied Europe was growing, there were still too many competing interests to launch a sustained campaign against Ploesti; Allied leaders had not yet agreed as to the best way to use their burgeoning air forces.

* * *

Many years before the huge Ploesti raid, military leaders in the United States belatedly came to understand the lessons that Billy Mitchell had sacrificed his career to impress upon them. Through the 1930s, using many of his principles, they developed plans and spent considerable energy and money to build a strategic air force. The centerpieces of this air force were fast and heavily armed bombers that were designed to be able to fight their way through enemy fighter defenses and bomb select targets with precision from high altitude. The predominant thinking was that these bombers would be so fast and well armed that a fighter escort would be an undesired redundancy; the fighter would be rendered obsolete by these fortified sky-giants. The B-24 and B-17 were designed and built to fill this role. The equipment and tactics to effectively outfit and employ them were especially and energetically developed by some of the brightest minds in the military, and in the aviation industry.

The Army Air Corps also developed a doctrine to employ their bombers. This doctrine took various turns during the years preceding the American entry into the war, but throughout its development it held that destruction of the enemy's ability to manufacture the goods and materiel required to wage war was the most effective way to hit him from the air. Further, there was discussion as to the effects of sustained bombing campaigns on the civilian populace of an enemy nation. All of the studies recognized the extremely complex relationships between the different industries that make up an economy, and there was considerable debate about the web or fabric that made up these relationships. Regardless, air power proponents declared that not only were strategic missions executed by heavy bombers the most effective method of striking from the skies, but that they were outright the most economic and effective means to winning a conflict.

During July 1941 the Air War Plans Division (AWPD) was created and charged with formulating a blueprint for a strategic air war against the Axis. In a bare month's time, the division presented AWPD-1: *Munitions Requirements of the Army Air Forces to Defeat Our Potential Enemies.* In it the Air War Plans Division identified the target sets upon which the emphasis for destruction should be most heavily placed. In order of priority those target sets were the Luftwaffe, to include aircraft and engine plants as well as aluminum and other metal manufacturing complexes; electric power producing stations; transportation targets; petroleum targets; and the morale of the enemy's populace.[1] The crippling of these targets would in turn surely cripple the enemy's ability to wage war.

Within a year—following America's entry into the war—a second plan was produced. AWPD-42: *Requirements for Air Ascendancy, 1942* maintained the same strategic objectives as APWD-1, but the target sets and priorities were altered slightly in light of observations made rather than experience gathered; at this point in the war the Army Air Forces had yet to mount any significant strategic attacks.

Parallel to the Army Air Forces' efforts, Britain's RAF had also developed sophisticated doctrines and forces for conducting a strategic air war.[2] The British, like the Americans, believed that striking the enemy's ability to manufacture war goods would yield decisive results, but they placed considerably more emphasis on the effects of strategic bombing on enemy morale.

When experience early in the war proved that their unescorted and lightly armed RAF bombers were little more than butcher's meat in the face of defending fighters, the British were forced to turn to the relative safety of the night. These night strikes enabled them to continue their operations with a more sustainable loss rate, but it cost them dramatically in terms of carrying out their pre-war strategic objectives. The same darkness that provided some measure of protection from enemy fighters also shrouded intended targets. The early radar bombing equipment was crude, little better than nothing. So, rather than being able to find and bomb a steel mill or an oil storage complex, the RAF bombers had difficulty even locating the town or city where the targets were sited. They had no recourse but to drop their bombs in the general area and hope to damage the target collaterally or indirectly by killing, frightening, or demoralizing the workers employed at the target. It was an indiscriminate, wasteful, and arguably ineffective practice.

*   *   *

When the Americans began to arrive on the scene during 1942 the British were openly skeptical of Yankee plans to adhere to daytime precision bombing. The Americans countered that their tactics and more heavily armed bombers would make the difference that would enable them to do so. In any event, despite intense pressure by ranking British officers to force the Army Air Forces bombers to operate at night alongside their own forces, the two Allies agreed to disagree.

* * *

Among the many important agreements and statements that came out of President Roosevelt's meeting with Prime Minister Churchill at Casablanca in January 1943, one of the most important was the Casablanca Directive. This put to paper the conventional wisdom that the purpose of the Allied aerial offensive was to destroy the German military, industrial and economic system as well as demoralize the German people to such an extent that their ability to produce goods would be significantly eroded.

The Casablanca Directive also carried a provision that allowed the Supreme Commander, Allied Expeditionary Forces, to use strategic air assets as he saw fit in order to prepare for the invasion of Europe—then being planned for the spring of 1944. With this directive serving as a broad-brush guideline, the Allied air staffs joined to produce a plan for what became known as the Combined Bomber Offensive, and which was ultimately codenamed POINTBLANK.

The plan borrowed heavily from the existing plans, recommendations, and documents. Because Britain had been so savagely handled by German U-Boats, submarine pens and related facilities and material were given high priority. Otherwise, the plan was not dramatically different from the earlier ones. The priorities, in order, were the German aircraft production plants and infrastructure, submarine yards and support activities, ball-bearing plants, petroleum production and refining facilities, synthetic rubber production, and military transportation. American air forces were directed to concentrate by day on prioritized targets from the developed lists, while RAF bombers were to support the prosecution of those targets with night raids. In practice, however, American and British interpretations of priorities did not always match up. Subsequently, when it officially began during June 1943, the Combined Bomber Offensive was more of a mutually agreed upon, loosely coordinated effort, rather than a closely choreographed aerial assault.[3]

At the conclusion of the Casablanca Conference, the American presence in Europe was still just a hint of what it would ultimately become. The British therefore were not reluctant to "share" their expertise with their American allies; after all, they had already mounted missions in excess of one thousand sorties. The Americans didn't even have that many bombers in Europe. The British continued to apply pressure to have the Americans join them on night missions to further increase the damage they were inflicting with their increasingly destructive terror raids into Germany. The Americans did not waver.

* * *

Aside from German defenses, the biggest enemy to the Combined Bomber Offensive was the dilution of the effort caused by the employment of the strategic bombers against other than strategic targets. Commanders in England were regularly frustrated when forces were commandeered to meet bombing requirements outside of the strategic target sets contained in the POINTBLANK plan. The invasions of North Africa and Sicily, and the low-level Ploesti raid were typical of the sorts of missions that bled the strength from carefully marshaled strategic forces. Though Ploesti was a strategic target, the mission was not part of a protracted and organized campaign. Indeed, the raid was considered by some critics to have been a sort of stunt.

* * *

The British and Americans both agreed that the number-one priority and greatest threat not only to their strategic air forces but also to the eventual invasion of Europe was the Luftwaffe. At the time of the Casablanca Conference, German air superiority over the Continent was unquestioned. Accordingly, its destruction was given the highest priority.[4] Early USAAF missions were short-range raids escorted by British-made Spitfires that suffered only relatively light losses so it appeared that Yankee confidence in their aircraft and tactics was not misplaced. It wasn't until the bombers went on longer raids, beyond the reach of fighter escort, that they began to suffer.

The British point of view that daylight raids could not be executed without prohibitive losses was vindicated on August 17, 1943. During miscued attacks at Schweinfurt and Regensburg, unescorted VIII Bomber Command B-17s and B-24s were savaged nearly as badly as the B-24s over Ploesti had been only a couple of weeks previously. Out of just more than 300 bombers, 60 were shot down. It was a loss rate that couldn't be sustained. Regardless, another 45 bombers were lost on a single mission to Stuttgart on September 6. For all that, the Americans would not relinquish their doctrine and another 60 bombers were lost on a repeat raid to Schweinfurt on October 14.

Although the attacks were effective, the loss rate was impossible to sustain. The bombers were subsequently used on shorter raids, within range of escort fighters, until something could be done to ameliorate the losses sustained over the more distant targets. It appeared that the Americans would need a miracle to continue long-range, daylight operations.

*   *   *

The miracle came to pass that same year as a combination of new tactics, new technology, and new equipment. The two front-line American fighters, the Lockheed P-38 Lightning and the Republic P-47 Thunderbolt, were designed as point-defense interceptors. Effectively adapting them to the escort fighter role wasn't easy because they simply didn't carry enough fuel to start a mission with the bombers and escort them all the way to the target and back.

A system was devised where successive relays of fighters met the bombers along the bomber route. Once joined with the bombers, the fighters crisscrossed overhead in a protective formation. It was an effective defense, but it also consumed fuel at a much higher rate. Turning and weaving to fend off attacking German aircraft, the escort fighters remained with the bombers until they in turn were relieved by another formation of fighters.

More experience with their aircraft also taught the American pilots how to increase their range by using different combinations of fuel mixtures and engine settings. Although the improvements were incremental, every extra mile the fighters flew with the bombers saved airplanes and lives.

The big boost that dramatically improved the escort fighters' ability to penetrate deep into Europe with the bombers was the introduction of the external fuel tank. The "drop tank" was so-called because once the fuel inside had been used, or upon engaging with the enemy, it could be dropped and the fighter could fly unfettered.

The external tanks were first used operationally on escort missions in July 1943. Originally made of a resin-impregnated compressed paper, they suffered from reliability problems that were largely fixed as more familiarity was gained. Later tanks were constructed of metal and proved much more dependable.

With their improved range, the P-38s and P-47s were able to range much farther afield—into Germany itself. Nevertheless, there was still a point on some missions at which the bombers flew beyond where the fighters could range. Unescorted bomber formations were often savaged—as was the case at Schweinfurt, Regensburg, and Stuttgart.

*   *   *

That changed with the introduction of the North American P-51B Mustang fighter. During 1941 North American had been approached by the British to build P-40s for them under license. The American company demurred and countered with an offer to design and build a completely new fighter. The result was what was eventually designated the P-51A. With its new laminar flow wing and other new technologies, it was a handsome, fast, and fairly nimble fighter with fantastic range. Nevertheless, its Allison-built engine limited its performance at high altitude. The British used it primarily for low-altitude ground-support and reconnaissance.

All of that changed when the Mustang airframe was mated with the superb British Rolls-Royce Merlin engine. This was the same engine that powered the legendary British fighter, the Supermarine Spitfire. Performance at all altitudes in all regimes surpassed even the most wildly optimistic expectations. With its new engine the Mustang was possessed of performance that equaled or exceeded that of defending German fighters. But more importantly, with jettisonable fuel tanks mounted under its wings, the P-51 could escort bombers all the way to Berlin and back. And it could knock down the best of the German fighters while doing so.

*   *   *

This is what Spaatz had needed. He knew American industry's productive capacity and he knew Germany's. He knew that in a war of attrition Germany could never hope to match the United States—even if the exchange in planes and crews was on a one-for-one basis. The new American equipment and crews gave him better than that. Germany was going to lose the air war.

As 1944 got underway, General Arnold established the United States Strategic Air Forces (USSTAF) in Europe and put Spaatz in charge. Composed of the Eighth and Fifteenth air forces, USSTAF was charged with carrying out the strategic air war against Germany. It was right where Spaatz needed to be. From his new post he could direct the employment of his forces in order achieve his ultimate objective: The destruction of the Luftwaffe.

*   *   *

Experience to this point in the war showed that wherever and whenever the Americans put a significant mission aloft, the Germans would resist it to the best of their ability. Spaatz and his planners were counting on this when they designed a plan to lure the Germans into the sky against heavily escorted bombing missions. During a series of massive, all-out efforts from February 20, to February 26, 1944, the Eighth and Fifteenth air forces put more than 3,500 bomber sorties into the sky. Targeting primarily aircraft-related plants, the bombers were met by intense fighter opposition. These German fighters were roughly handled by the escorting American fighters. The end of the effort saw the German fighter defenses badly mauled, and German aircraft manufacturing capability badly damaged. More than 600 enemy aircraft were claimed destroyed by the Americans, and many skilled and irreplaceable German pilots were killed. That the Americans lost 226 bombers was significant, but it was not a disaster. America could replace her losses, and more. Germany could not. The operation, which came to be known as Big Week, was a major watershed in the decline of the Luftwaffe, and further marked the transition of air superiority over Europe from Germany to the Allies.

*   *   *

Spaatz kept the pressure up. The Germans were so badly weakened that they became selective about the raids they opposed. Spaatz and his staff designed bombing missions not so much around the damage they would cause, but rather around the likelihood that the Germans would rise to oppose them. They had learned that if the Germans came to fight, the American fighter escorts would beat them. And as they were successively beaten, the quality and quantity of the German airmen deteriorated.

* * *

As 1944 drew on and preparations for the invasion of Europe intensified, Gen. Dwight D. Eisenhower, the supreme allied commander, had to make a decision about how best to use the forces under his command. Operation POINTBLANK had been terminated on April 1, 1944, and he had been given direct control of all Allied air forces. There were strong competing interests for the heavy bombers of the USSTAF. Spaatz and his staff argued that oil-related targets should be hit.[5] They held that a Nazi military starved of oil would be unable to move or fly, and that a similarly starved economy would be unable to produce. Further, the targets were big, difficult or impossible to disperse—and most importantly—were sure to be heavily defended by German fighters. German pilots killed over oil targets would be unable to oppose the Allied invasion force.

The RAF Air Chief Marshal Sir Arthur Tedder, who was also Eisenhower's deputy, contended that a concerted campaign against oil targets would take too long to have an effect—if it was effective at all. He favored the use of the bombers against transportation targets, particularly railroad marshaling yards in France and Germany from where German troops could mobilize to oppose the invasion. Further attention would be directed against bridges that would serve to choke or funnel German troop movements. Tedder's opponents declared that such targets were too numerous, too small, and too easily repaired. Further, the casualties sustained by civilians, particularly the French, would be enormous.

Eisenhower weighed all the options and decided in favor of Tedder and the transportation plan. Beginning in April, intensive efforts were undertaken, not by just the USSTAF, but indeed by all the Allied air forces in Europe to strike out against transportation-related targets. Both the Eighth Air Force based in England, and the Fifteenth based in Italy, hit such targets throughout Western Europe. By the end of May 1944, much of the German-held rail system was in ruins, and a concerted effort had dropped many of the most important bridges. Nevertheless, the Germans were able to move men and equipment, albeit at a reduced rate.

* * *

Spaatz never did give up on his "Oil Plan." At the same time that Eisenhower sided with the advocates of the transportation campaign, he also gave permission for Spaatz to pursue oil targets insofar as resources and circumstances permitted. On June 8, 1944, Spaatz declared in an order to the commanders of the Eighth and Fifteenth air forces, that their primary strategic mission was the denial of oil to the German military.

Chapter 10

Buildup

BIG WEEK, D-Day, and the real commencement of Spaatz's Oil Plan were all months away when the Fifteenth Air Force was activated at Tunis on November 1, 1943. The Fifteenth was born of necessity, in large part to prepare for the invasion of France the following year. During planning for the invasion, General Henry Arnold, chief of the Army Air Forces, was concerned that the Eighth Air Force alone would not be able to provide the strategic air power necessary to execute the Combined Bomber Offensive and support the planned invasion. His British counterpart, Air Chief Marshall Charles Portal, concurred and directed Arnold's attention to southern Italy.

The area around Foggia and Bari—just above the heel of the Italian boot—was quite suitable for air operations and had already been somewhat developed before being abandoned by retreating German forces. Strategic bomber bases in Italy would allow attacks on German targets from a different axis than missions launched from England. Additionally, when Allied air forces in England were weathered in, there was a good possibility that the forces in Italy might have more favorable weather.

Arnold embraced the concept and wasted little time in developing it further. In early October he submitted a plan to the Joint Chiefs of Staff to create the Fifteenth Air Force. Their stamp of approval was immediate, and the Combined Chiefs of Staff, composed of the U.S. and its allies, gave their go-ahead on October 22, 1943.

Placed under the command of Lt. Gen. James H. Doolittle, the nucleus of the new air force was formed by redesignating Headquarters, XII Bomber Command, as Headquarters, Fifteenth Air Force. The new air force was composed initially of the 5th Heavy Bombardment Wing with four B-17 groups (2d, 97th, 99th and 301st,) and two B-24 groups (98th and 376th). Two medium bombardment groups, and a fighter wing rounded out the Fifteenth. It would grow and transform considerably.

*   *   *

Following the movement of the veteran heavy bomb groups from North Africa to Italy were arrivals directly from the United States. To merely note that the Fifteenth continued to increase in size with the arrival of new units would be an omission that would leave the story of the Ploesti campaign only partially told.

The hazards associated with the journey from the United States to North Africa were noted earlier in the recounting of the Halverson Project's trail blazing efforts. That undertaking involved twenty-three aircraft and crews, and ended amazingly enough with the safe arrival of all. This was not to be the norm. More typical was the odyssey of the 459th Bomb Group—a B-24 unit that departed Mitchel Field, New York, after receipt of orders in early January 1944.[1] Four squadrons, the 756th, 757th, 758th, and 759th, totaling sixty-two B-24Hs and approximately 2,500 personnel made up the 459th. The itinerary for the bombers and their crews called for staging from Mitchel Field, to Morrison Field, Florida. Once in place the crews were to make their way individually to Italy via Trinidad, Brazil, Senegal, Morocco, and Tunisia. On the other hand, the bulk of the support personnel were manifested aboard various transport ships to be convoyed across the Atlantic, through the Mediterranean, and thence to Italy.

One of the first aircraft to leave Morrison Field was a 756th Squadron B-24 piloted by 2dLt. Charles F. Webb. The airplane, with a crew of ten, plus four passengers never arrived at Trinidad. A subsequent search effort conducted by trailing aircraft from the 459th turned up no trace of the Webb crew.

Two days later another 756th B-24 that had diverted into Puerto Rico after a fruitless search for the missing bomber was damaged beyond repair when its nose wheel collapsed while taxiing. The fuselage had buckled behind the flight deck when the front of the bomber struck the ground, and, though the aircraft was a loss, fortunately no one was injured.

On January 14, only five days after Webb's bomber had disappeared, a B-24 from the 757th piloted by Lt. Edward Hodge suffered the same fate on the same route to Trinidad. Searchers turned up no trace of the missing bomber or its crew.

Within the next week or so, two aircraft from the 759th were lost to airfield accidents in British Guiana. Fortunately, no lives were lost, but both B-24s had to be written off. The attrition rate for the 459th's crossing was alarming—and the first bomber had yet to reach Italy!

*   *   *

The 459th's support personnel had in the meantime been transported to Hampton Roads, Virginia, to be loaded aboard four different Liberty ships. By January 14, they were headed out into the deep waters of the Atlantic. Accommodations were poor—the enlisted men were bunked in racks stacked six-high. "You have to crawl into your bunk sideways, they are so close together," one man complained. Matters were made worse when a storm tore at the convoy over a three-day period. Water rushed over the decks and tore lifeboats loose from their davits, washing them out into the open ocean. Men became seasick, and the sour stench of vomit permeated everything in the poorly ventilated quarters below deck. The decks were slippery with the sickening bile.

Following the storm the rest of the trip was relatively smooth. The men occupied themselves by playing cards, writing letters, and washing laundry by hanging it over the side and letting the cold ocean water wash through it. The convoy was not molested by the German U-boat fleet, for at this time of the war, the German submarines were on the defensive.

*   *   *

The B-24 crews continued their journey, encountering conditions wholly foreign to them. The checkerboard farms of the States were replaced by steaming green carpets of South American jungle. Too, the tropical storms they encountered were totally unlike anything they had experienced in training. Lieutenant Leo Fletcher tried to navigate across the Mato Grosso of Brazil by flying beneath a particularly vicious rainstorm: "At 300 feet, we still couldn't see the ground at times, or anything else for that matter, and with such a big ship, I couldn't get lower."

The tropical nature of their stopover bases was particularly exotic to the airmen; most of them had never ventured outside of the United States. Natives approached them to sell all sorts of wares—and services. One crewman who was intent on keeping a mascot bought a monkey. During the long flight across the Atlantic from Natal, Brazil, to Dakar, Senegal, he began to feel sorry for his furry friend cooped inside its tiny cage. He saw no harm in letting it out for a bit of exercise and soon the little simian was joyfully bounding about the different fuselage stations, finding no shortage of handholds and perches. The rest of the crew, bored by the long over-water flight, laughed at the monkey's clever antics. The amusement was not long-lived, for after a time the blissfully happy little mascot launched itself through the open waist window and into the void of miles of empty space.

The long flight across the Atlantic from South America to Africa was the most unnerving part of the journey. Fuel was short, the weather was unpredictable, and the crew was wholly at the mercy of the navigator, who had no tools other than his sextant, charts, chronometer, and a compass—not much different than the captain of a sailing ship. That these navigators were likely only a year or two removed from their days of hanging out at the malt shop made their successes all the more remarkable.

And the B-24 itself could be the crews' worst enemy. Lieutenant Colonel Phil Warren, the commander of the 759th, had one of the most hair-raising experiences of his career during the crossing: "Shortly after we reached midpoint, and not long after we had emerged from some clouds, all four engines quit! Suddenly, I wasn't flying an airplane anymore—I was on the front porch of a house that had just fallen off a cliff. But good emergency training stood by us, and in less time than it takes to tell about it, I shut off the autopilot, switched the four fuel boost pumps on, dropped the nose of the plane to maintain air speed, called the navigator to send an SOS with our position to both Natal and Dakar, and ordered the crew members to prepare to ditch." Then, just as suddenly as they had quit, the engines on Warren's ship caught again. No explanation for their misbehavior was ever identified, but once they had safely made Dakar all four engines were changed—just in case.

Once in Africa, with the danger of the Atlantic crossing safely behind, the remainder of the trip to Italy seemed less daunting, but it still was not without its hazards. Sadly, another collapsed nose wheel incident not only destroyed another B-24 but claimed the life of a crew member and injured several more. This time the accident occurred at the airfield at Oudna, Tunisia. The nose wheel failed just as the bomber was about to lift off. Instead of getting airborne, the B-24 careened off the end of the runway and dug into the sand. The big ship was nearly cracked in two behind the flight deck, and the fuselage and tail stuck into the air at a steep angle. Burns from the ensuing fire killed the flight engineer, while the rest of the crew suffered from a variety of serious injuries.

* * *

It wasn't until February 3, 1944, nearly a month after the 459th departed Mitchel Field that its first B-24 touched down at Giulia Field in Italy. Located roughly twenty miles southeast of Foggia, Giulia had been constructed by the Germans and was intended for use by Ju-87 Stuka dive-bomber units. It was abandoned before it was put into operation when the British Eighth Army swept over the area the previous October.

The long-awaited arrival was marred when one of the first B-24s to land struck another on the runway and sheared away its aft fuselage with a wing. No one was injured.

When the last bomber of the 459th finally arrived at Giulia Field a *month* later, on March 3, the final tally was shocking. The aircraft loss rate was eight of sixty-two—a stunning 13 percent. It nearly equaled the worst losses the 459th would sustain in operations against the enemy. Further, thirty-eight lives had been lost. The number of aircraft damaged but returned to service was not tallied.

The main portion of the 459th's personnel—the ground echelon—was a week or so behind the first aircraft, and was worse for the wear. They had endured an air attack during the transit of the Mediterranean, and while disembarked at Taranto, a transport truck plowed into their formation and sent eight men to the hospital. Finally, on the night of February 12—during a rain shower—the ground echelon arrived at Giulia Airfield.

* * *

This build-up of forces from the Fifteenth Air Force in southern Italy was enormous. By May 1944 there were twenty-one heavy bomber groups, each with four squadrons of approximately sixteen aircraft each. So closely packed were the different airfields that mission commanders had to be careful not to overfly neighboring bases when assembling their formations for a mission. And added to this mix of heavy bomb groups were seven fighter groups and a number of light and medium bomber groups, as well as a reconnaissance unit. Further crowding the skies was a large number of light and medium bomber groups, and fighter groups, from the Twelfth Air Force, as well as a host of RAF units.

* * *

The logistical requirements to support the Fifteenth Air Force were enormous. The length of the supply chain alone was an extraordinary challenge. Goods from all over the United States were shipped along a route that spanned the Atlantic, threaded the passage at Gibraltar, and terminated in Italy. The port at Bari in southeastern Italy handled much of the load, and as such was the target of a special German aerial attack on the night of December 2, 1943—one day after Jimmy Doolittle had moved his headquarters to the port city.

The raid—executed by more than a hundred Ju—88 twin-engine bombers was a spectacular success for the Germans. Seventeen Allied ships—five of them American—and 39,000 tons of cargo were destroyed and at the same time more than a thousand lives were lost. Almost half of the casualties were caused by mustard gas released from a 100-ton cache of chemical bombs aboard a stricken merchant ship. The gas had been brought into theater for retaliatory use in the event the Nazis resorted to gas warfare. Ironically, the Nazis never did use poison gas on the battlefield; the only American gas casualties in World War II were caused by American gas.

German attacks aside, the largely unsung and under-appreciated supply men ensured that stocks of the basics—fuel, food, bombs and ammunition—were never seriously short. In concert, the transportation men made certain that those supplies reached the appropriate destinations on time. Although other commodities might be less plentiful, there was always something kill the enemy with.

To put the efforts of the logisticians into perspective it is interesting to note what the very basic requirements in just fuel and ammunition were to put one heavy bomb group into the air: A 36-plane mission needed 96,000 gallons of gasoline, 360 500-pound bombs, and 187,000 rounds of .50-caliber ammunition. All of this was operated, loaded, and maintained by approximately 2,400 men.[2]

And all of these men had to be fed, watered, clothed, and otherwise cared for. When one realizes that the typical mission involved ten or more bomb groups—and that missions were almost a daily affair—the enormity of the efforts required of the logisticians becomes apparent.

Chapter 11

Loophole

WHEN SPAATZ was made commander of the United States Strategic Air Forces—comprised of Eighth and Fifteenth air forces, Doolittle was relieved of command of the Fifteenth in Italy and given command of the Eighth in England. He was replaced by Lt. Gen. Nathan F. Twining, previously the commander of the Thirteenth Air Force in the South Pacific.

As the head of the most powerful air forces in the world, Spaatz was professionally obsessed with his plan to execute a concerted campaign against Germany's oil production centers. He was certain that such an effort was the quickest way to destroy the Luftwaffe, and thereby, Germany.

Eisenhower was not totally sympathetic to Spaatz's convictions, and on March 25, 1944, he sided with his deputy, Air Chief Marshall Tedder and directed Spaatz to concentrate the efforts of his strategic air forces against Germany's transportation infrastructure. Spaatz could not bring himself to accept this decision as each day that went by saw Germany's fuel production increase.

On April 5th, 1944, Spaatz stuffed the Fifteenth through a technical loophole and hit Ploesti for the first time since the low-level raid of August 1, 1943. The intelligence annex for the mission's field order—in keeping with the spirit of the transportation plan—mentioned nothing about the oil complexes at Ploesti. Instead it stated: "The Ploesti

[Marshaling Yard] is key point in rail lines to Moldava. Current tactical situation on Russian Front makes this target an important and active communications center for the German Army."[1] What isn't mentioned is that the Ploesti marshaling yards were also adjacent to the Astra Romana oil refinery.

The strike would be the first mission over Ploesti since the TIDALWAVE mission. It was to be nearly three times the size—made up of nine groups of B-24s and four groups of B-17s. And unlike the TIDALWAVE mission, it would have fighter escort for much of the flight into and out of Romania. This escort was important as it was estimated that the enemy could oppose the strike with up to 225 fighters. Worthy of note is that the mission to Ploesti wasn't the only effort that the Fifteenth was fielding that day; a bomb group of B-17s was tasked with hitting the marshaling yards at Nis, and four bomb groups of B-24s were assigned to attack targets in the Romanian capital, Bucharest.

This April 5 raid was William H. Harvey's first. He was a fresh-caught lieutenant recently arrived from the States. Assigned to the 450th Bomb Group at Manduria, Harvey was trained as both a bombardier and navigator, and remembers well that the aiming point for this mission was indeed the marshaling yards. But he also remembers that "It was obvious that the aiming point on the marshaling yard was right next to a refinery and loading station—and that no one would be upset if the whole damned place went up!"[2]

Once airborne and headed northeast, the bomber force began to run into trouble in the form of weather. The 304th Bomb Wing's four groups of B-24s encountered a cloud layer at approximately 8,000 feet over the Adriatic Sea. A series of climbs and turns and descents were made to try and clear the clouds and keep the formation together. It was to no avail, for nearly a third of the force returned to bases in Italy when the 304th aborted the mission. Communications were difficult, however, and some of the force continued to the target. Further along the route the 5th Bomb Wing shed a number of B-17s in the clouds that also returned to Italy with their bombs.

Bill Harvey's B-24—*Maiden U.S.A.*—wasn't among those that turned back. In fact, because the 304th Bomb Wing had aborted, the 450th Bomb Group—at the head of the 47th Bomb Wing—had to assume the responsibility of leading the entire Fifteenth Air Force. It was well before the formation reached its initial point when a gaggle of what was likely Romanian IAR 81s began to peck away at the bombers. The crews identified these aircraft as German FW 190s, however records do not support this. According to Harvey, the enemy fighters "bird-dogged us for a time and made a couple of feeble firing passes."[3] After a while, however, the enemy fighters were joined by another group of ten to fifteen fighters. It was then that the attacks began in earnest.

The Axis fighters climbed to a position above and in front of the bombers—the position technically labeled twelve o'clock high. They then dove head-to-head on the big ships, their wingtips and cowlings sparkling with the flashes of machine gun and cannon fire. The bombers in turn blasted back with every .50-caliber gun that they could bring to bear. Once finished with their firing passes, the fighters dove safely below the B-24s, then started a wide, right arcing turn to a position above and parallel to the bombers, on the left side of the formation. This was a perfect position for a classic high-side firing pass.

The Romanian pilots took advantage of the position and continued their attacks. For Harvey, it was an eye-popping introduction to combat. Amid the blasting of his own ship's guns, the fire of the enemy fighters, and the screams and shouts over the radio and intercom, he was responsible for ensuring that the bomber was properly set up to release its load of high explosives. This demand for his concentration was competing with the drama of aircraft dropping out of the sky—some on fire or in pieces, or both. The claustrophobic clamp of the oxygen mask over his face, the freedom-inhibiting grasp of his heavy clothing, and the tight confines of his crew position all contributed further to the terror of the attack.

After reaching the IP, the 450th picked up a southeasterly heading for the marshaling yards. Shortly, the intensity of the defending flak guns began to reach furious levels. The enemy fighters drew back while the big bombers were dealt a beating from the ground. The sound of shrapnel banging, clattering, and punching holes through the thin skin of the B-24 helped punctuate the experience for Harvey—as if he needed it.

Flying off to the sides of the formation were enemy twin-engine aircraft—Me-110s and Ju-88 bomber-killers. These big fighters swung their noses around to point at the bomber stream to launch aerial rockets. The rockets were much longer-ranged than machine-gun or cannon fire but were horribly inaccurate. Harvey recalls, "The rockets seemed to go everywhere but straight—mostly arcing upwards."[4]

On approach to the target, Harvey could see that the Germans had ignited smoke pots. Despite the smoke screen and the clouds the target was still visible when the formation let loose its deadly cargo. "We really clobbered them that day. Flames shot high in the air and we could see secondary explosions in the refinery and loading areas."[5]

As soon as the formation cleared the target, however, the enemy fighters were back. Wounded aircraft were given special attention, as noted by an after action report: "The customary GAF [German Air Force] tactic of attacking stragglers was used in the course of these operations. Attacks were made by groups of 3-4 a/c in repeated maneuvers, closing from beneath in a climb and then diving away. A few attacks were executed singly and in pairs, and mass frontal attacks were made from above by groups of approximately 20 e/a."[6]

These attacks notwithstanding, Bill Harvey survived his first combat mission to Ploesti. But he would be back. For its part as the ad hoc strike lead, the 450th Bomb Group received a Distinguished Unit Commendation.

The results of the April 5 raid were impressive. Post-mission assessments showed that the majority of the 588 tons of bombs released had gone wide of the marshaling yards. Instead, the Astra Romana complex had been hit hard and its production capacity had been significantly compromised. The raid had been costly, though; 13 of the 230 bombers that had made it through the weather had been shot down.[7] This was a loss rate of nearly 6 percent. Nevertheless, in the grand scheme, the results justified the costs, and many more attacks would follow.

*　　*　　*

On this mission, escorting P-38s from the 1st, 14th, and 82d fighter groups, and P-47s from the 325th—limited by fuel—failed to down any enemy fighters. Instead, two P-38s were lost.[8] The weather that had turned back many of the bombers also made it difficult for the fighters to rendezvous with the bombers. The fighter escort was ineffective. Harvey saw no friendly fighters whatsoever until the return trip, when his formation was joined by a handful of P-38s over Yugoslavia. The relatively short-legged P-47s would fly only one more escort mission to Ploesti before being replaced by more suitable P-51s.

*　　*　　*

In the spring of 1944, the P-51 Mustang had only just arrived in theater. Although it outperformed every other American fighter on almost every count, one of its disadvantages was its similar appearance to the German Me-109; from time to time P-51s were mistakenly shot down by the very bombers they were charged with escorting.

Following one such incident, a Mustang was sent to the 449th Bomb Group's airfield at Grottaglie so that the B-24 crews there could get a good look at the new fighter. Upon arrival the eager pilot started a series of low, fast passes—all the better for impressing his audience. Tragically, he overtaxed his skills and flew into a dirigible hangar. The resultant explosion and fire completely destroyed the deadly fighter, and the pilot's shredded body was found where it was thrown—a few yards from the wreckage.[9]

There was seemingly no end to the number of ways that death was visited on the men of the Fifteenth. Five mechanics of the 97th Bomb Group were killed in their sleep in the early morning hours of April 17. An RAF Wellington that was out of gas smashed into their tents. A sixth man lost his leg.

These two accidents were characteristic of the significant number of casualties that were sustained that were not even remotely related to enemy fire.

*   *   *

Two more attacks against marshaling yards at Ploesti on April 15 and April 24 yielded results similar to the attack of April 5. The bombers seemed unable to deliver all of their bombs on the designated transportation targets. Inexplicably, many of their bombs seemed to fall into major refineries. Results were immediate; German imports of petroleum products from Ploesti during April 1944 were only 56 percent of what they had been during March.[10]

Eisenhower wasn't an idiot. He saw through Spaatz's subterfuge and called him on it. In subsequent meetings Spaatz came into line and directed major efforts against the Transportation Plan target sets—among others as needs arose. At the same time Eisenhower and Tedder made concessions to Spaatz and approved limited strikes against oil targets.

The implementation of the Oil Plan was underway. And the destruction of Ploesti was the cornerstone of that plan.

Chapter 12

Downed

IMPLEMENTATION OF the Spaatz Oil plan may have been officially sanctioned, but operations against Ploesti at this point were still masquerading as part of the transportation plan. The intelligence annex of the field order for the mission of May 5, 1944, hints at this:

> Ploesti remains the most important communications target in the Balkans. New line from Pitesti bypasses Bucharest, but all traffic for the front must go through East yard at Ploesti and virtually all must also pass through either the N[orth] Yard or S[outh]. Station. Attacks to date have caused great damage to refineries. It is estimated that modern capacity has been reduced from eight to three million tons per year. Astra and Standard groups are out of action and Concordia Vega damaged. In view of this situation, substantial bonus of damage may be expected from spillage at Romana Americana and Concordia Vega—only major refineries in city still active. . . .[1]

The mention of the collateral damage to the refineries that could be expected from strikes against the adjacent rail facilities—and its description as a "substantial bonus"—suggests that the choice of this particular target was largely driven by Spaatz's pursuit of the Oil Plan. The intelligence annex is also interesting because it gives the impression that the complexes at Ploesti had been largely destroyed. The three raids executed since the start of the campaign *had* caused extensive damage, but much of it was repairable or not significant to the production or refining processes. This was borne out by the fact that the campaign would require a further twenty missions to effectively shut the complexes down.

*   *   *

Second Lieutenant Robert K. Barmore, of Verona, New Jersey, had arrived in Italy only the previous month.[2] As a member of the 451st Bomb Group based at Castellucia, the 23-year-old was assigned as the co-pilot aboard *Devil's Duchess* on May 5, 1944, one of seventy-one B-24s from the 47th Bomb Wing that were assigned to hit the main Ploesti marshaling yards. As the formation departed its assigned initial point and turned onto the bombing run, its crews could only barely make out the preceding formation as it punched through an unbelievably thick cloud of antiaircraft fire. A moment or two later, Barmore and the rest of the *Devil's Duchess* crew was flogging through the same barrage of flak bursts.

The B-24 crew dropped their bombs on target and the pilot, 2dLt. Paul Krueger, put the bomber into a left turn for the rally outside of the target area. It was then that the ship was caught by several bursts of flak. Immediately it became apparent that the bomber had been mortally hit, as every engine but the left outboard had to be feathered. Barmore remembers, "I knew that we were in trouble now. Paul Krueger gave me the controls, rang the emergency alarm bell—the signal to bail out—and was out of his seat fast. His oxygen had given out and he went to the radio table to get oxygen. After I took over I knew for sure that we would not get home."

Barmore's oxygen supply had also been cut off. As he ripped his mask from his face, the rest of the crew started to leave the bomber. The nose gunner bailed out almost immediately, along with the navigator and bombardier. A moment later SSgt. Charlie Joines, the engineer, stumbled down from his position in the top turret. His face and hands were covered with blood. Barmore left his seat and tended to Joines's wounds, which turned out to be largely superficial face and head cuts caused by splintered glass from the turret.

By now, with no hydraulics and all but one engine shot out, the plane was spiraling downward, out of control. Nevertheless, Lyle Clark, the ball turret gunner, made his way up to where Barmore was tending

Joines. Both waist gunners had been hit and badly wounded, and they needed help. Barmore, Joines and Clark started back through the fuselage of the careening bomber. In the meantime, with the situation growing more desperate, Lieutenant Krueger bailed out through the nose wheel well.

Clark and Joines made their way through the bomb bay and jumped out through the camera hatch. Barmore, who was wearing a bulky seat pack parachute, got hung up in a bomb rack and couldn't move. Caught in the howling slipstream, he was soaked by an inflammable mixture of hydraulic fluid and fuel that spewed from torn lines. Finally he broke free. When he reached the waist position he found the tail gunner, SSgt. George McDonald, administering first aid to SSgt. Arch Eakins, one of the waist gunners. The other waist gunner, Sgt. Maurice Kelly, had been badly hit below the hips and couldn't move. McDonald was able to get Eakins out the camera hatch, and Barmore ordered McDonald to bail out as well. "I got Kelly's chute on and asked him if he could just pull the release if I pushed him out. He said he could, so I pushed him out the hatch."

With no time to lose, Barmore followed. "The ground looked awfully close when I went out, so I pulled the ripcord as soon as I felt wind in my face. When the chute opened the plane was on fire on the ground and I was certain that I would land in the fire."

Barmore landed close by, but not in the raging fireball that had been *Devil's Duchess*. He was the first one to touch down. Kelly and McDonald landed soon afterward, and he quickly made his way to where the wounded waist gunner was lying motionless. "He had nothing much left from his upper legs on down, but seemed to suffer no pain. I gave him a shot of morphine from the escape kit and tried to make him comfortable." The two men were soon joined by a group of Romanian farmers, one of whom brought up some water for Kelly. After a bit, McDonald appeared, limping from a rough parachute landing.

Two village policemen and some of the peasants eventually carted the three men to the local police station. Kelly was too far gone and died later in the afternoon. "A very old woman put candles in his hands, blessed him, and cried as though he was her own."

Barmore found out later that the other waist gunner, Arch Eakins, also died. He and the surviving crew members were imprisoned in a Romanian POW camp.

Bomber formations evolved as the war progressed and sometimes differed from one theater to another. A bomb group formation of the Fifteenth Air Force typically was made up of three boxes of six aircraft each, flying in an inverted-V configuration, leading three more identical boxes. The six aircraft that made up each box mirrored the larger group formation with two, three-ship elements in an inverted-V configuration. Altitudes within the entire formation were varied, as they were within each box. This configuration provided the best defense against attacking fighters and ensured a reasonably tight bomb pattern.

*   *   *

Lieutenant Victor McWilliams and his crew from the 455th Bomb Group were on their third trip to Ploesti that day.[3] The 455th was a B-24 unit based out of Cerignola. Some would argue that three trips to Ploesti was a stiff test of the odds.

The flak on this mission—as described by nearly all the participants—was particularly fierce. McWilliams's ship was hit in the right wing almost as soon as the formation came under fire. Both engines were knocked out, and almost immediately the B-24 started down in a right-hand spiral.

Reacting quickly, McWilliams pulled back the power to the two engines on the left wing in an attempt to regain control of the aircraft. At the same time he salvoed the bombs in an attempt to lighten the wounded ship. When one of the waist gunners called up and reported that the aircraft was on fire, McWilliams gave up on the idea of saving the ship and ordered the waist gunners to help the tail and ball-turret gunners out of their positions, and to bail out. Next he ordered the crew members in the forward section to jump clear.

Finally he was alone in his doomed ship. At this point an Me-109 attached itself in formation alongside the bomber. McWilliams remembers that, "The pilot motioned for me to get the hell out of there. I thought it was decent of him." McWilliams knew he was wounded in the left wrist and leg, but it wasn't until he tried to stand up that he realized that his leg below the knee was only barely attached. Nevertheless, he managed to exit the bomber and deploy his parachute.

He landed in a tree, below which stood an elderly Romanian woman tearfully fretting at the situation. Eventually he was dragged out of the tree, and loaded into a car. Unfortunately the car blew a tire and the frightfully injured McWilliams had to endure a stream of curious onlookers until another vehicle arrived to take him to a hospital in Bucharest. There his leg was amputated and he was given little chance of recovery because of all the blood he had lost.

Amazingly he did recover. After an extended recuperation he was overjoyed when he was moved to a regular Romanian prison camp and learned that every crewman aboard his ship had survived.

*   *   *

Lieutenant John Plummer was a pilot with the 99th Bomb Group, a B-17 unit based out of Tortorella.[4] The Ploesti mission of May 5 was a memorable one for him as well; it was a day that didn't start out as well as he might have liked. First off, Plummer nicked himself quite badly while shaving with cold water; it took him some time to staunch the flow of blood. Then, while getting dressed, he noticed that his right foot felt peculiar in its boot. He pulled the boot off and discovered that scores of centipedes had made it their home the evening prior. They were now little more than a nasty mess that fouled his foot, sock, and boot. After cleaning up the wriggling glop, his spirits were lifted slightly by a hearty breakfast of creamed beef gravy on toast washed down with grapefruit juice and coffee.

After a normal brief and pre-flight, things began to sour again. Plummer had trouble getting his right outboard engine, number-four, started. He called the crew chief onto the flight deck. After some work, the engine was started, but Plummer wasn't satisfied with it. The oil pressure was at the lower limit of what was acceptable, and the cylinder head temperature was at the upper limit of what was acceptable. Too, he noted that the engine seemed to be running slightly rough, an observation that was confirmed visually—the engine's cowl flap was vibrating just enough to be noticeable.

Plummer's dilemma was one that pilots loathed. It would have been much better had the engine been obviously malfunctioning. In that situation he could have aborted the mission without any questions being asked. In this instance he had an engine that was technically within limits even though his experience told him that it might not last through the mission. If he aborted, his motivation might be questioned, particularly since the target was known to be a tough one. The last thing he wanted was a cowardly reputation. As an aircraft commander he was expected to make tough decisions, and the decision he made was to press on with the suspect engine.

The oil pressure on the number-four engine continued to deteriorate throughout the flight. Two hours from the target a telltale streak of oil was streaming back from the engine atop the right wing, but Plummer continued on; the engine was still operating within limits, and he and his crew had three tons of bombs aboard that needed to be delivered.

The situation only grew worse. About 25 miles short of the IP the ship took flak hits that set one of the bomb bay door motors afire. By the time the flight engineer was able to extinguish it, the bad engine had pumped oil all over its nacelle, and the oil pressure had dropped below acceptable limits. It was time for Plummer to make another command decision. He was past the point of no return; the technical solution was for him to secure the engine by feathering the propeller and shutting it down. But to do so would mean that he would likely drop out of the protective formation and fall prey to enemy fighters.

Plummer decided to keep the engine running. He briefed his co-pilot that in the event the oil pressure dropped to 20 pounds per square inch, he should secure the engine. Then, just after starting the bomb run—with no warning whatsoever—the left inboard engine, number-two, failed. The co-pilot quickly feathered the number-two propeller, while Plummer advanced the power on all three remaining engines, including the oil-starved number-four. Despite having added nearly full power on the remaining engines, Plummer's ship inevitably began to fall behind. As he slowly slid to the rear of the formation, he also descended in order to keep his speed up. It was a risky place to be. The danger from being hit by the higher formation's bombs was very real.

The ship survived that danger, and the bombardier dropped their bombs along with the rest of the formation. Their luck didn't hold, however. Only a few miles after passing over the target the number-four engine finally caught fire. The propeller was quickly feathered and the engine was shut down. But there was now absolutely no way that Plummer was going to be able to stay within the protective cover of the rest of the bombers. Despite his best efforts, he lost altitude and the formation soon disappeared from view. Worse, there were no friendly fighters to protect them from the enemy aircraft that had come into view.

Plummer could hardly maneuver his big bomber like a fighter, but he racked the ship around in a series of turns in order to make it as difficult a target as possible. In doing so he was operating at the very edge of controllability. It was while pulling through one of these turns that he encountered turbulence. The B-17 staggered and stalled, then fell off into a left-hand spin. Evidently the enemy fighters wrote the ship off, for they abandoned their pursuit.

Fighters or not, Plummer's situation was desperate. The B-17 was not designed to spin, and Plummer and his co-pilot had to resort to the basic spin-recovery techniques they had practiced during their primary training in tiny, single-engine aircraft. After retarding the throttles of the two good engines to idle, the two pilots applied full right rudder and stuffed the control yoke forward. The crew must have been terrified as the horizon spun crazily to the right while the bomber plummeted out of the sky. This was nothing that any of them had ever trained for.

After a few turns the spin slowed, then finally stopped. Plummer released the pressure on the right rudder and brought the yoke back, but that wasn't enough to bring the big Flying Fortress out of its dive. With the airspeed well over 300 miles per hour the aircraft was in real danger of coming apart, and the control yoke was useless against the tremendous forces. The pilots had to resort to use of the elevator trim tabs in order to get the bomber's nose to start up out of its dive. Finally, Plummer and his co-pilot were able to level the aircraft at about 8,000 feet.

There was little thought that the crew was going to be able to nurse the stricken ship all the way back to Italy. Instead, Plummer turned his attention to stabilizing the two remaining engines, getting as far out of Romania as he could, and setting the aircraft up for a controlled bailout.

From a point well north of Bucharest, he started toward Yugoslavia. That there were no enemy fighters to finish them off was a blessing. Seeking to lighten the airplane and increase its chances of clearing the mountains into Yugoslavia, Plummer ordered everything tossed overboard, including the ball turret. Lightened as it was, the airplane's performance began to improve and the two pilots were able to reduce the power on the remaining two engines—lowering the odds that they might fail.

Finally, after a nerve-wracking flight that wound through high mountain passes, Plummer and his crew brought the ship across Yugoslavia to the Adriatic. Plummer was now faced with a final command decision: Should he bet on the remaining two engines and risk the nearly two-hour flight back across the Adriatic? Or should he put it down along the beach and hope to join up with friendly partisans?

Plummer pressed on and ultimately landed back at his base—the last airplane to return.

It wasn't a bad ending to a day that began with a boot full of centipede guts.

*   *   *

The attack of 5 May was the largest raid mounted against Ploesti to that point. An intensive effort put 166 B-17s and 319 B-24s into the skies over Romania. These were escorted by 153 P-38s and 42 P-51s—the largest escort effort to date. Losses totaled 18 bombers and 2 P-38s.[5]

*   *   *

Any discussion of the campaign against Ploesti must be put into perspective. At the time, the rank and file crewmen did not consider the missions to Ploesti to be a part of a special campaign. They were just considered tough missions. It must be remembered that the bomb groups flew several times a week; missions to Ploesti were tucked in between missions that were conducted all over southern Europe. One day might see a group sent to targets in France. Two days later it could be ordered to attack enemy positions in Yugoslavia or Bulgaria. A day later might see it hitting German troop concentrations in northern Italy. A mission to Ploesti could be assigned for the following day, and after a short rest to regroup and conduct maintenance the group could very well be ordered on a mission to Austria or southern Germany.

Indeed, some crewmen considered the heavily defended targets in Austria and Germany to be even more fearsome than Ploesti. Sam Marie, a bombardier from the 465th Bomb Group, was one of those. "Based on my experiences Ploesti couldn't hold a candle to Munich; there, the natives were narrow-minded and mean. In all the many missions my squadron flew to Ploesti, we never lost a plane. On the other hand, we lost eleven over Munich."[6]

A review of the 187 missions flown by the 485th Bomb Group bore this out. The group flew a total of six missions to Ploesti and lost only one bomber over the target, and that loss was not to enemy fire, but because the airplane was struck by the bombs of higher-flying aircraft within the formation. The group's missions to Ploesti seem unremarkable when compared to some of the other targets, where it was much harder hit.

The 485th's experiences over Romania were not the norm. The Ploesti defenders claimed a huge toll of American equipment and men, and gave it a deserved reputation as one of the most fearsome targets of the entire war.

*   *   *

The attack of May 5 was followed by another attack that same night. The RAF's 205 Group sent 38 Wellingtons and 5 Halifaxes to the marshaling yards at Campina. This attack was in turn followed up by 135 B-24s from the 304th Bomb Wing. The raids caused significant damage, but the 304th lost six ships and the RAF lost three.[7]

Chapter 13

DEFENSES

AMERICAN LOSSES to anti-aircraft fire increased throughout the Ploesti campaign, while the percentage of losses to defending fighters decreased. This was not solely due to the beating being experienced by the Romanian and German fighters. Rather, it was in large part due to increasing numbers of flak guns brought into the defense, as well as improvements brought about by experience and better equipment.

At the official start of the campaign—marked as the April 5, 1944 strike against the Ploesti marshaling yards—there were 142 heavy flak guns in place. Before the last American bomber dropped its load on the Dacca Romana refinery on August 19, 1944, that number had nearly doubled to 278. What had been a wicked concentration of enemy firepower was, at the end, absolutely murderous.

The defenders wasted no time bolstering the number of heavy antiaircraft weapons, an action that reflected the importance of the target. By April 14, the number had already grown to 178, and photo-reconnaissance showed 234 big guns in place by May 5. The final 44 guns were put into battery during the next three months.

There were areas in Europe that were defended by greater numbers of antiaircraft batteries; the huge area of Berlin and its environs was one of them. But no other target had such a large number of guns concentrated in such a small area. Ploesti was a compact city, and the refineries that defined its perimeter were so close together that the defenders' task was made that much easier.

The types of guns emplaced around the city were predominantly of three types. The most prevalent was the legendary "Acht-Acht," or 88. Firing an explosive shell with a diameter of 88 millimeters, it had an effective range of over 25,000 feet, and if necessary could get shells up above 30,000 feet—albeit with less accuracy. It had an effective rate of fire of approximately fifteen rounds per minute, and fired an explosive shell weighing almost 21 pounds. There were approximately 210 of the deadly 88s arrayed around the city.

The next most numerous of the heavy guns was the 105mm cannon, of which there were approximately 50. It fired a shell weighing just more than 35 pounds, and its effective range of well over 30,000 feet could reach even the highest-flying bombers. Despite its larger size, its rate of fire of about fifteen rounds per minute was similar to that of the 88.

The monster at Ploesti was the 128mm antiaircraft gun. It hurled a shell weighing 57 pounds that could reach well over 40,000 feet. Its rate of fire was slightly slower than the others, twelve rounds per minute. Fortunately for the Americans there were fewer than thirty of these brutes incorporated into the defenses. In fact, these enormous guns were mounted on the cars of an armed train that also incorporated sleeping cars, electrical generators, ammunition cars and other supporting rolling stock. As such, it was somewhat mobile—though with its complex fire support system and supporting apparatus of all sorts, it was hardly an affair that was chugged around from place to place at a moment's notice.

The emplacements varied in their sturdiness and sophistication. In some cases, they simply sat in the dirt surrounded by scraped-earth revetments. More permanent positions were dug into the earth and surrounded by lumber-reinforced earthen breastworks approximately twelve feet wide at the base and four feet wide at the apex. Yet more robust preparations included six-inch-thick concrete retaining walls with adjoining concrete personnel structures and ammunition storage bunkers. The fire control and billeting arrangements were usually wood plank structures near, but not exactly collocated with the guns.

The railcars mounting the 128mm guns could also be detached from the train and pulled into special revetments. These, along with inch-thick steel armor gave them especially good protection. Also, the gun-carrying rail cars could be locked into place directly to the rails on any portion of the line. Stabilizing legs were lowered to provide the required support.

The heavy guns were augmented and protected by nearly 300 lighter guns—mostly 20mm cannon. With high rates of fire, these could be devastating to low-flying aircraft, as had already been demonstrated by the TIDALWAVE mission.

The flak defenses surrounding Ploesti were part of a system made up of many components. First, the American formations had to be detected as early as possible. There can be little doubt that the Germans had intelligence operatives on the ground in Italy who provided intelligence on Fifteenth Air Force operations. But they were just one element in a many-layered command, control, and defense system that ultimately terminated with antiaircraft rounds bursting among the bombers.

Once airborne, the American bombers were detected almost immediately by German radar stations arrayed down the coasts of Yugoslavia and Albania that had been erected following the ejection of the Nazis from southern Italy. These installations plotted the formations as they moved northeast across the Adriatic. As the tactical picture matured, it became apparent which targets were more likely to be hit, and the appropriate defenses were alerted—by radio and telephone.

As the bombers approached Romania, more German radars—Wassermans, Freyas, and Wurzburgs—continued to plot their progress. These radar tracks were augmented by visual observations from Romanian personnel posted throughout the cities and the countryside. Data from sonic detectors was incorporated into the information net. All the reports were processed and plotted by Centre Sensible—the primary Romanian command-and-control node, in Bucharest.

The radars that were used fell into two different categories—long-range detection and tracking, and targeting. The FUGM 80 Freya system was Germany's basic long-range detection radar. Characterized by a thirty-three foot-tall rectangular antenna, it had a detection range of approximately seventy-five miles. While it had no good height-finding capability, its antenna could be rotated in any given direction, and it had otherwise decent performance.

A further development was the FUGM 402 Wassermann. A huge device, it was essentially eight Freya antennas cobbled together and mounted on a nearly two hundred foot-tall rotating tower. With a detection range of one-hundred-and-fifty miles, it was one of the finest early warning radars used by either side during the war.

The Freyas and Wassermanns were complemented by the Wurzburg targeting radars, of which each battery was equipped with at least one. It was a smaller set characterized by a parabolic antenna. The Wurzburg operated at a much higher frequency than the longer-ranged radars, and was capable of providing more precise targeting data. The shorter-ranged Wurzburg's were tied directly to the flak batteries and gave them the capability to accurately fire through smoke, clouds, or darkness.

For every measure in warfare there is a countermeasure. Especially during the infancy of electronic warfare, the development of equipment, techniques, and tactics was such that there was a continual leapfrogging of capabilities and counter-capabilities. The Americans deployed several counters to German radar, of which two were especially effective.

Window (also known as chaff) was as effective as it was primitive. Essentially very thin metallic strips roughly one foot in length by a half an inch in width, chaff could be cut to counter certain radar wave lengths. It was carried in bundles or packets by attacking bombers and jettisoned overboard by hand along the approach routes. The subsequent clouds of metallic litter reflected German radar waves and created havoc with their ability to track the formations. Innumerable false targets were generated and it became almost impossible to sort the real thing from the rest of the mess.

Another effective tool that the Americans put into use was a jamming device codenamed Carpet. Typically mounted in one or more aircraft within a formation, the jammer was tuned to the bandwidth of the Wurzburg radars. When tuned appropriately—and this was difficult because the radars could use more than one frequency—the jamming device was quite effective. In combination with chaff, Carpet jammers could force battery commanders to abandon their radars for less effective visual targeting methods.

The electronic war was fluid, and the Germans developed counters to the countermeasures the Americans employed. Nurnberg was a modification that used radar returns from propeller modulations. Wurzlaus was a counter that used Doppler effect, a difference in the speed of a radar return relative to surrounding radar returns. Wizmar was a technique that shifted the frequencies of the radars and was specifically designed to foil jamming by carpet. All three of these German counters demonstrated some degree of efficacy, though the use of Wurzlaus and Nurnburg cut the effective range of the radar by nearly half.

It must be remembered too that the technology was in its infancy and not readily understood or trusted by everyone who used it. It also was prone to breakage and malfunction, and it required skilled technicians to maintain it. There were also special considerations for its employment. For instance, a Wurzburg antenna needed to be positioned at least a couple of hundred meters away from the guns it supported; otherwise it was prone to damage or jamming from muzzle blasts.

*   *   *

When the bombers were approximately 150 miles from Bucharest and Ploesti, the first warnings—by siren—were delivered to the general populace. Protection of civilians had taken on increased importance since the mission of April 4, 1944, against Bucharest's marshaling yards; more than four thousand civilians were killed when American bombs fell outside the target area.

Also at this time, final defense preparations were made; defending fighters were staged as the situation dictated and antiaircraft batteries were readied for immediate action. Final warnings were given at approximately 40 miles, and at approximately 20 miles the outermost batteries began to fire.

Low-level attacks were more difficult to detect by radar because of the masking provided by mountains, hills, and other terrain. Still, the two low-level penetrations that were conducted were ultimately picked up and tracked by German radar stations—as well as by visual observers. In both cases there was enough time to stage a withering defense.

The bomber formations were continuously tracked to help ascertain their ultimate destination, but also to effect fighter intercepts as far out as possible. First contact with Axis fighters was sometimes made before the formations had crossed the Adriatic.

As effective as the defending fighters were, it was the flak guns that took the highest toll of attackers. Using data from their Wurzburg radars, the fire control crews at each battery continuously developed firing solutions for the formations overhead. The radar data was augmented and refined with information from visual range finders and sound locators. The reliance on the radar for firing solutions varied from battery to battery and situation to situation—depending on a number of factors. These included the individual battery commander's confidence in—and experience with—the radar; the state of repair of the equipment; and whether or not smoke, cloud cover, or darkness precluded him from using any other data. Too, American countermeasures could negate the effectiveness of the radar.

It appears that the most successful battery commanders used a combination of the fire-control modes available to them. For instance, because the radar was designed to track the approximate center of a formation, the plotting crews sometimes used visual tracking to refine their data so that the leading elements of a formation could be targeted. Or if the radar set was nonfunctional or degraded by countermeasures, the crews, if conditions allowed, could rely completely on visual tracking. Another option was the use of data from other batteries; connected by both radio and telephone. This web of connectivity was one of the greater strengths of the defenses around Ploesti.

*   *   *

A review of accounts finds frequent mention of German aircraft—very often twin-engine fighters—that simply shadowed the American formations rather than attacking. These were recognized for what they usually were—aircraft sent aloft to establish the exact altitudes of the bomber streams. American airmen nicknamed them "stool pigeons." Their information was relayed to flak batteries, which could then fuse their antiaircraft shells more accurately.

The German antiaircraft rounds were designed to explode at a predetermined altitude or upon contact with a solid object. A precise determination of the bomber formation's altitude obviously improved the probability of success. It was well worth the risk to send aircraft to do just this. The mission was dicey, however, because the pilots ran a very real danger of being bagged by escort fighters. They often scooted in and out of clouds, or maintained enough separation from the bomber escorts to stand a decent chance of escaping if the American fighters gave chase.

*   *   *

There was one antiaircraft development the Germans never fielded that bears mentioning if only to illustrate what a close thing the American bomber victory over Europe was. That development was proximity-fused antiaircraft ammunition. The proximity fuse was an American-developed device fitted into the nose of an antiaircraft projectile that emitted a radio signal. When that signal was reflected back from an aircraft in great enough strength it triggered the projectile to explode. This enabled an antiaircraft battery to shoot down a target without scoring a direct hit, or without the relatively inaccurate guesswork associated with fusing a round to explode at an airplane's estimated altitude. It turned near-misses into hits.

The proximity fuse was a closely held secret and was first used operationally by the U.S. Navy on January 6, 1943, at Guadalcanal. In fact, the Allies were so fearful it might be compromised that it wasn't until the British were confronted with V-1 guided missile attacks in June 1944 that it was released for use over land.

*   *   *

Germany's antiaircraft defenses were enormously expensive. The guns were difficult and costly to produce, as was the specialized ammunition. During 1944, 20 percent of Germany's ammunition production went to antiaircraft stocks, and 30 percent of its heavy-gun production went toward flak defenses. Too, the defenses were labor intensive; the draw on manpower was so heavy that later in the conflict, with so many able-bodied men needed at the front, the antiaircraft system was manned by a significant number of boys, old men, and trustworthy POWs. That so much money, resources, and expertise was directed toward the defense of the skies no doubt hastened the outcome of the war on the ground.

*   *   *

Flak and fighters were the threats that the American airmen feared the most, but these same airmen never aborted, or even wavered from executing an attack because of the danger. Precisely the opposite; from afar the formations appeared to be an unstoppable machine. The machine might appear ragged—shedding pieces of itself as it marched through the sky—but it always reached its target. And it reached its target because the airmen—fearful as they were—had the guts to fly it there.

Nevertheless, no matter how courageous the men were, if they could not locate and accurately bomb the target, their courage was for nothing. The Germans tried to make it for nothing with all the energy and ingenuity they could muster. They based their efforts on producing as much smoke as possible in order to deny the Americans the use of their Norden and Sperry bombsights.

Some would argue that generated smoke was the most effective defense the enemy fielded. Several missions had to be repeated because of poor bombing results caused—in part if not in whole—by smoke obscuration.

The devices the Germans and Romanians used to generate the smoke screens were often referred to as "smoke pots." This simplistic term conjures up an image of an open, oil-filled vat or container that was set afire to produce a sooty, dirty veil of smoke. In reality, producing the smoke screens was the responsibility of four specialized military units totaling nearly 2,000 men who maintained and operated an equal number of chlorosulfonic acid generators.

These devices were comprised of a large barrel capable of holding 400 pounds of chlorosulfonic acid, and a large bottle of compressed air. When fully charged, the air bottle had a capacity of 6,000 cubic feet of air under a pressure of 2,200 pounds. Air from the bottles was delivered through lines to the acid barrels at a pressure of 90 to 100 pounds per square inch. The smoke created by the resultant chemical reaction was exhausted to the atmosphere through a projector pipe. The units were placed so as to provide the maximum coverage to a given area depending on the prevailing wind.

Each generator was provided with a spare barrel of acid and a spare bottle of compressed air. The units were operated singly by one individual, with no interconnection of units or provision for a central control or distribution center. The generators were usually put into action about forty minutes to an hour prior to an anticipated attack. Their use was strictly intended for use against formations of aircraft rather than single reconnaissance types. Of course, due to the nature of the beast, the generators were often put into operation when attacks failed to materialize or were directed against neighboring facilities.

A set of one barrel of acid and one bottle of compressed air, under normal use, would last approximately three and a half hours. The spare assets at each point doubled this time. Nevertheless, a strong breeze required an increased rate of emission and cut the time of coverage accordingly.

Either by design or mistake, the Americans significantly reduced the defenders' ability to create effective smoke screens by the end of the campaign. The chlorosulfonic acid needed to create the screens was stored in existing oil storage tanks and was transported from these tanks as required to recharge the depots of the smaller units. As it developed, much of the existing supply and storage capacity for the acid was collaterally destroyed during attacks against the refineries. One reason that the missions at the end of the campaign were not so severely hampered by smoke was because of a shortage of chlorosulfonic acid.

As in the fight against the radar and flak guns, the Americans fielded different countermeasures to overcome the smoke screens, as well as cloud cover. One of these countermeasures was the H2X radar set. It was first used at Ploesti on July 15, 1944. Nicknamed "Mickey," it was a fairly new development—at the very forefront of radar technology—and was derived from the British H2S radar. Designed primarily for bombing in darkness or through clouds, the system was mounted in specialized bombers positioned at the head of the formations. Usually the equipment was mounted in place of the lower ball turret. The H2X had a spinning antenna and a range of approximately 50 miles. The pulsed energy that was emitted by the set was received back by the antenna and displayed on the operator's scope. A trained operator could become quite skilled at interpreting the returned signals; water provided almost no radar reflection at all, whereas bridges, bends in a river, islands, cities, and rail yards provided distinct, readily recognizable returns. It wasn't easy, and a variety of features or combinations of features could present themselves in a very confusing manner.

Using the picture on his scope, the operator would locate a preplanned, readily identifiable feature, and set up the bomb release over the target using a known bearing and distance from that feature. While not as accurate as visual bombing, it was certainly better than dead reckoning—that is, bombing blindly through smoke or clouds using nothing more than the time elapsed on a given heading to determine a position over the ground.

Offset visual bombing was a technique that didn't rely on radar equipment. Actually it was simply a tightened version of dead reckoning. Using a readily recognizable feature that was in the clear and hopefully in close proximity to the target, a formation would navigate from that feature—using a known bearing and distance—to drop their bombs.

Both of these methods involved intense preparation, particularly in terms of photo-reconnaissance. Approach strips from different axes needed to be shot and prepared, as did specialized navigational grids prepared to ease the task during the heat of combat. Special scope photography was also performed at night by single bombers. All of this material played a significant role in achieving the required accuracy.

The Americans also tried to thwart the smoke and clouds with weather reconnaissance aircraft, usually P-38s. These would fly overhead the intended target prior to each mission and pass weather and smoke information to the bombers. They would delineate which targets were obscured and which were clear, or mostly clear. This gave the bomber leaders time to change their target, if necessary, to one that was not obscured. This method was effective in more than one instance, and though the original primary target had to be hit later, the practice ensured that bombs were effectively dropped on targets of value.

Finally, one form of target obscuration was, in effect, a mixed blessing. That was the cover created by the successful strikes of the leading parts of a formation. The smoke from burning oil often reached up to the altitude of the trailing bombers, making a precision drop much more difficult. Still, the fact that the obscuration was caused by a successfully hit target helped ameliorate some of the frustration.

Chapter 14

MOUNTAINEERS

FROM APRIL 5, 1944, when the campaign began, until May 6, Ploesti was bombed six different times—including one night raid by the RAF's 205 Group. Losses had been heavy; 52 ships and crews had been downed. Still, the results had been very encouraging. This was reflected in the intelligence annex of the field order for the mission of May 18, 1944:

> Recent operations have severely damaged and rendered inoperative for several months Astra and Standard groups of refineries and damaged Concordia Vega. Columbia Aquila and Creditul Minier still inactive and unrepaired after August 1943 attack. Steau Romana at Campina badly damaged and out of operation after attack of 6 May. As a result, refinery capacity in Ploesti area reduced from about 10,000,000 tons per year of which 8,500,000 tons was modern capacity to about 2,000,000 tons. Plan for tomorrow [18 May] contemplates destruction of all remaining capacity and completion of job at Concordia and Unirea Sperantza. Objectives in each case are boiler and powerhouses, distillation and cracking units which if destroyed will render refineries inactive for 6 to 9 months. Axis oil output cut by Fifteenth and Eighth Air Force attacks to date is estimated as 35 to 40 percent. Successful execution of tomorrow's plan should raise the figure to over 50 percent— believed to be critical point in Axis war potential.[1]

It appears obvious that the mission of May 18 was planned to be the knockout blow that would put Ploesti out of the war. It would be the biggest effort to date. The plan called for a total of twenty-one bomb groups to attack the Romana Americana Refinery, the Unirea—Sperantza Refinery, the Xenia Refinery, the Conrcordia Refinery, the Redeventa Refinery and the Dacia Romana Refinery. And though Romanian refinery facilities had been hit since the beginning of the campaign on April 5, this was the first mission that *officially* assigned refinery targets to the different bomb groups. By now, the Allied leadership was satisfied with the amount of attention that the transportation target sets were receiving, and perhaps more importantly, the incidental attacks on Ploesti were showing tangible results.

Approximately 700 bombers got airborne to make the attack. Within a couple of hours, however, it became obvious that the mission was coming apart. Atrocious weather along the route made it almost impossible for the different groups to maintain their formations. Some of the groups were recalled, but others weren't, and still others missed their recall signals.

William E. Correll was a B-24 ball turret gunner assigned to the 449th Bomb Group based at Grottaglie, Italy.[2] His six-ship squadron formation was one of those that missed the call to abort the mission. Nonplussed, they pushed through the weather. They were going to take on one of the toughest targets in Europe.

Approaching the Unirea-Sperantza refinery, they broke out of the weather and into the clear. A black cloud of bursting flak loomed in front of them, and roiling, oily smoke rose up from the target, which had already been hit by the formations that preceded them. Disturbingly, smoke also rose from the crash sites of several bombers.

Correll anxiously watched the skies for enemy fighters as the formation steadied its course for the bomb run. But the danger came from the flak guns below. The ship just behind Correl's took a direct hit and was knocked out of the formation in a blinding flash, spiraling down to earth. A short time later Correll felt his own airplane jump as the bombardier toggled its load of bombs. Barely an instant later he was caught by surprise when another flash rocked his bomber, *Old Ironsides*.

Two engines were gone and the airplane was spinning out of control. Not sure whether to jump or stay with the plummeting ship, the crew hung on. Finally, after losing more than two miles of altitude, the pilots were able to wrestle the big ship back into level flight at about 8,000 feet.

Shaken, but still airborne, they managed to point the badly damaged B-24 back toward Italy. The damage they had sustained was severe and the flight engineer expressed his doubts about the ship's ability to carry them back to base.

Just then, the tail gunner called out "Bandits." Six Axis fighters swung into the attack, and the gunners onboard *Old Ironsides* tried to fend them off with their .50-caliber machine guns. In the ensuing fracas the crew claimed three of the enemy machines, but the onslaught was too much. An oil line in one of the ship's two remaining engines was hit, and the engine was lost. There was no way that the big ship was going to stay airborne. The flight engineer pointed this out and announced that he was going to jump. The pilot backed him up. He rang the bailout bell and hurriedly told the rest of the crew to stuff anything they wanted into their pockets and abandon ship.

All of this was quite a shock for Correll. He had checked into the squadron only two days earlier. Nevertheless he was ready to go and crawled out from his position in the ball turret. But there was a problem in the back of the airplane. One of the waist gunners had pulled the ripcord to his parachute too soon. It was flapping around in a tangled mess in the back of the fuselage. Correll and a couple of the others were able to calm the gunner down. They had him stand upright while they carefully folded the parachute back and forth through his outstretched arms. All of this took place in a bomber that was falling out of the sky. Finished, they handed him the small pilot chute and instructed him to release it as soon as he cleared the bomber. Out he went, and it was with great relief that the rest of the crew watched the parachute inflate fully.

Correll started to climb out of the stricken ship when he was reminded by the co-pilot to retract the guns to his ball turret. There was a danger that they might catch the parachutes of the crewmen in the front part of the airplane as they jumped. Quickly, he climbed back to his turret, brought the guns in, then made his way rearward, and jumped clear of the ship.

As soon as his parachute blossomed Correll spun around and tried to count the other parachutes around him. *Old Ironsides* drew his attention away when it smashed into a mountain ridge. The resultant explosion didn't hold his attention for long though, for small-arms fire cracked from the ground below, and a quick look revealed that several men were shooting at him. Desperate to make himself the most difficult target possible, he began to swing from side to side. When some of the panels in his parachute collapsed he immediately let go of the risers and curled himself into a ball to make himself as small as possible as he prepared to crash into some trees.

He fell into a wooded area and was jerked to a halt several feet above the ground. Suspended between two trees, he managed to swing over to one and struggled to get out of his harness. It was then that he heard someone approaching and, instinctively, he tried to hide behind the trunk of the tree. At the same time that he caught sight of an armed man coming directly for him, he realized how futile his attempt to hide was; the parachute in the branches above him marked his position. With no other good option, Correll raised his hands into the air. Inexplicably, the other man dashed back into the trees.

Wasting no time, Correll shucked his parachute harness and dropped to the ground. Dashing through the trees in his heavy flight gear soon exhausted him. As he stopped for a moment to shed some of it, he heard someone approaching. Again he attempted to hide behind a tree. Again he was spotted, and again he raised his arms.

His luck held. He had come down in Yugoslavia and was soon being embraced and backslapped by ten of Tito's partisans. They quickly hustled him out of the area—away from German forces and pro-German partisan units. Over the next two weeks, aside from being spat upon by an old woman who mistook him for a German, his treatment was as good as the harried partisans could make it. Within two weeks, he and a group of fifty-three other airmen were flown out of a makeshift landing area by a flight of two C-47s. Before leaving, most of the rescued men stripped to their skivvies and donated their clothing and shoes to their rescuers. It was a surprised pair of Red Cross ladies who met the semi-nude men with coffee and donuts upon their return to Italy.

William Correll returned to operations and flew his next mission on June 10, 1944, only 23 days after being shot down over enemy territory.

*   *   *

Of the approximately 700 bombers that got airborne to participate in the May 18 attack, only 206 actually crossed the target. Enemy fighters were particularly aggressive as parts of the bomber escort were lost or separated by heavy clouds along the route and over the target. Losses for the raid tallied out at fourteen bombers and two fighters. And of course the flak defenses were fierce; they were always fierce.

The mission was hardly the crushing blow the planners had hoped it would be. Rather, it was almost an embarrassment when actual results were held up against the original heady intent. And though some damage was inflicted, it would take three more months and seventeen more missions before the job would be finished for good.

* * *

It has been said before in many other places but it bears repeating that the aircraft maintenance men were largely unheralded heroes in this war. They worked extraordinarily long hours in all types of environments and conditions. Quite often they put maximum effort into getting an aircraft ready for a mission only to see it return in tatters—or not at all. This took a psychological toll. Particularly if they began to second-guess whether something they did or didn't do played a part in the airplane's loss. But there was nothing for them to do except pick up their tools and move on to a different airplane. And that's what they did.

It wasn't only the airmen that became casualties in this war, though. Accidents claimed many ground crewmen. Jess Akin was a B-24 assistant crew chief with the 485th Bomb Group. It happened that the bomber he was assigned to, as assistant to the crew chief, Lloyd Arnold, burned to the ground on its hard stand at the airfield. An inquiry was held and Arnold was cleared of wrongdoing, but it was determined that Arnold would benefit from some rest. Accordingly, he was put aboard an aircraft bound for Rome. After only a few minutes the plane crashed, killing everyone on board. Jess Akin was promoted to crew chief.

If the world at large did not appreciate the work that the crew chiefs performed, the aircrews certainly did. Typical are the memories of Winfield S. Bowers, a pilot with the 455th Bomb Group. He praised the work of Cpl. John Lutz:

> Lutz was one of the men assigned to the crew chief for *Pin Down Girl*. As Frank Fox, our flight engineer, used to say, "they just don't make many as solid as *Pin Down Girl*." Lutz felt the same way. Busy as he was, Lutz salvaged plywood from bomb bay luggage carriers and cut the plywood to exactly cover the carpet on our flight deck. As soon as the aircraft landed and was parked, he would quickly put the plywood down on the flight deck, before anyone could track mud on our carpet. He would remove it again just before

takeoff. Thus, our carpet was always nice and clean on all bombing missions.

Another thing that Lutz did in his spare time was polish the instrument panel! There was no polish available so he used clean engine oil. It made the panel look awfully nice, but I had to stop him from doing that because going down the runway the shiny instrument panel would reflect on the windshield, thus hindering my vision.[3]

Bowers was one of many pilots who said that they wished they had taken more time to thank more people for the superb support work they performed. He and others like him know that there was no way that they could have done their jobs as well as they did without the dedication of millions of people like Corporal John Lutz.

Chapter 15

BOMBARDIERS

THE UNITED States put its faith into two separate bomb-aiming systems—one developed by Norden, and the other by Sperry. Both of these were much more than rudimentary bombsights. In fact, they were arguably the most advanced computers of their time. Rather than simple aiming devices, they were entire bombing systems that incorporated gyros, autopilots, and automatic bomb-release features.

Bombardiers underwent lengthy and extensive training to operate these complex systems. To attempt a thorough and detailed explanation of the theory and operation of the Norden and Sperry sights is beyond the scope of this work, but a brief description and overview of their employment is important in the context of the Ploesti campaign.

The bombardier's job typically began well before the takeoff itself. Once the target was known he conducted pre-flight preparations—taking into account the axis of the attack, planned altitude and speed over the ground for the bomb release, forecast winds and cloud-cover, and the types of bombs to be used—among many other important factors. One of his most important duties was familiarizing himself with the primary and alternate targets. This was accomplished primarily with intelligence photos. These were studied carefully, because no matter how sophisticated the Norden and Sperry systems were, in the end they were still dependant on the human eye. If the target was not correctly identified, the mission would be a failure.

The bombardier turned on his bombsight prior to flight, allowing the gyros to spin up so that he could check it for proper operation.[1] Additionally, he checked that the bombs were correctly loaded and that the arming pins—which kept the bombs from exploding in the event that they were inadvertent dropped—were installed. Then he checked the guns and ammunition and lent assistance elsewhere as was required.

Once airborne the bombardier made his way back to the bomb bay and pulled the arming pins. This ensured that the bombs were armed and, barring malfunctions, were set to explode at the right time upon making contact with the target.

Provided that the navigator and pilots had properly done their jobs, the bombardier visually acquired the target and provided steering guidance to the pilot. At about this point the bomb bay doors were opened. The drag from the airflow in and around the bomb bay made the airplane more difficult to handle, so it was important that the pilot had enough time to settle the ship prior to the bomb release. Once the track was aligned with the target, the bombardier directed the pilot to "clutch in" with the autopilot. This in effect put the control of the airplane into the bombardier's hands, via the computer-controlled autopilot. Using a set of knobs, he kept the sight's cross hairs positioned over the target.[2] That this fine-tuning was possible, even in turbulence and heavy flak, was due primarily to the stabilization provided by the system's gyroscopes.

As the airplane approached the release point, a drop line at the bottom of the sight began to travel up the vertical line of the two crosshairs. When the drop line reached the intersection of the crosshairs, the bombs were automatically released. At this point the bombardier called "bombs away"—despite this being obvious to everyone on board—and closed the bomb bay doors.

The importance of the bombardier's job is self-evident; in reality the only airman doing any real bomb aiming in a given formation was the lead bombardier. Much of the time, to ensure adequate coverage of the target and to preclude mid-air collisions, a formation dropped its bombs on the cue of the formation leader. In effect, when the bombardiers in the formation saw their leader release his bombs, they released— toggled— their own. This underutilization of the bulk of the bombardiers' training struck a chord of irony among their highly trained ranks. "A monkey could have done what we were doing," grumbled one of them. They often called themselves "toggleers."

The training was necessary. If the formation leader aborted or was shot down, or if his equipment malfunctioned the alternate flight leader would have to lead and execute the bomb release. And if the alternate flight leader were unable to do the job, the next crew in line would have to take over. These types of situations were not uncommon. Also, the role of lead bombardier was shared—one bombardier couldn't fly every mission. Finally, as lead bombardiers were lost in combat or rotated home, they needed to be replaced. So even though many bombardiers did not use their training to the fullest, that training was probably justified.

Several features of the sights could be used regardless of where in the formation a particular ship was. For instance, the bombardier could settle the horizontal crosshair of the sight across his assigned portion of the target. Releasing in this manner would ensure that the bombs did not fall long or short.

A common boast of the day was that the Norden was capable of dropping a 500-pound bomb into a pickle barrel from 20,000 feet. Although the Norden's were generally accurate, no system—even today—is capable of such precision. More common was a circular error probable—or CEP—of about 1,000 feet. This meant that half of the bombs dropped from any given B-17 or B-24 would fall within a circle with a radius of 1,000 feet.

The errors could be attributed to any number of factors. Human error—especially in the face of enemy flak and fighters—was probably one of the most significant. The maintenance of the equipment was another major factor. The systems—ruggedized though they were—couldn't be tuned to factory specifications after weathering dozens or more missions. Further, elements as mundane as winds aloft, propwash from preceding aircraft, the assembly of the fins on the bombs, even the finish of the paint on the bombs could induce errors.

An error of 1,000 feet was not a particularly gross shortcoming. When one considers the size of a typical target, the numbers of bombers employed, and the dispersion of bombs required to achieve the desired effects, the system was *accurate enough*. Ruined Axis industrial complexes across the whole of Europe testified to this fact.

One of the factors that confounded accuracy the most was obscuration of the target by clouds. The bombardiers couldn't hit what they couldn't see. And they couldn't hit a target if weather conditions were such that they couldn't even get to it. That this was a factor is borne out by an excerpt from records of the 97th Bomb Group, a B-17 outfit. At the beginning of the campaign—the strike against the Ploesti marshalling yards on April 5, 1944—one of the group's squadrons lost the formation and returned without dropping its bombs. Nevertheless the bulk of the formation pressed on to the target where heavy cloud cover and smoke over the target made an accurate drop very difficult. The bombers released their loads even though the obscuration of the target made real-time hit assessment nearly impossible. As it turned out, even though the marshalling yard did suffer some damage, the nearby refinery facilities were hit much harder. A stroke of luck? A planned mistake? The answer is still unclear. Regardless, later strikes would not fare so well against obscured targets.

*   *   *

Finally, a good bombardier was important not just for the effect that well-placed bombs would have on the target, but also for keeping the formation exposed to enemy fire for the briefest time possible. A bombardier who was thoroughly familiar with his target and equipment stood less chance of setting the formation up poorly for the bomb run. If a faulty run at the target couldn't be salvaged, the entire formation was sometimes wheeled back around and set up for another run through the same flak and fighters that it had just fought through. It was as bad as flying two missions. Sometimes it was worse than two missions, not only because the defenders already had their guns zeroed in, but also because of the danger and difficulty inherent in flowing back into the stream of trailing groups of bombers. Midair collisions over the target were a constant hazard without even attempting this sort of maneuver.

*   *   *

The Fifteenth Air Force put an unconventional tool into the pockets of its fliers over Ploesti. Radio operators who were fluent in German were assigned to the lead aircraft of various bomb groups on certain strikes. These men monitored enemy fighter nets and used the information they gathered to predict the time, location and strength of the expected attacks.[1] The information provided by these specialists was just one more part of the overall effort that, when combined with all the other pieces, helped to ensure that the campaign against Ploesti would be a success.

Chapter 16

TEAMWORK

WHEN LIEUTENANT Russell Christesen arrived at the 463d Bomb Group's base at Celone on May 20, 1944, he was part of one of the very first replacement crews to join the unit; the 463d operated B-17s and had started combat operations only a few weeks earlier. Having just delivered a brand-new B-17G from halfway across the globe, the replacement crewmen were already feeling as if they were making a contribution to the effort.[1]

The officers in the crew were assigned to a tent that was empty only because its occupants had been lost over Ploesti two days earlier. As they settled in they couldn't help but wonder at the hopes and lives and dreams of the men they were replacing. It was an awkward sensation, and they felt like intruders. After getting their bedding and personal belongings into place they made their way around the squadron area to meet some of the unit's veteran airmen. The veterans' tales further whetted their appetite for operational training.

At this point in the war the Fifteenth Air Force was short of crews and reasoned that there was no better training for combat than actual combat. Christesen was nearly stunned when, the day after arriving, he found his name on the mission orders for the following day, a strike to Avezzano, Italy. The orders didn't stop coming. Over the next nine days he flew six missions to targets in Austria, France, Italy, and Yugoslavia. Just over a week after arriving he was nearly as combat-experienced as any navigator in the group.

The 775th Squadron operations staff posted the flight schedule and battle orders for the May 31 mission on the evening prior. Christesen noted his name on that list with some apprehension; his group had lost seventeen aircraft—nearly 30 percent of its total complement—in its first month of operations; and the losses had continued to mount since he had started his tour. He was exhausted; the mission over Zagreb that same day had been especially tough. Still, there was nothing to do about the assignment, so he went to bed just after sunset. His tent now felt as much a part of his life as any other place he had slept. But his sleep was fitful. He spent much of the night tossing and turning in apprehension of the next day's mission.

It is likely that the other airmen who made up the crew to which Christesen was assigned were also uneasy. Fortunately for them their roster had been left nearly intact; the trust and confidence that they had developed during the previous several months—in training and in combat—had made them a more effective team. And a more effective team was a more survivable team. But leaving crews intact was not always possible in the bomb groups of the Fifteenth Air Force; sometimes replacement crews had to be broken up to fill holes in established crews.

As it was, this crew's original pilot, Lt. Charlie "Chuck" Grogan, was moved to the right seat so that he could gain experience prior to captaining an airplane in combat. The pilot's seat was filled by an outsider, Lt. R. J. Lauper, who had just finished his stint as a co-pilot in which he had demonstrated the skills and maturity that were required to lead in combat. The original co-pilot, Lt. Jack Flenniken, was the only member of the crew who was reassigned. He was sent to another crew so that, like Grogan, he could gain experience prior to commanding the crew of a ship in combat. The rest of the crew included the bombardier, Lt. Al D. Richards; the engineer and top turret gunner, Sgt. Jack F. Haymaker; the ball turret gunner, Sgt. A. Orville Schuette; the radio operator, Sgt. Jesse M. Jones; the right waist gunner, Sgt. Jim R. McGlynchey; the left waist gunner, Sgt. Harvey L. Pearson; and the tail gunner, Sgt. Carl D. Lester. And of course Christesen, who remained at his position as the navigator.

*   *   *

Up to May 31, it had been nearly two weeks since the Fifteenth Air Force had attacked Ploesti during the day. Over the course of the campaign that spring, the Axis would enjoy only one other such respite. The German and Romanian defenders used the time to their advantage to repair their fighters and increase their state of readiness. It is also certain that repair crews worked furiously to patch up bomb damage to the refineries.

Nevertheless, Spaatz and his planners had not forgotten Ploesti, nor the importance of its destruction as one of the cornerstones of his Oil Plan. Recent strikes by the Eighth Air Force had successfully hit Nazi synthetic oil plants in Northern Europe. These strikes had caused real damage and equally real concern to German war planners, to whom it was obvious that the Allies were mounting a systematic effort to deny Germany the fuel it needed to fight. The intelligence annex to the field order for the May 31 mission neatly detailed recent progress and the importance of operations against Ploesti:

> Successful attacks on Wiener-Neustadter complex have raised oil to high priority. Detailed analysis of results to date indicates that destruction of remaining active capacity at Ploesti will create critical situation for entire Axis war effort and make possible further important inroads through attacks in Austria, Hungary, Yugoslavia and Italy. Eighth Air Force has now damaged all but 2 of the major synthetic plants in its area making it possible for Fifteenth to destroy sufficient refinery and synthetic capacity to raise total cut in production close to 75 percent. Destruction of vital installations in targets selected will immobilize Ploesti capacity for several months.[2]

* * *

The wake-up call came to Christesen's tent at 0330. He and his tent-mates put on their khaki uniforms—complete with full insignia—and strapped on shoulder holsters with .45-caliber pistols. One of Christesen's rituals on mission days was to place a small New Testament in his left breast pocket, over his heart. It had a metal cover with an engraving: "May this keep you safe from harm," and had been given to him by his parents the previous Christmas.

The sleepy men made their way to the officer's mess, where they had a breakfast of powdered eggs, warmed Spam, fresh baked bread with orange marmalade, powdered milk, and coffee. After eating they returned to their tent and pulled on their bulky flying pants, jackets, and boots. They laced their regular shoes together and carried them in the event they had to bail out. The shoes were much better for walking than heavy flying boots.

Next, they boarded a troop truck for the trip to the group's briefing shack, where military policemen stood guard outside. They took seats on makeshift benches of planks supported by bomb crates. At the front of the room was the ubiquitous map covered by a dark blue curtain. On another makeshift easel was a sketch of the formation, indicating aircraft and squadron positions.

They snapped to attention as the group commander, Col. Frank Kurtz walked to the front of the room and barked out, "As you were, men!" After the men settled back into their seats the curtain was drawn back from the map, and there was the long, red yarn—stretching all the way to Ploesti. The room was filled with muffled groans. "Men," Kurtz said, "our target for today is the Xenia Refinery at Ploesti."

The group operations officer gave the details. One of two B-17 groups from the 5th Bomb Wing—the other was the 301st—the 463d was ordered to attack the Xenia Refinery. A number of B-24 bomb groups would be attacking other targets in the Ploesti complex, to include the Romana Americana, Concordia Vega and Dacia Romana refineries. This was to be the first attack since the disastrous mission of May 18, the same mission that had claimed Christesen's tent's previous occupants.

Their formation would be augmented by special pathfinder aircraft. These were radar-equipped B-17s that were designed to be able to find the target in the event it was obscured by smoke or clouds. Each airplane was loaded with twenty, 250-pound GP bombs. They also carried three cartons of radar-reflective "window," which was designed to confuse the enemy radars. This was to be jettisoned overboard from just before the IP until they cleared the target. Their bombing altitude was to be 23,000 feet.[3]

After the operations officer's brief, the intelligence officer stepped up to the platform. His brief was not encouraging. The enemy situation had changed little, and the airmen could expect intensive flak and fighter opposition. He did note that the fighters lately seemed to avoid closely flown formations and instead tended to pick on stragglers. This was heartening, except of course in the event that a crew's airplane became a straggler.

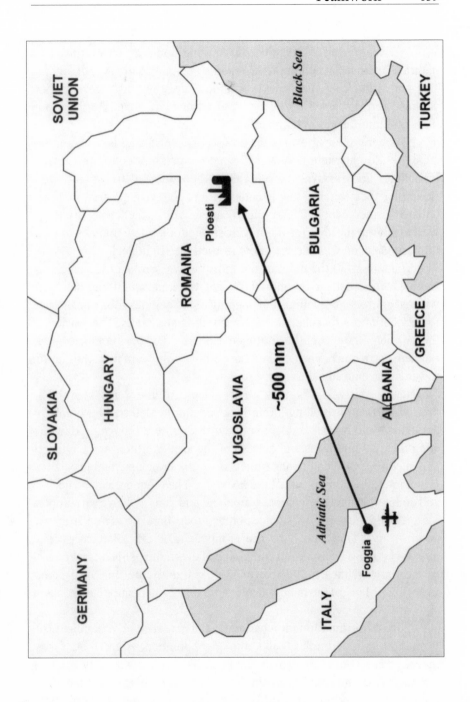

The weather brief predicted outstanding bombing conditions. This naturally meant that conditions would also be outstanding for defending flak and fighters. Following the weather brief they all "hacked" their watches and dispersed into separate briefings conducted by the group navigator and the group bombardier.

Following their briefings the crew's officers made their way to the supply building where they were issued oxygen masks, life preservers, parachutes and survival packets. They then boarded trucks and were driven to their aircraft hardstands. There, the ground crew and six enlisted airmen, who did not typically attend any of the formal briefings, were readying the ship for flight. Christesen took a few minutes to brief the rest of the crew while the pilots readied the flight deck.

At about 0530 the quiet of the morning was broken by a crackling rumble as more than a hundred Wright Cyclone radial engines were whirled to life. The cracking and popping of the engines soon transitioned to a smooth bass roar that shook surrounding structures. The tension of the airmen—now tightly buttoned aboard the big bombers—was ratcheted up a notch when a green flare climbed skyward from the control tower. It was the signal to taxi.

Nearly thirty B-17s took their places in line for takeoff. The prop wash from preceding aircraft rocked and jostled trailing bombers. Too, dirt, sand, grass, and smoke blew through the lightening dawn to sting the eyes and faces and nostrils of the airmen. Pilots and engineers kept a close eye on engine instruments—at the same time taking care not to run into other aircraft or off the taxiways. The other crewmen checked and double-checked the charts, equipment, and guns at their own stations.

At 0545, just at first light, another green flare was fired from the control tower, the signal for the group to take off. At thirty-second intervals the big ships roared and bounced down the pierced steel planks of the runway, then broke free of the earth and climbed to join their formation. Many of the men said silent prayers as their ships carried them skyward.

Assembling the formation was not just a matter-of-fact exercise. The formation was complex, and the big bombers were not easily maneuvered. Too, each airplane looked alike, and it was only by their markings that one could be distinguished from another. Even then, each bomber generally flew in a different position from mission to mission. The danger of mid-air collisions was very real, and not particularly

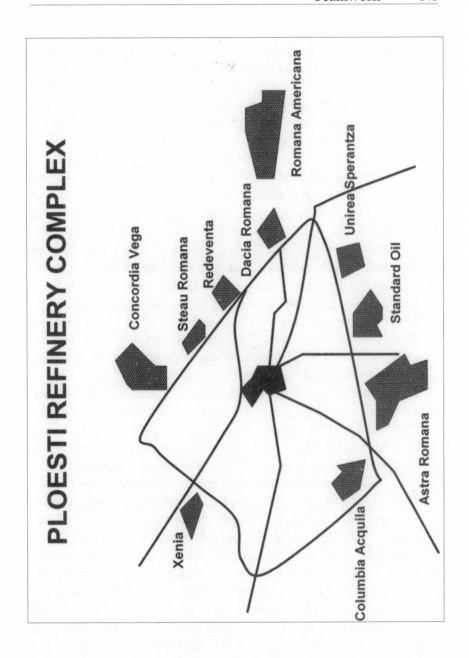

uncommon. Through the course of the war significant numbers of airmen were killed before they ever started for their targets.

On this day, the 463d assembled without incident, and more than an hour after getting airborne joined on the 301st Bomb Group at an altitude of 5,000 feet for the trip to Ploesti. The 301st was assigned to lead the two groups. Once over the Adriatic, the gunners let loose a few rounds as they test-fired their weapons. At about 0740 the two groups were intercepted and joined by weaving formations of P-51 and P-38 escort fighters from the 306th Fighter Wing.

The flight across the Adriatic and then across Yugoslavia, Bulgaria, and into Romania was largely uneventful for the 463d. The group reported no encounters with enemy fighters, though other groups airborne that day were receiving more than their share of attention. It was the flak that had the attention of Christesen and the rest of his crew. As the formation approached Homoraciul—the IP—from the southwest, the airmen could see thick clouds of black antiaircraft fire to their right—a sparkling mass of smoking black blossoms. It was only a few minutes later that they hit the IP and swung south, directly toward those deadly clouds. Christesen hadn't seen flak like this before.

They watched the formation in front of them disappear into the black cloud of flak explosions. Then it was their turn. Exploding ordnance beneath them lifted the airplane. Nevertheless, on the bomb run they had no choice but to fly straight and level and sweat it out. The explosions from especially close bursts of flak cast shadows that unnerved the airmen. Along with the shadows came red-hot shards of shrapnel.

The airplane was suddenly jolted by a direct hit—seeming almost to stop them in mid-air. Lauer called out "What the hell was that?" Jack Haymaker, in the upper turret, shouted out, "Hit on the right wing, we're losing no fuel!" The right wing had a hole blown clean through it, a direct hit on the outboard fuel tank between the two engines. Fortunately, the tank was empty. The antiaircraft round had malfunctioned and hadn't exploded until it passed through the wing, but it peppered the top of the bomber with shrapnel holes. The crews luck was considerable; if the shell had fused as it was supposed to, it would have blown their wing off.

Shaken, but not deterred, Lauper and Grogan maintained control of the airplane and held their place in the formation as they continued the bomb run. The bomb bay doors were opened, and at 1029, Al Richards called out "Bombs away!" The airplane surged upward as the two-and-a-half tons of high explosive bombs left the vehicle and fell away toward the refinery.

As was standard practice, the bomb bay was visually checked after the target run to make certain that all of the bombs had been safely dropped. It was not an infrequent occurrence for bombs to hang in place after the release. This could be extremely dangerous as the bombs could fall out over friendly territory, or onto other bombers. Worse—and it had sometimes happened—the bombs could break loose and explode when the aircraft landed.

As luck would have it, Haymaker discovered that one of the bombs on the lower left side hadn't fallen clear. It was hung up on the rear bomb rack. Adding to the danger was the fact that the front arming impeller—a small propeller that was designed to spin in the slipstream and drive the bomb's firing pin into place—was turning freely. Once the impeller completed its rotations, the bomb would be armed and could be exploded by a blow to the fuse. The bomb had to be broken loose. Russ Christesen recounted how the bombardier, Al Richards worked together with Jack Haymaker:

> Haymaker immediately got down into the open bomb bay and pinned the impeller, preventing the fuse from being armed. Next, Richards made his way back to the bomb bay to help formulate a plan with Haymaker. With the shackle on the outside set of racks and the bomb bay doors stuck open, there was nowhere to stand while trying to get rid of the bomb. The two of them waited until we were over the Adriatic before getting to work; there was no sense dumping the deadly missile on some poor peasant's head. By then we were also lower, so the temperature was not quite so bone-numbing cold.
>
> Richards then quite literally put his life into Haymaker's hands: He had Haymaker slip his right arm through the parachute harness on his back and wrap his left arm around the inside bomb rack. Then he had Haymaker suspend him over the jammed bomb. And also over two miles of empty space! It typified the trust that we had in each other.
>
> Working in that eye-watering wind blast, Richards banged away with a hammer and chisel on that shackle for what seemed quite a long time. It was an exceedingly difficult job as the bomb bay was cramped and his flying clothes were bulky—and he had to be careful not to drop his tools. Besides, he was hanging nearly upside down. Poor Haymaker used every ounce of his strength to keep the two of them inside the airplane. With Richards banging away on the

shackle, one slip would have sent them both tumbling out. But the two of them worked well together, and the bomb finally fell free into the water. I think their teamwork really typified what made our crew so effective.

That teamwork continued to serve the crew in good stead. Christesen went on to complete four more missions to Ploesti and successfully finished his combat tour. Likewise, every other man of the team made it home.

* * *

The May 31 mission might serve as evidence for those who would argue the superiority of the B-17 over the B-24 in terms of ruggedness. None of the 53 B-17s sent over the target was lost, even though they sustained heavy damage from flak. Of the 27 bombers from the 463d that made it over the target that day, 24 were hit. Conversely, of the 428 B-24s that made it over the target, 16 were shot down. Granted, the skies over Romania were hardly a sterile test environment, and the B-17s didn't encounter the same fighter resistance as the B-24s, but the evidence adds fuel to the perennial argument. In fact, an analysis of losses over Ploesti during the campaign of 1944 shows that the percentage of losses for the B-24s, at 5.1 percent, was more than twice the 2.4 percent loss rate of the B-17s.[4]

* * *

Regardless, the May 31 mission was the only time that B-17s went to Ploesti and returned with no losses. Overall, bombing results were mixed because the smoke screen had a detrimental effect on bombing accuracy. The Axis put more than 120 fighter sorties into the air. P-38 and P-51 escorts claimed to have shot down 22 of those fighters for a loss of six of their own.[5]

Chapter 17

Romanian

THE MISSION of June 6 was interesting because it marked the first really large-scale attempt by the Americans to spread out the enemy fighter defenses in Romania with a geographically dispersed bomber force. In fact, some of the B-17s that attacked Galati Airdrome were based out of the Soviet Union as part of Operation FRANTIC.[1] Communications and transportation targets were the objectives of six different bomb groups. The intelligence annex noted the growing importance of the Danube River as a transportation route for Ploesti's petroleum "as most oil from Ploesti must be shipped west over Danube for refining."[2]

The Romana Americana, Dacia Romana, and Xenia oil refineries in Ploesti received the attentions of a further eleven bomb groups, and the marshaling yards in Brasov were hit by four bomb groups. The Germans and Romanians, even working together, were unable to defend against so many attackers. Nevertheless, 14 of the 310 bombers sent aloft were brought down.[3]

* * *

Romanian Air Force Lt. Ion Dobran was one of the many hundreds of fighter pilots from that nation who were largely unheralded and whose actions until very recently were relatively unknown.[4] Dobran, who was born in Valeni Podgoria in 1919, first trained in fighters during 1941. He was placed in an operational squadron during 1942, and by June 1944 had scored five aerial victories over various Soviet types while engaged in combat on the Eastern Front.

It is June 6, 1944—D-Day—and the Allies are storming the beaches at Normandy. It is unlikely though that Ion Dobran is aware of the far-away action. In fact he is in a dugout playing cards with fellow squadron mates. He is assigned to the Romanian 9th Fighter Group, now flying Me-109Gs. A veteran of many air battles against the Soviets, he has yet to fly in combat against the Americans. He won't have to wait long. Today, as part of the campaign against Ploesti, the Americans are striking many related targets across Romania.

Suddenly word reaches the airfield at Tecuci that an American bomber formation is inbound. Eagerly, Dobran races out to his aircraft and spins the engine to life. Wasting no time, he signals one of his squadron mates to join on his wing as he roars airborne. As the two fighters climb overhead their base they are able to monitor the progress of the American bombers. Their radio controller—"Albatross"— broadcasts that the Americans are headed toward Independenta, a railroad station to the south, along the Siretul River, not far from the important transportation hub of Galati.

Climbing southbound, Dobran tries without success to catch fighter formations that have gotten airborne ahead of him. In the distance he catches sight of the bombers: "Suddenly, I vaguely see the American formations like sparkles." Soon afterward the bombers release their loads on the airfield at Galati. He is too late.

But just as the bombers finish their run, Dobran catches sight of another formation of four fighters, below and to his left. With their red-painted noses, he is unsure if they are from a sister squadron, or perhaps enemy ships. He advances his engine to full power and climbs above them, parallel to their path. After a short time he recognizes them as P-51 Mustangs, the most dangerous of the American fighters. The P-51s have taken up a position to the rear of the bomber formation, and Dobran has in turn slid into position behind them. The entire procession is headed northeast now, into the Soviet Union, just east of Bolgrad.

Dobran is at nearly 20,000 feet now, well above the Americans, but he is alone; somewhere he has lost his wingman. He is eager to fight, particularly since he has an altitude advantage, and because it appears that the Americans are not yet aware of his presence. He pushes his fighter over into an attack, gaining airspeed and closing the distance. He drops slightly below the Mustangs, then pulls up, and takes aim on the right-hand ship. The Americans are oblivious and continue flying in a perfect parade formation.

Dobran closes the range. With his thumb he opens fire with his fighter's 20mm cannon, and with his forefinger he triggers the two 7.62mm machine guns. Using the track of the tracer rounds, he corrects the spread of his fire and watches rounds pepper the Mustang. For a moment there is no reaction from the Americans, but then the stricken ship arcs left under the rest of the formation, while the other three fighters start a protective climb to the right.

Dobran follows his smoking prey into a left turn for just a moment before he breaks off his attack and presses on toward the bombers. He has his engine in full over-boost, but he has lost some airspeed and is aware that the other three American fighters are in hot pursuit—and gaining. Desperate not to share his victim's fate, Dobran abruptly throws his fighter into a steep dive. As his airspeed approaches 500 miles per hour, he pulls back on the stick and climbs into the, sun hoping that the Americans won't be able to match him.

It's no good. "I see them climbing like glass pearls—one, two, three—after me." The lead fighter opens fire on Dobran. The P-51 is in perfect firing position—directly centered behind him in the climb. As his airspeed slows, Dobran has no choice but to head downhill. He kicks left rudder and hangs in space as his ship slowly exchanges nose for tail and starts back to earth. In the meantime the following Mustang—there is only one now—climbs past him to the right and executes his own reversal.

Dobran is shaken by the skill of the American pilot, and by the superiority of the P-51. "He is good. I execute a spin—as if I were hit. But it is in vain." Desperate, he makes a short series of sharp turns, then, turning so hard that vapor streams from his wingtips, he exhausts his entire retinue of aerobatics. It does no good. "I cannot get rid of him and the anger blinds me—a red curtain covers my eyes for one moment. I am boiling with rage. If we were face-to-face I would fight him without reason, but here in the sky I can do nothing."

Dobran climbs for the sun again but to no avail. His fighter has been hit and is streaming glycol. There are other hits, but fortunately his aircraft doesn't explode. Instinctively he reaches for the canopy. It's time to bail out, but he stays with his ship.

As the fighter descends, suddenly the canopy ices over. Hardly able to see, he makes sharp, short, zigzags, hoping to throw off the American pilot. They are low now, and even though Dobran's speed is very slow, the P-51 is still stuck to his tail. Finally, he pulls his fighter into a stall then recovers at less than a thousand feet.

With no good option he lowers his landing gear and makes for a barley field, hoping to land and clear the airplane before the American can set his ship afire. "I fasten the seat belts and I land—frightened out of my wits—waiting to roll over on the soft ground." As soon as the Me-109 stops, Dobran leaps clear and looks skyward, sure that the P-51 will be hurtling down in a strafing run. There is nothing but the distant fading rattle of an aircraft engine. Dobran is ecstatic with this unexpected gift of life. "Then from inside, like a huge river, an unspeakable joy—the joy of a man who can see again the sky, the sun, and the grass. The wind is caressing me. Oh God, how beautiful is life when you start from broken pieces. After all, we are modern gladiators—one of the two fighters should die. Who pointed the thumb up for forgiveness?"

*   *   *

Ion Dobran fell to American fighters once again during a fierce air battle on July 26—he was uninjured. He survived the war after scoring ten aerial victories and having been shot down three times.

*   *   *

Of all the aircraft types that Germany and her allies used to defend Ploesti and its approaches, the most effective and the one used in greatest numbers was the German Me-109. Produced in greater numbers than any other fighter in history, the original design was nevertheless ten years old in 1944. It first reached production in 1936 and it was in that same year that the world was stunned by its appearance overhead the Berlin Olympics. Its sleek and efficient lines—and its performance—were unlike anything else in the world. There was nothing else in production anywhere that could hope to match it.

When the Nazis launched their war in Europe in 1939, the Me-109 swept everything out of its way. It quickly underscored its reputation as the finest fighter in the world. It wasn't until it met the newer British Supermarine Spitfire over France that its unrivaled superiority came to be challenged. The two aircraft were nearly evenly matched in almost every respect. Over the next several years the graceful Spitfire managed to hold the line in the West long enough for the Americans to arrive in strength with their newer fighter designs.

In order to keep up with the aircraft being fielded by its foes, the Germans expended considerable energy and resources to further develop and modernize the Me-109. Perhaps the most recognized, and certainly the most produced variant was the Me-109G. The "Gustav," as it was popularly known, was powered by a Daimler Benz DB 605 A-1, V-12 liquid-cooled engine that produced 1,475 horsepower. With this engine it had a top speed of just over 400 miles per hour—nearly identical to the American fighters that opposed it. It was produced in many sub-variants that were armed with a variety of different machine guns and cannon. It was the Gustav that was used in several different variants by Ploesti's defenders in 1944.

The Me-109G had several strong points. It was relatively fast, and decently well armed. It could absorb some amount of battle damage and still bring its pilot home. Too, it was more maneuverable than the P-38, and was, in experienced hands, at least competitive against the much more modern P-51. It's small size made it more difficult to see than larger types, and a tougher target to hit. Above all, Germany and its partners had the equipment and workers available to produce it in huge numbers. Even Romanian license-built aircraft augmented the German-built planes that its air force operated.

But the Me-109G also had its shortcomings. The design was getting older and heavier—it shared hardly any components with the models fielded several years earlier. It wasn't easy to fly. Accidents were commonplace, and it is likely that as many aircraft were lost to poor flying as were lost in combat. This was very important as the quality of Axis pilots deteriorated badly during the war's last years.

The quality of the aircraft's construction was also inferior to that of the American fighters. With its limited access to resources Germany was hard pressed to provide the specialized materials needed to construct high-performance engines and aircraft. Too, the quality of the slave labor used to produce many of the components was inferior. Adolf Galland, the commander of the German fighter forces, marveled at the performance and reliability of captured American fighter engines compared to their German counterparts.

Perhaps the design's biggest shortcoming was its lack of range. When it was engineered during the 1930s, extended range operations for pursuit fighters weren't a major consideration for most air forces. This was not necessarily a severe disadvantage when it was used to defend point targets—for instance the refineries at Ploesti. But it limited the type's versatility for longer-ranged operations that might have hit the bomber streams further out, or ambushed and disorganized the escorting fighters. Even used as a point-defense fighter, its limited range often dictated when and where it had to attack rather than allowing its pilots the luxury of choosing precisely the right time and place to engage.

Despite its shortcomings, the Me-109 was a formidable opponent. It was the type flown and favored by most of Germany's highest-scoring aces. It was also the fighter most favored by Romania's fighter pilots—preferred even over the locally produced IAR 80/81 series. Over Ploesti it shot down a considerable number of American bombers and fighters, and it killed a not-inconsiderable number of American men.

*   *   *

The Me-109 was also commonly known as the Bf 109. The two letters were derived from the Bayerische Flugzeugwerke complex in Augsburg, Germany, where Dr. Willy Messerschmitt led the team that designed and produced the successful fighter. Seeking to capitalize on Messerschmitt's name, the company was incorporated in 1938 as Messerschmitt AG (Aktien Gesellschaft). Subsequently, the Me-109 designation began to appear. The Germans tended to use the original Bf 109 designation more often, although they also used the Me-109 designation. (Me-109 is seen more often in American and British writing.)

Regardless of the designation, American crewmen all over Europe were learning the hard way that the Axis fighter plane was an efficient killing machine.

Chapter 18

Lightning

THE MISSIONS during April and May 1944 had scored some significant successes against many of the major refinery complexes, but the Romana Americana refinery on the east side of Ploesti had so far escaped serious damage. A number of factors, including an especially effective smoke screen, had combined to protect it from more significant destruction. As the largest and most productive of the Ploesti plants, this situation was intolerable to Spaatz's Oil Plan men; the Romana Americana refinery alone was producing nearly 15 percent of the total Axis petroleum supply.[1] In an effort to negate the effects of the protective smoke screen that had spoiled previous high-altitude attacks on the critical refinery, a plan was devised that borrowed a page from the TIDALWAVE play book.

*   *   *

Ploesti would be attacked from low-level. But this time, rather than striking with B-24s—something that had never been seriously considered since the last low-level raid—Ploesti would be attacked by P-38 Lightnings. The Lightnings would ingress at low altitude until just prior to reaching the target, at which time they would climb several thousand feet and execute a dive-bombing attack.

There were several reasons why it was thought that massed P-38s would be able mount an effective low altitude strike without suffering intolerable losses. First, the P-38 was faster than the B-24. Cruising just above the nap of the earth at about 230 miles per hour, the Lightnings stood a better chance of arriving in the target area undetected. Once they got into the target area, they could push their speed up at least another 100 miles per hour, making them much more difficult for antiaircraft guns to hit. The P-38 was a much smaller airplane than the B-24. Common sense held that a smaller target was a more difficult target. The P-38 was a fighter. Even laden with extra fuel and a 1,000-pound bomb, it would still be more maneuverable than a B-24, and would be better able to defend itself against enemy fighters. Whereas the smoke screens put up by the defenders around the refinery had foiled the high-altitude heavy bomber attacks, it was felt that the surprise arrival of a low-level P-38 strike would deny the defenders the time necessary to create an effective smoke screen.

And even if a smoke screen was generated, it was believed that the P-38 pilots, climbing to only about 6,000 or 7,000 feet, would be able to see well enough to dive bomb through the choking, gray pall. The P-38s would be flying out of bases from around Foggia, only half the distance from Ploesti that the Benghazi-based Liberators had traveled nearly a year earlier. This meant that a fighter escort could be provided for the bomb-laden P-38s. It was decided that the P-38s executing the strike would be accompanied by a like number of P-38s unfettered with bombs. It was to be an all-Lockheed Lightning show.

The P-38 was the best choice between the two fighters available to the planners; the P-51 Mustang was the other type on hand. Both fighters had the required range to fly at low altitude from Foggia to Ploesti and back. But the P-51 was a smaller aircraft than the P-38 and the 1,000-pound bombs that were required may have been too difficult to carry over such a distance. Also very likely considered was the fact that the P-51 was a single-engine aircraft. Because the target was heavily defended by antiaircraft guns the P-38, with its two engines, was probably more survivable than the P-51.

*   *   *

The bombing portion of the mission was assigned to the three squadrons of the 82d Fighter Group (95th, 96th, and 97th) and the 1st

Fighter Group was tasked with providing the escort with its three squadrons (27th, 71st, and 94th). Both were veteran units, having come to North Africa via Great Britain in 1942. The two groups subsequently played significant roles in the advance from North Africa, across the Mediterranean, into Italy, and now into southern and central Europe. They counted a number of aces among their ranks and were considered more than equal to the task. Their respective staffs were given preliminary no-note briefings in the days before actual orders for the mission were issued. Like TIDALWAVE, this mission depended on security and surprise; everyone was admonished to treat the plans with the utmost secrecy.

Tasking orders were issued on June 9, 1944, only the day before the mission was to be flown.[2] Immediately the staff and crews of both groups went to work. Coordination for the rendezvous between the groups was worked out, as well as the formation for the low-level ingress. A route was chosen that promised to "effect maximum surprise and receive minimum reaction from the hundreds of antiaircraft guns in the area."[3]

The 82d Group pilots were briefed that evening and given time to study mosaics and photographs of the target, with particular emphasis on the three key aiming points: a boiler house, distillation units, and the cracking plant.[4] At the same time, they reviewed the tactics and procedures they would use to deliver the 1,000-pound bombs—weapons they were unaccustomed to using.

At Vincenzo, home of the 82d, the entire base was locked down due to the sensitive nature of the upcoming strike. There was too much work to do anyway. Mechanics and support personnel threw themselves into an all-out effort to get as many aircraft ready for the mission as possible. Especially critical to the success of the operation was the mounting of the big 300-gallon external fuel tanks on the 82d's fighters. These were absolutely essential; with a 1,000-pound bomb slung underneath the other side of the fuselage there was no way that the heavily loaded P-38s were going to make it without the extra fuel provided by the oversized external tanks.[5]

There were problems though. The big tanks, normally used only for ferrying the aircraft over long distances, and not for combat, didn't arrive until June 9. Worse, they came without their required special strut sockets. Fortunately the service squadron managed to produce the essential parts, and the last tanks were successfully hung only a few hours before takeoff.[6]

*   *   *

Lieutenant Colonel Ben A. Mason was the deputy commander of the 82d, and was excited at the prospect of taking part in what was obviously such an important mission. Mason had completed his flight training in 1934, when most of the young officers in the group had still been in grade school. When the war broke out Mason had been among the first to put in a request for assignment to a combat command. His initial request was denied—as were the next several. He languished at Stateside units as an instructor while his superior officers told him to forget about flying fighters in combat, because he was too old. Mason wouldn't stand for it: "If I'm good enough to teach these youngsters to fly in combat, you can be damn sure I'm good enough to lead them in combat."[7]

His protests didn't do him any good. The closest he got to combat was when he wangled an assignment to ferry a P-38 to North Africa during 1943. Later that year, he was formally transferred back to North Africa where he served on various staffs. Early 1944 saw him assigned to the operations office of the Mediterranean Allied Air Force at Cacerta, north of Naples. Finally, he couldn't stand it any longer. He flew to Fifteenth Air Force headquarters in Bari and made a personal appeal for a combat assignment to General Nathan Twining. It worked. A couple of weeks later Mason was assigned to the 82d. He had only been there a short time when he bagged his first enemy aircraft, an Me-109, on May 10, while escorting bombers to Wiener Neustadt. Too old for fighters indeed!

The precedent at the 82d—and at many other units—was that the group commander and the deputy group commander did not fly on the same mission. This precluded the group being left without senior leadership in the event both were lost on a particularly rough mission. Mason was able to convince the 82d's commander, Lt. Col. William P. Litton, to make an exception for the mission to Ploesti. It was an important one, and Litton no doubt recognized that Mason's leadership would be a stabilizing influence.

Before turning in for the evening, Mason made note of the tremendous effort the ground crews were putting in.

*   *   *

At the 1st Fighter Group's base at Salsola, just north of Foggia, only select members of the staff and senior pilots were yet aware of the nature of the next day's mission. As the escorts, their part of the mission would require no special target planning. Therefore, the rank-and-file pilots had little or no idea of what was in store for them the following day.

*   *   *

The pilots of both groups were up very early for their mission briefings. Target assignments were reviewed for the individual squadrons of the 82d. The 95th's pilots were to hit the main distillation plant; the 96th's were tasked with hitting the main boiler house; and the 97th's were to attack the main cracking plant. If those three critical points could be destroyed, production at the Romana Americana refinery would be gravely impaired.

The 1st Fighter Group pilots were caught by surprise when the mission was laid out for them. Nothing similar had ever been attempted. There was a consensus of relief when they learned that the 82d was charged with dive-bombing through the flak at the refinery. As the escorts, they felt that their chances of survival were much better than those of the dive-bombers.

They were wrong.

Shortly after the briefings were concluded the lead aircraft from both fighter groups got airborne with the first light of dawn, shortly after 0500. The 82d put forty-six aircraft into the air, while the 1st managed to launch forty-eight of the twin-boomed fighters. At 0540 the two groups rendezvoused over the Gulf of Manfredonia at 2,000 feet. Once joined, Lieutenant Colonel Litton of the 82d swung the formation around and took up a heading of 068 degrees. Cruising now at low altitude above the Adriatic, the next landfall would be Yugoslavia.

*   *   *

Almost as soon as aircraft became airborne they began to abort. The P-38 was blessed in that it had two engines. If one was hit, the other was powerful enough to take the airplane home. The P-38 was also cursed because it had two engines. With two engines there was twice as much to go wrong, particularly when those two engines were the 12-cylinder Allison V-1710 inline types that powered the P-38. The Allison engines had their proponents, but few would argue that they were as reliable as the Pratt & Whitney radials that powered a number of types including the P-47, or even the inline Packard-built Merlins that pulled the P-51. If one engine went bad on a P-38 it was cause to abort a mission.

Evidently a lot of engines went bad. Of the forty-six aircraft that the 82d sent aloft, seven returned to base—six of those for mechanical reasons.[8] For its part, the 1st sent back nine aircraft before reaching the target area.[9] The two-group formation would shrink from ninety-four aircraft to seventy-seven before it crossed into Romania.

Litton led his low-level formation across the Adriatic and through the mountains of Yugoslavia. Here, the 82d's pilots could feel how differently their heavily loaded aircraft responded. The 1,000-pound bomb—mounted on the left fuselage shackle, and the 300-gallon fuel tank—mounted on the right fuselage shackle, together weighed 1,000 pounds more than the two 165-gallon fuel tanks normally carried. The pilots could actually feel the gas in the large external fuel tank sloshing about as they maneuvered through Yugoslavia's mountainous terrain. The sluggish response of the aircraft to control inputs at low altitude made many pilots uncomfortable.

Ben Mason almost aborted, but it wasn't for engine trouble. He was suffering from a bout of gastrointestinal distress, a malady that was not particularly uncommon throughout the Fifteenth Air Force. But this particular episode was very nearly crippling him. He carried on. "I'd be damned if I was going to abort the mission just because I had to relieve myself!" At any rate, as the formation reached Yugoslavia and the tension began to increase, his discomfort passed. There were other things to concentrate on.

There was only one incident of note during the flight through Yugoslavia. Unable to continue for unknown reasons, Lt. Walter Leslie of the 95th squadron pulled his aircraft up and away from the rest of the formation and bailed out.[10] The pilotless P-38 exploded as it hit the ground. Leslie was subsequently picked up by a partisan group and returned to Italy two months later.

Once across the mountains, Litton dropped his fighters right down to the deck and across the short northwest spur of Bulgaria and into Romania. He was at the head of the 96th Squadron. Behind him was the 95th, followed by the 97th, to which Mason was attached. Upon reaching the Danube, Litton angled slightly to his right and picked up a more easterly heading of 086 degrees. The flight then roughly paralleled the river until it reached the eastern end of Lake Balta Greaco, just north of the Danube and about 30 miles south of Bucharest. The lake was the designated IP.

The 1st Fighter Group rode herd on the 82d—offset to the south on their right side. Lead squadron of the 1st was the 27th, led by Lt. Armour Miller.[11] To its north was the 71st, and trailing the other two was the 94th. Nearly three hours after getting airborne, and two-and-a-half hours since effecting their join-up, the two groups had covered more than five hundred miles.

*   *   *

The mission planners had determined that one of the chief elements required for the success of the attack would be surprise. This element wasn't achieved. German *Freya* and *Wurzburg* radar units—and most probably observers on the ground—detected the formation in time for fighter controllers to order a scramble.

For his part, Capt. Dan Vizante, commander of the ARR's (*Aeronautica Regala Romana*) 6th Fighter Group, was stunned when the alarm was sounded at 0800; American raids rarely occurred before 1000.[12] He rushed outside with his alarm pistol and fired a green flare, the order for an immediate scramble. In short minutes the Romanian IAR 81 fighters of his group were joining over the field. They climbed and carved a wide arc through the sky as they pointed toward their staging point northwest of Bucharest, nearly seventy miles distant.

At the same time that Vizante was rushing to get his group airborne, units of all other types were flushing their aircraft into the sky from various airfields. No one knew what the Americans were up to, and they didn't want to be caught flat-footed on the ground. By the time the two P-38 groups reached Lake Balta Greaco, Romanian and German aircraft of all types were stampeding skyward.

*   *   *

What happened after the formation of P-38s reached the IP is a jumble of conflicting recollections, claims, and unintentionally perpetuated confusion. The following account is the result of an extensive effort to untangle the many differing descriptions. It is by no means the last word on this engagement—no account ever will be—but it has been prepared after a careful study of multiple sources and is an honest effort to reconcile, or at least note, the differences.

*   *   *

The three squadrons of the 1st Fighter Group started their turn to the north before the 82d's bomb-carrying aircraft. The 1st checked back east to redress the formation and, at about the same time, the 82d started its turn north. Again, the squadrons of the 1st turned back north, but in the process of so many turns, the different units became spread out, with one flight of the 71st Squadron becoming completely separated from the rest.[13] At about this time the escorting aircraft of the 1st jettisoned their external tanks and started to climb in preparation for contact with the enemy.

Almost immediately after settling down on a northerly heading the P-38s encountered the first of what would be a constant stream of enemy aircraft. The larger portion of the 71st quickly dropped down on six Do-217 twin-engine bombers. The enemy aircraft didn't stand a chance against the heavy weapons of the P-38s, and all of them were quickly hacked out of the sky.[14]

It was probably very close to this moment when Romanian commander Dan Vizante received his second surprise of the morning. He was racing to the head of his fighter formation when "I heard in my headset: 'Attention Paris Attention Paris, Turkeys over the nest.' I recognized the voice of Traian Garriliu, chief of the command post at the airport Papesti-Leordeni, telling me that the American fighter planes [turkeys] were heading for the airport. Simultaneously I could see, at very low altitude, wave upon wave of Lightning fighter planes with twin bombs coming from the east, heading straight for our airport."

Vizante and his group couldn't have had a better home field advantage.

The formation Vizante had spotted was the three-flight grouping (twelve aircraft) of the 71st, which was by now trailing the other two squadrons of the 1st Fighter Group by several miles. The twin bombs Vizante describes were the standard 165-gallon external fuel tanks slung underneath the fuselage.[15] Flush from the excitement of scoring six quick victories, the P-38 pilots were caught low, slow and unaware. Vizante led twenty-three IAR 81s down from 4,600 feet in a slashing head-on attack. Three P-38s went down on the first pass. The subsequent engagement was an incredibly wild melee that took place only hundreds of feet above the floor of a wide, shallow valley. So tight, low, and close was the fight that several aircraft were lost to collisions and to crashes into the ground. To make matters even more confusing, antiaircraft units on the ground fired indiscriminately into the entire mess.

In its description of events after the initial attack, the 71st Fighter Squadron's mission report details how the three flights stayed together and attempted a turn to the right, an effort that was frustrated by superior numbers of enemy aircraft. The enemy attacked simultaneously from all directions with flights of varying size. The report relates the caliber of the Romanian pilots: "The enemy was aggressive, skillful, courageous."[16]

The single-engine Romanian fighters played havoc with the P-38s. With the speed and altitude advantage that they held from their first diving pass, they were able to nip in and out of the fight with remarkable agility. This sort of fighting suited the maneuverable Romanian machines well. The arrival of a few P-38s from the 27th Squadron furthered the ferocity of the fighting. In only a few minutes nine Lightnings had crashed or been blown out of the sky. Vizante, an ace with fifteen aerial victories to his credit, claimed two more.

The fight wasn't entirely one-sided. At least three Romanian machines went down, either from gunfire or collisions. The valley floor was littered with the burning wreckage of American and Romanian fighters.

*   *   *

This particular engagement is striking because of the large discrepancies between claims made by both two sides regarding aerial victories. The claims are over-inflated when compared to records of actual losses. By any measure, the 71st took a beating. The squadron lost at least seven P-38s in this initial melee alone, and the 27th also lost two. But the Romanians claimed that they downed twenty-three Lightnings, and described an engagement that involved nearly a hundred of the American fighters. Clearly, they overstated their successes, particularly when they had the advantage of being able to count the wrecks that had fallen on their own countryside.

American claims were also exaggerated. The 71st Fighter Squadron's mission report officially details some of these claims. The report states that a total of six FW 190s were destroyed—five by Lt.

Herbert Hatch and one by Lt. Carl Hoenshell. It credits Hatch with probably destroying another FW 190 as well as damaging a separate FW 190. Lieutenant John Shepard is also credited with damaging an FW 190. Also, a CR. 42 was credited to Lt. William Armstrong.

In all, American pilots were credited with eleven confirmed victories for this engagement, whereas the Romanians allowed that they lost only three ships. The disparity is difficult to reconcile, inasmuch as the Romanians did not have a reputation for downplaying their losses. The differences can probably best be attributed to confusion on all sides during the frenzy of the battle. An indicator that the fighting was indeed frenzied was the wide range of reports from American pilots relative to the size of the attacking force; descriptions of the numbers within the enemy formation ran from twenty aircraft all the way up to a hundred.

*   *   *

An interesting sidebar to this engagement is that the Americans misidentified their adversaries as German FW-190s. This misconception was perpetuated for several decades and only relatively recently has it been corrected. The Romanian IAR 80/81 type was little known at the time, and it bore a marked resemblance to the German fighter.

The IAR 80 was actually a Romanian derivative of the Polish P.Z.L. P.24E fighter that was being license-built by the Romanian Aeronautical Industry factory in Brasov during the 1930s. The resulting design was distinctly modern, and when the first production models were completed at the end of 1940, they were the equal of the British Hurricane and the American P-40, if not the German Me-109.

The IAR 80 was fitted with a license-built Gnome-Rhone 14-cylinder radial engine producing 1,025 horsepower. It was capable of powering the aircraft up to 320 mph, and gave it a ceiling of nearly 35,000 feet. Through the aircraft's career, the installed armament varied, but it never really suffered from being too lightly armed, as was the case with many of its contemporaries. By all accounts the aircraft handled very nicely, was extremely maneuverable, and with its wide-tracked landing gear was easy to handle on the ground, especially during takeoff and landing.

Despite its wonderful handling characteristics, continued development of the IAR 80 and a slightly more powerful version, the IAR 81, was slow. It simply wasn't able to keep pace with better designs—including the Me-109. Although they occasionally managed to score well, they more often received worse than they gave and were clearly outperformed by the newer American fighter types. In all, just less than 450 examples of the two types were produced before the Romanians switched to construction of license-built Me-109s in 1944.

*   *   *

It is also likely that the American fliers may have mistaken the Romanian aircraft for German FW 190s for another reason. The Romanians were not considered to be as skilled or formidable as their German counterparts, and it may not have occurred to the Americans that the pilots who had handled them so roughly could have been anything but German.

The IAR 81s weren't the only misidentified types. The Italian-built CR. 42 biplane discussed in the 71st's mission report is totally out of place. It was most likely an IAR 38-type army cooperation aircraft. This was a common occurrence during the campaign over Romania. Obscure Romanian machines were commonly assumed to be Italian-built aircraft, probably because the recognition training provided to the American pilots was weak on the Romanian types. And previously, if their opponents hadn't been German, they had been Italian.

*   *   *

At about the time that the 71st was getting butchered, one of its sister squadrons, the 94th stumbled into an assortment of types that included Do 217s and various biplanes. The P-38s made quick work of them, downing two of the bombers and four of the biplanes. These biplanes, like the one discussed earlier, were initially identified as Italian-built CR. 42 fighters, but they were also IAR 38 variants.

While the squadrons of the 1st Fighter Group tried to save themselves from the Romanians, the bomb-carrying P-38s of the 82d continued to press north around the eastern side of Bucharest toward their target, where they too encountered a mix of enemy aircraft. Though they were under strict orders not to engage in aerial combat—lest they become thwarted in their primary dive-bombing mission—a few of the pilots scored running kills. Claims were put in for a mixed bag of Me-109s, an Hs 126, an Me-210, and an He 111.[17]

Ben Mason, at the head of one of the 97th's flights—exercised extraordinary self-control when he saw an Me-110 approach from his eleven o'clock position. When the German fighter opened fire, Mason resisted the urge to turn and engage, a move which might have broken up the formation. "When I saw his guns start to fire, I pulled up quickly to spoil his aim in case he got lucky." Mason and his flight passed unhurt, and none of the Axis aircraft they encountered pressed their attacks with any vigor.

The element of surprise had been lost early. By now it was obvious to the Romanians and the Germans that something big was afoot. Antiaircraft guns were manned and smoke screens initiated. Past Bucharest, and only a few miles from the Romana Americana complex, the P-38 pilots of the 82d pushed their throttles forward and started to climb. The plan called for them to reach an altitude of 6,000 or 7,000 feet before they rolled into their dives.[18] Climbing above them as high cover were most of the flights of the 27th and 94th squadrons.

Antiaircraft fire intensified as the P-38s approached their target. Augmenting the fire of the smaller caliber weapons was a box barrage put up by heavy guns—a gauntlet the fighters would have to penetrate both on the climb up and the dive down. Supplementing the barrage was an effective smoke screen. While it was not cloaking the entire complex, it was thick enough to make it difficult for the pilots to find their aim points.

The 96th Squadron, first on the scene, offset slightly to the east then rolled in on the target on a generally westerly heading. Its target—the boiler house—was partially obscured. Nevertheless, in part due to careful pre-mission study of target photos, the pilots were able to distinguish the structure by means of its two smoke stacks—one shorter than the other.

Smoke completely covered the main distillation plant, the 95th's target. Its pilots used a large nearby storage tank as a reference point from which to drop their bombs, the effects of which could not be ascertained at the time due to the heavy smoke.

Last to arrive overhead was the 97th. The flak was so heavy by this time that its commander brought the squadron around to the north, where it appeared that the curtain of enemy fire was less dense. This target—the main cracking plant—was less heavily screened by smoke and its pilots reported at least one bomb hit.

Lieutenant Colonel Mason, still with the 97th, had dropped his external fuel tank by now in preparation for his attack. Dive-bombing was not something the P-38 fliers practiced often. Mason increased the angle of his dive as much as he dared to ensure better accuracy. His aircraft—named *Billy Boy*, after his son—had taken hits in the horizontal stabilizer and both engine cowlings before he started his dive. Now, hurtling toward the ground, he ignored the enemy fire and devoted his entire concentration to putting his bomb into the cracking plant. "On that mission we learned just what the heavy bombers had to go through every day!"

Mason released the bomb while passing through about 2,500 feet, and felt his aircraft jump—suddenly lightened as it was. At the same time he pulled the nose of the fighter up and turned east and south away from the refinery. The official post-mission narrative noted that his bomb had scored, causing an explosion. "After I made my dive I pulled out just above the smoke screen. After getting clear of the smoke, I got as low as possible and headed for our assembly point. On the way I suddenly saw, at about a thousand yards directly in front of me and about fifty yards wide across my path, what looked like a row of blinking lights." Recognizing the antiaircraft guns for what they were, Mason dropped the nose of his P-38 and sprayed the emplacements with fire from the four .50-caliber machine guns and single 20mm cannon mounted in his fighter's nose. The antiaircraft gun crews tended to be much less effective when they were taking cover!

Mason escaped with his aircraft more or less intact, but several of his comrades did not. Lieutenant Charles Welch was caught by antiaircraft fire over the target and suffered a fiery death. Captain Elwyn Jackson's P-38 was hit in both engines. After dropping his bomb and clearing the smoke screen he bellied his aircraft into a field and was immediately nabbed. Lieutenant Tom Hodgson was flying on only one engine when he released his bomb. He threw himself into a duel with a flak battery. It wasn't a good idea; he was hit again and crashed in front of another gun emplacement, where he was immediately captured—fortunately with only minor injuries. Two other fliers, Lt. Bill Jefferson and Lt. John McMonegal were also downed—Jefferson on the way to the target and McMonegal after dropping his bomb. Both men survived and, along with Jackson and Hodgson, became POWs and were later repatriated.

* * *

German accounts record an attack at about this time by two *Staffeln* of Jagdgeschwader (JG) 53 Me-109s based out of Targsorul.[19] As aerial clashes had been nearly constant for the previous sixty or so miles this may not have been recognized by the Americans as a separate attack, and there is no specific mention of it as such. Nevertheless two 82d Group pilots claimed an aerial victory apiece over Me-109s encountered south of the refinery (the Germans admitted one loss). At the same time, the Germans claimed several victories during this attack, but American records do not support this. Normally quite fastidious regarding victory credits, the German fliers may have been credited with aircraft downed by antiaircraft fire.

*   *   *

Portions of the Romana Americana refinery were burning from those bombs of the 82d that had found their mark. Smoke and fire from the flaming plant climbed skyward. Thick and black, it was easily distinguishable from the smoke screen. Of thirty-six P-38s from the 82d that had turned north from the IP near the Danube, only three didn't deliver their bombs on the refinery complex—one pilot jettisoned his bomb during an aerial engagement, another put his into a three-story factory-like structure, and the third pilot's bomb failed to release.[20]

Once clear of the refinery, the American fighters hastily picked up wingmen of opportunity, mutual support being the best way to survive.

Home was still 600 miles away when Lt. Charles Lagenour of the 96th shut down his left engine, which had been hit during the attack. Soon he was joined by squadron mate Lt. Al Mikes and five more ships from various other squadrons. Mikes led Lagenour while the others weaved overhead in a protective formation. About fifteen minutes after setting a course for home the small grouping of Lightnings was attacked from above by Me-109s from JG 53's 2 *Staffel*. The Americans numbered the enemy force at about fifteen aircraft. In the ensuing fight Lagenour went down in his crippled ship and was killed.[21] The Germans made additional claims, but records do not confirm them.

*   *   *

The 71st's mission report outlines an event that illustrates how the exigencies of combat force cruel decisions on men:

P-38, battle letters BI, of the 82d Fighter Group escorted Lt. Shepard safely out of danger while he was flying on single engine. Aircraft battle letters, BN or BM of 82d Fighter Group came out of target area with Lt Ferguson, but fell behind and could not be escorted because Lt Ferguson and other members of his flight were short on fuel.[22]

One can only imagine the sinking feeling all participants felt as the flight of 71st Squadron fighters pulled slowly away from their wounded 82d brother, leaving him to his fate.

*   *   *

The flight home was more of a running battle than a carefully scripted egress. The Lightnings eventually outran the defending fighters and made their way back to Italy in small bands. Most of them fanned out at low level and attacked whatever targets presented themselves. Pilots of the 82d strafed twelve trains. But it was dangerous work—close to the ground and within the range of just about every weapon the enemy could field. Several more Lightnings were lost while strafing during the trip home.

Ben Mason was one of the pilots who shot up anything that appeared to have any military value. Coming out of the target area, he joined with two other Lightnings and, after making a couple of turns to look for other P-38s, he took the lead for the trip back to Italy. Heading west, the three P-38s shot up a locomotive, some trucks, and a couple of small airfields. Approaching another airfield near Craiova, Mason lined his guns up on an airplane that had just landed. An instant before he was about to fire he spotted an Me-110 nearing the field from his two o'clock position. "As we closed, he started a turn toward me." Setting up for a 30-degree deflection shot, Mason held his fire as long as he dared, because he knew that he didn't have much ammunition remaining. "I fired a one-second burst and my guns were empty." Mason pulled up and rolled to his left in time to see the German twin-engine fighter roll right and fall to the ground. Congratulations from one of his ad hoc wingmen were immediately forthcoming: "Good shooting, Colonel!" Mason thanked him, and suggested that they fly directly home. He didn't like being in Indian Country with empty guns.

*   *   *

Mason wasn't the only one out of ammunition. Lieutenant Herbert Hatch and Lt. Carl Hoenshell, of the 71st, had survived the massacre that the Romanians had dealt much of the rest of their squadron. In fact, Hatch had fought like the devil and would later be awarded official confirmation for five victories for the day, while Hoenshell would be awarded four. But now, at the start of their homeward leg, they were out of ammunition.

Soon after joining, the pair picked up Hatch's wingman, Lt. Joe Morrison. They had been separated during the fight and Morrison's plane was pretty badly shot up; he was staying aloft on only one engine. The three fighters pointed toward home and were soon joined by the P-38 piloted by Lt. John Allen, of the 94th. After shepherding Morrison and his wounded ship through various hazards, including some fairly intense flak, the flight crossed into Yugoslavia at about 12,000 feet.

It was while he was weaving over Morrison that Hatch spotted of group of six Me-109s, high above them at their eight o'clock position. Hoenshell directed Morrison to put his crippled ship into a dive, away from the enemy fighters. Morrison wasted no time and stuffed the nose of his P-38 toward the undercast that shrouded the mountains below them.

Hatch described how the remaining three pilots—with no ammunition—turned to take on the Me-109s. "Carl, Allen, and I held the turn as best we could and, when the 109s broke formation and came at us from six o'clock we turned into them hoping to scare them off by looking like we were ready for a fight—but they didn't scare worth a damn."

When it became obvious that the ruse wasn't going to work, Hoenshell shouted at Hatch to dive away. Hatch did just that with an Me-109 in hot pursuit. "The Me-109 was chasing me, and I had nothing left to fight with, so I went through that undercast so fast I didn't even see it. I was hitting close to 600 miles per hour when I came through the bottom into a valley between two high ridges." Hatch had lost the Me-109, but had also lost the rest of his flight. After he climbed back up and searched for the others, he turned and headed for Italy alone.[23]

Hatch was the first pilot in his squadron to return to base. Joe Morrison nursed his shot-up aircraft to the airfield at Bari, and found ground transportation back to Salsola. John Allen also made it back to base. Carl Hoenshell had last been seen with several Me-109s fast on his tail. He was gone.

*   *   *

The survivors of the mission continued to trickle into their own bases and alternate fields throughout Allied—occupied Italy. Some aircraft simply were too damaged or too short on fuel to return to their own airfields. Lieutenant Colonel Ben Mason—the man who was "too old" for combat—managed to make it back to the 82d's base at Vicenzo. Ironically, the gastrointestinal problems that had nearly forced him to abort the mission seemed to have been cured by the terror and excitement of the day.

The loss rate was horrible. At nearly 30 percent, it very nearly mirrored the loss rate of the all-B-24 TIDALWAVE mission of the year before. Naturally, and fortunately, the loss of life was far smaller. When the final cost was counted it was found that the 1st Fighter Group had lost fourteen P-38s and the bomb-carrying 82d had lost nine. It was the worst day in combat that either unit ever experienced. Further, it was the worst loss rate sustained by any significant P-38 formation during the entire war.

The damage that the P-38s had caused to the Romana Americana refinery was not as severe as the planners had hoped, but it was an incremental contribution to the overall campaign—much as the damage caused by each high-altitude, heavy-bomber mission was tallied as an incremental contribution. Ploesti was not going to be shut down by a single silver bullet. It was going to take the concerted effort—and lives—of many men over a period of time.

*   *   *

Spaatz had followed the mission, and sent the following message to General Twining later that day: "Initiative displayed in the planning and execution of today's fighter bomber attack on Ploesti is most gratifying. Operating at a range hitherto considered impractical for fighter-bombers your fighters have demonstrated anew the flexibility of our air forces. The determination to find and exploit a new method of attack reflect great credit on you and the forces under your command. Please pass to all participating units."

Germans

THE AMERICAN airmen were experiencing hurtful losses, but the pilots of the defending fighters over Romania were also taking a beating. At this point in the war, the Allies enjoyed air superiority in nearly every aspect on nearly every front. Just about everywhere they went—and they went wherever they pleased—Allied airmen outnumbered their defending Axis counterparts. Too, the quality of the Allied equipment and the training of their airmen exceeded what the Axis was able to field.

The situation for the Germans only worsened with time. As seasoned pilots were lost they were replaced by youngsters who didn't have nearly enough training. When these replacements were subsequently killed their places were, in turn, taken by pilots with even less training. Proving Spaatz's theorem, the scarcity of fuel caused by the continuing campaign against Ploesti and other oil targets meant that less and less fuel was available to train those same replacement pilots that were required to defend Germany's refineries. Ironic was the fact that German industry was actually producing more aircraft than ever. But it just didn't matter because there weren't enough skilled pilots to use them effectively. It was a death spiral from which the Luftwaffe never recovered. The situation could have been even worse, but most of the fighting took place over Axis-held territory, so, Axis pilots who were shot down—but not killed or badly injured—could be thrown right back into the fight.

This was the situation with which Hauptmann Helmut Lipfert found himself dealing during the late spring of 1944.[1] Leader of 6 *Staffel* of *II/Jagdgeschwader* 52, an Me-109 unit, Lipfert was a veteran of the Eastern Front and had scored more than 125 aerial victories. He was the exception, for many of his pilots were newcomers and not nearly as experienced.

The unit had only arrived in Romania in May, after losing nearly all of its aircraft and a good many of its pilots during the disastrous German defeat in the Crimea. Newly reequipped, the *staffel* had flown with some success against Soviet units since then. But it wasn't until June 11, 1944 that Lipfert led his Me-109s against an American bomber attack.

When word of the American penetration arrived, Lipfert and his unit left their base at Manzar, close to the Black Sea, and flew northwest to the airfield at Zilistea, nearer Ploesti. All sixteen fighters were immediately refueled and airborne again just in time for the ground controllers to vector them onto a formation of the big bombers. These bombers were after oil storage and railway facilities at Giurgiu, on the Danube, south of Bucharest. This was along the route that the P-38s of the 1st and 82nd Fighter Groups had used just the day before.

The sight was nearly overwhelming; the masses of bombers and swarms upon swarms of protecting fighters were marked by innumerable, thick, brilliantly white condensation trails. The procession of bombers would have been impossible to miss even without ground control. Nothing in his experience against the Red Air Force had prepared Lipfert for this inexorable wave of airborne American machinery. The *Dicke Autos* (*Luftwaffe* radio code for heavy bombers) astounded him not just with their size, but by their numbers as well.

Lipfert turned and climbed, searching for just the right position from which to mount his attack. He noted that his small band of fighters didn't seem to cause much of a stir so long as it stayed away from the big bombers. At one point, as they climbed right through a formation of American fighters, there was no reaction whatsoever. Perhaps they were mistaken as friendly.

Just after reaching 20,000 feet Lipfert caught sight of a lone B-17 flying a thousand feet below him. He started down on the big ship with his friend Heino Sachsenberg close aboard. The German concentrated on the four-engined bomber—he had never attacked such a machine. As he dove, Lipfert was surprised that the B-17 was holding its fire. Perhaps again, he was misidentified as a friendly aircraft.

If that was the case, it was a costly mistake. The German pilot unloaded the guns and cannon of his Me-109 into the fuselage and engines of the solo ship. In short order two of the engines were on fire. He broke off only when tracer fire from Sachsenberg's guns came streaming over his canopy. Upside-down Lipfert watched his wingman fill the bomber with gunfire until it was completely enveloped by flames. He counted five parachutes as the bomber fell in pieces toward the ground.

American fighters screamed down on the two German ships. They were too late to help the bomber and its crew but were no doubt bent on revenge. Lipfert dove away and slow-rolled his airplane all the way to the deck, where he was able to outdistance his opponents. He raced all the way to the Danube, then cautiously climbed and made his way back to Zilistea. There, four other Me-109s—one damaged—were already waiting for him. In the end, Lipfert's *staffel* lost three pilots killed in the day's action. The loss rate was just short of 20 percent, a rate no unit could sustain.

*   *   *

As effective as the gunners aboard American bombers were, they were notorious for over-claiming victories against enemy fighters. The reasons for this were manifold. First, an airplane attacking an American bomber formation took fire from a great many guns. Virtually every gunner on every bomber who had an opportunity to open fire did so. If the attacking fighter was hit, duplicate claims for aerial victories were made by many of those same gunners. Determining who actually hit the aircraft was usually impossible. And just because a ship was hit, didn't mean that it was mortally damaged. Few of those enemy aircraft caught by the bombers' guns exploded immediately. Most of them dove clear of the formations and were able to make it back to an air base, or at least crash land. The gunners—often under multiple attacks—hardly had time to watch and see if an enemy airplane fell four or five miles to the ground.

The Me-109—the most numerous enemy type in the skies over Romania—also had a unique trait that caused American gunners to over claim kills. Its Daimler Benz engine belched a distinct black stream of smoke when the throttle was quickly advanced. This smear of smoke was often erroneously interpreted by defending gunners as an indication that the enemy had been hard hit and was going down. What was more likely was that the Axis pilots—their firing runs complete—were shoving their throttles forward to make as quick an escape as possible.

Finally, it should be noted that the defending gunners were very young men. As such, they were excitable and wanted dearly to strike out and kill those who were trying to do the same to them. In the split-second, fire-thrashing hell of aerial combat it was easy to make mistakes.

The debriefing officers were left in a difficult position. Who were *they* to argue with the adrenaline-stoked young warrior who insisted that he had shot down two or three, or more, enemy fighters? After all, it wasn't the intelligence officers who had had their ships nearly shot out of the sky. And it wasn't the intelligence officers who had just seen their crewmate blown to bits. They had been safe on the ground in Italy. They often felt they had little recourse but to accept the claims of the young gunners, even though they knew that they could hardly be valid. The final tallies officially filed were done so later—by necessity—after more detached analysis.

*   *   *

Shell casings from spent machine gun rounds—friendly and otherwise—also posed a hazard to the bombers. These could get lodged in engines, or smash into windscreens, or penetrate gun positions. Casings falling into propeller arcs were known to come hurtling out at tremendous speed, causing serious damage and injury. The number of ways to die in the sky above Europe seemed infinite.

Above: 2d. Lt. Russell Christesen's B-17 crew, based at Celone, Italy, as part of the 463d Bomb Group. Despite being sent to Ploesti five times, the airmen finished their 50-mission requirement and completed their combat tour intact. Standing, from left: 2d. Lt. Charlie Grogan, Pilot, 2d. Lt. Jack Flenniken, Co-pilot, 2d. Lt. Russell Christesen, Navigator, 2d. Lt. Al Richards, Bombardier, Sgt. Jay Haymaker, Upper Turret, Sgt. Jesse Jones, Radio Operator, Sgt. Harvey Pearson, Left Waist Gunner, Sgt. Jim McGlynchey, Right Waist Gunner, Sgt. Orville Schuette, Bottom Turret, Sgt. Carl Lester, Tail Gunner.
Russell Christesen

Left: A bare-breasted beauty graced the tail of *Never Satisfied*.
James Patton

A B-17 falls from the sky over Ploesti. *I. W. Williams*

Romanian antiaircraft crews and guns on parade. *Dénes Bernád*

Ion Dobran was a leading Romanian ace. Here, pictured in the cockpit of an Me-109G, Dobran was shot down by American P-51s on June 6, 1944. He was one of the few high-scoring Romanian aces who survived the war. *Dénes Bernád*

The Me-109G was the favored mount of the defending pilots over Romania. These two Romanian fighters are readying for takeoff. *Dénes Bernád*

Above: First Lieutenant Arthur Fiedler shot down three Me-109s over Romania during the Ploesti campaign. He finished the war with eight aerial victories. *Arthur Fiedler*. *Below*: Mickey Mouse adorned the cowling of this Me-109G. *Dénes Bernád*

IAR 81s at readiness. The Romanian fighter was marginally inferior to the American types it encountered, yet its pilots enjoyed, literally, a significant homefield advantage. Romanian pilots who were shot down and survived uninjured could be put immediately back into service. Too, the "Gypsy" pilots would often attack the American bomber streams as they flew into Romania, then quickly land, refuel, rearm and get airborne again. The Romanians acquitted themselves reasonably well in this type of craft. Note its strong resemblance to the FW-190 (below). *Denes Bernad*

Photographed at Lesina, Italy, this captured German FW-190 was painted with U.S. markings and used to familiarize American crewmen with the type. The quite capable Focke Wulf made few appearances over Ploesti, yet U.S. crews constantly claimed encounters with it when they misidentified the similar-appearing Romanian IAR 80/81. Note its similarity to the Romanian IAR 81s (top photo). Also note that it may have been difficult for the U.S. maintenance crews to keep the type shod with wheels. *Art Fiedler*

Above: Massive contrail streams marked the paths of advancing bombers, which greatly assisted the defending fighters and antiaircraft gunners. *1st CCU via 450th Bombardment Group. Below*: A view of the B-24 co-pilot's station. *450th Bomb Group*

The P-51D Mustang was the dominant fighter over Ploesti. This example, *Helen,* was Art Fiedler's mount. *Below*: Two P-51Ds of the 317th Fighter Squadron in flight. *Both courtesy of Arthur Fiedler*

A straggling bomber knows no strangers. Here, note that a B-24 (lower left) has somehow lost his own formation, and joined with a formation of 2d Bombardment Group B-17s for protection. *Charles Hollenberg*

Charles Hollenberg of the 2d Bombardment Group was a B-17 tailgunner. He took this photo of the flak over Ploesti on July 31, 1944. *Charles Hollenberg*

Above: This photograph from the ball turret of a B-17 shows Ploesti and its smoke screen in the background. *George Guerre*

Below: This target photo of the Americana Romana refinery was taken on the next-to-last mission against Ploesti on August 18, 1944. Note the pockmarks of earlier raids that were obviously well off the mark. The causes of these inaccuracies were many and varied. *Russell Christesen*

The markings on these B-24Js were still incomplete when Art Fiedler snapped this photograph. The "J" model was no prettier than its predecessors, yet saw plenty of action over Ploesti. These ships were likely close to base as the ventral, or bottom, turrets have been retracted. *Art Fiedler*

An IAR 80 burns at an airfield in Romania. *Dénes Bernád*

Above: The waist gunner's position on the B-24 was cramped and dangerous. *450th Bombardment Group.*

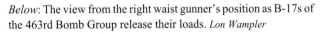

Below: The view from the right waist gunner's position as B-17s of the 463rd Bomb Group release their loads. *Lon Wampler*

These Romanian fighter pilots are speaking the language of fighter pilots around the world. *Denes Bernad*

This B-17, part of the 463rd Bomb Group, has feathered the propeller on its number-three engine. Note the B-24 flying below her in the lower-left corner of the photo. *Russell Christesen*

Above: *Bottoms Up,* a B-24 of the 450th Bomb Group, shows the wear-and-tear typical of rough conditions and hard use. *Lieutenant Fred Reinke. Below:* American POWs welcome Soviet troops into Bucharest, late August 1944. *Woody Marks via Robert Ken Barmore*

American POWs chat with their former Romanian enemies as they wait to be airlifted back to Italy. *Woody Marks via Robert Ken Barmore*

Above: An exceptionally fine view of a P-51D from the 325th Fighter Group. This remarkable photo was taken during August 1944, the month Ploesti finally fell. *Art Fiedler*

Below: Many Romanian palaces and government buildings were destroyed by German bombers in the days immediately after King Michael overthrew dictator Antonescu and changed his country's allegiance from Hitler to the Allies. *Woody Marks via Robert K. Barmore*

Above: On August 22, 1944, this Romanian soldier was guarding American POWs in Bucharest. A few days later following Romania's change of allegiance from the Axis to the Allies, he was not. Here, he poses with his family for the camera of former POW Woody Marks only days after the two were enemies. *Woody Marks*

Below: Elated American and British POWs pile aboard B-17s for their hasty and dangerous evacuation flight back to Allied territory in Italy. The codename for this prisoner exodus was right on the mark: OPERATION REUNION. *Woody Marks*

Chapter 20

Selflessness

DURING THE two weeks following the P-38 raid of June 10, 1944, the heavy-bomber groups of the Fifteenth Air Force were sent against other critical and well-defended targets including Vienna, Innsbruck, Bucharest, and Turin. They were able to mount these attacks despite being grounded by weather for several days.[1]

The field order for the June 23, 1944, mission called for more than two hundred aircraft from the 5th and 47th Bomb wings to hit the refineries. A total of six groups were to bomb the charmed Romana Americana refinery, and two groups were charged with striking the Dacia Romana complex. Additionally, nearly one hundred bombers from the 55th Bomb Wing were tasked with hitting oil storage facilities at Giurgia, and the 304th Bomb Wing was to send an equal number of aircraft against the rail junction at the Bucharest Chitila station yard.[2] It was hoped that the wide-ranging, simultaneous attacks would dilute the fighter defenses and make for a more effective strike at Ploesti.

The refineries were not hit as hard as had been planned. The entire 47th Wing, which was to have put four groups over the Romana Americana complex, aborted due to weather. On the other hand, the 5th Bomb Wing put 139 bombers across both the Dacia Romana and Romana Americana refineries and scored some success with more than 283 tons of bombs.[3]

The escorting fighters from the 31st, 52d and 325th Fighter groups posted an impressive score as well. Claims were made for 25 Axis fighters destroyed.[4] The Romanian units in particular took a beating; the commanders of two of their four fighter groups were shot down and killed. The loss of these two experienced fliers when tallied with the men already killed since the opening of the campaign in April was a blow that unnerved the increasingly hard-pressed Romanian Air Force.

*   *   *

This day also included the action that resulted in the first award of the Medal of Honor over Ploesti since the disastrous low-level attack of August 1, 1943. It was an award that wasn't won cheaply.

Second Lieutenant David R. Kingsley entered the service from Portland, Oregon, and was assigned to the 341st Squadron of the 97th Bomb Group, based out of the airfield at Amendola. This well-liked and respected twenty-five-year-old bombardier had twenty missions under his belt when pilot Edwin R. Anderson and co-pilot William C. Symons lifted the B-17 *Opissonya* into the air to rendezvous with the rest of the 97th's ships. Originally assigned as the last airplane of their squadron's formation, *Opissonya* assumed the lead of the unit's second "V" of aircraft when the original ship aborted. Weather over Yugoslavia caused a breakup of the larger formation, and when the men of the 97th Bomb Group flew out of the clouds they found themselves alone.

Their assigned target was the Dacia Romana refinery complex at Ploesti. Clouds covered the target area, so radar was used to lead the group from the initial point to the bomb-release point. Preceding formations had already successfully hit the refinery, and heavy black smoke billowed up through the contrasting white carpet of the undercast. Flak was heavy, and black smears from the exploding shells spotted the otherwise blue sky. Amidst it all, Axis fighters made concerted attacks on the formation despite a covering escort of P-38s that—for whatever reason—failed to come down to provide protection.[5] These attacks sent down the two bombers just off *Opissonya's* right wing. Despite the flak and damage from the fighter attacks, Anderson held his position.

About a mile to the right, a twin-engine German fighter cruised on a parallel course, probably relaying information to the flak batteries. Antiaircraft fire knocked out *Opissonya's* number-one engine, and soon it began to lag the rest of the group. Compounding the crew's difficulty was damage caused to the control surfaces on the right wing and a fuel tank that had been torn out of its mounting. Notwithstanding their quickly deteriorating situation, Anderson and Symons kept the B-17 on course until Kingsley released their load of bombs over the target.

Clear of the target, but now alone, the crippled ship came under immediate attack from three very aggressively flown Me-109s. There was no help from escorting fighters. Making more than a dozen individual firing runs on the big ship, the enemy fighters racked it with cannon and machine gun fire. The tail gunner, Sgt. Michael J. Sullivan, was hit in the head and arms when a 20mm cannon shell exploded in his position. Unable to call for help, he crawled forward from his position. The two waist gunners—Sgt. Harold James and Sgt. Martin Hettinga, pulled him around the hole left by the shot-out tail wheel, and forward to the radio operator's station. Here, Lieutenant Kingsley immediately set to work tending the wounded man's considerable injuries.[6]

The three German fighters left without downing the big ship. Anderson ordered the crew to jettison whatever they could in order to stay aloft. Meanwhile, the pilots and flight engineer did what they could to stabilize the stricken ship. For a time it looked like they might make it back to Italy. They had the misfortune though, of unwittingly flying overhead the airfield at Karlovo, Bulgaria. This was where Germans helped to train Bulgarian airmen for combat in the Me-109.

Opissonya was set upon immediately by eight Me-109s. Sergeant Stanley J. Kmiec, who had moved from the ball turret into the blood-spattered tail gunner's position to cover the airplane against attacks from the rear, was wounded. Like Sullivan before him, Kmiec made his way forward to the radio room where Kingsley treated his injuries in the increasingly cramped space.

One of the waist gunners, Harold James, also tried to man the tail gunner's position. Leaving Martin Hettinga to cover both waist positions, he made his way to the rear of the ship, where he found one gun jammed and the sight blown away. It was a bloody mess. He returned to his waist position, where he could do better work.

That the airplane was still aloft was barely believable. The top turret was out of commission, and aside from the number-one engine being shot out the number-two engine was badly damaged. The wings were so thoroughly ripped and torn that the whole airplane was shuddering violently. It was obvious that it was not going to hold together much longer. *Opissonya* was not going home to Italy.

With his ship obviously doomed, Anderson rang the bailout bell and ordered the crew to parachute from the bomber. The waist gunners were the first to leave, out the open bomb bay. Lieutenant Kingsley then helped the wounded Kmiec out of the aircraft, and the rest of the crew followed until only Anderson, Kingsley, and Sullivan remained. Anderson stayed with the ship as long as he dared before it fell out of control. He was knocked down, but was able to crawl to the nose hatch and escape. He fell alongside the lurching bomber for a short while before he had enough separation to pull his ripcord. With a full parachute nearly stopping his descent, Anderson watched *Opissonya* fall away.

Only Kingsley and Sullivan remained. There was no way to survive now but to follow the others out of the falling wreck. Sergeant Sullivan recalled what happened next: "After everyone had cleared the ship, Lieutenant Kingsley attempted to locate my parachute harness. He discovered that it had been ripped by cannon fire." Without hesitating, Kingsley quickly slipped out of his own harness and, amid all the blood and torn clothing and other debris, managed to fit it onto the wounded gunner. That he was able to do this in the cramped, careening carcass that was what was left of *Opissonya* is nothing short of incredible. "Carrying me in his arms, the lieutenant struggled to get me through the door into the bomb bay and told me to be sure to pull the ripcord after I had cleared the ship."[7]

Sullivan was the last man to see Kingsley alive. As he tumbled away from the dead B-17 he could see the lieutenant watching him from the bomb bay. He pulled the ripcord of the lieutenant's parachute and felt a sharp jerk as the canopy deployed. He looked up and saw *Opissonya* fall into a spin, whereupon it hit the ground, exploded, and burned.

When the big bomber hit the ground it not only took the life of David Kingsley, but also killed a family picnicking in the shade of a tree. Mother, father, and daughter were killed instantly.

*   *   *

American women worked for the Red Cross at many of the airfields. They typically ran small canteens that served doughnuts and coffee, and sold small comfort sundries such as candy, chewing gum, and cigarettes. Just the sight of these women was a comfort to many of the men, and their kindness is remembered fondly. Norval Seeley of the 97th Bomb Group recalls a Red Cross worker called "Flip" who worked at the base at

Amendola, and how she would wait to serve them after mission debriefings. "No one would tell her who was missing, but somehow she always knew and cried a little," remembered Seeley. "She had a book that you got to sign after your last mission, and I was certainly looking forward to that event."[8]

Chapter 21

Bulgarians

SIX MISSIONS were mounted against the Romana Americana Refinery from May 18 to June 23, 1944—including the special P-38 raid. It was a resilient and vexing target. Fifteenth Air Force intelligence officers were unsure if it was dead yet, so another strike—part of a multi-pronged attack—was scheduled against it for June 24. Two B-24 groups were tasked with striking the Romana Americana complex, four B-17 groups were charged with hitting marshaling yards at Craiova, and two B-24 bomb groups were to hit the Piatra rail bridge. Planners were further testing their theory that the attacks—geographically spread out as they were—would overwhelm and confuse the German and Romanian defenses.[1]

* * *

The intelligence annex on enemy fighter defenses for this mission started with a discussion of Bulgaria-based Me-109s: "Estimate enemy can put up 35/40 Me-109s from Sofia airfields. These aircraft will probably intercept en route to Craiova and may follow to target area there." The estimate was not far off the mark.[2]

Manning one of those Bulgarian fighters was Lieutenant Stoyan Stoyanov. Since scoring his first aerial victory against a B-24 retiring from the TIDALWAVE mission nearly a year earlier, Stoyanov had become one of Bulgaria's leading fighter pilots.[3]

Like their Romanian counterparts, the Bulgarian fighter pilots and their actions in the skies of World War II are little known or understood. Probably because their front-line fighter was the German Me-109, American pilots almost always assumed that the fighters they encountered over Bulgaria were German, and there were, indeed, German fighter units based in the country. Nevertheless, the significant Bulgarian fighter force was a very real threat to the bomber formations and did score some successes against their much more numerous American adversaries.

*   *   *

Air raid sirens sounded in Sofia at 0700 on June 24. Stoyanov and his squadron mates manned the cockpits of fourteen available Me-109Gs. They listened to loudspeakers as the fighter control station at Boyana, situated north of the capital, broadcast the progress of the American raid. Stoyanov was on edge: "Today again the number of enemy planes was a record—more than six hundred of them!"

The order to launch came, and at 0800 the squadron was scrambling airborne and climbing for altitude. They were vectored to join with a German flight of eleven Me-109s. Once rendezvoused, Stoyanov's commander complied with the order to hand over control of his flight to the German flight leader.

This order did not sit well with the Bulgarian pilots. They had long regarded the Bulgaria-based Germans as only half-hearted allies whose interests did not lie so much with protecting Bulgaria as with protecting the oil complexes at Ploesti. When Allied bombers came, it seemed that the Germans had little interest if the target was Sofia or another Bulgarian target.

The pilots listened carefully as the ground station plotted the course of the American formation that was south of Sofia and heading northeast. The German flight leader kept the formation headed north, rather than toward the heavy bombers. Stoyanov couldn't stand it. "Demonstratively, I left the German planes and turned my flight back to the south where our capital city was, thus finishing this joint air operation." The rest of the Bulgarian fighters followed Stoyanov, leaving the German formation on its own.

The Bulgarians, with Stoyanov at their head, continued their climb as they passed Sofia and pressed southward. As they approached the mountains of southern Bulgaria, they spotted the long column of American bombers and escorting fighters. "One by one, the formations followed each other as if they were making a military parade, and we watched them from our side." Stoyanov and the rest of his flight counted nine groups of twenty to thirty bombers each—all of them guarded by Mustangs and Lightnings. "Part of the fighter planes flew higher than the Fortresses with constant changes in their flight direction, watching carefully from above which gave encouragement to the bomber crews. Some more groups of forty to sixty fighter planes flew like a swarm of bees in a ball-shaped mass, ready to fight against any attacker from any direction or altitude."

The Bulgarians watched as the last formation of Americans passed by. They were still unsure of the best way to mount their attack. They maintained their position and altitude—about five thousand feet above the bombers—and watched as a formation of American fighters started to climb toward them. "A group of them slowly came nearer to us, but probably believed that we would watch them peacefully, so they returned to the column. So then, we continued to fly parallel to them, but stayed a good distance behind."

Carefully calculating the position of the protecting fighters, Stoyanov led the Bulgarians nearer to the trailing formation of bombers. Judging that they could make an attack unmolested, they finally dove down, firing, and left two of the bombers seriously damaged and smoking. Once through the formation, they climbed and made a quick escape, though on a course that paralleled the American bombers.

"As we just relaxed for some minutes, one of our pilots reported that a bomber plane was following our flight direction some few miles behind us. I saw myself this airplane and wondered what his mission was to fly alone. If it had engine problems it should return to base. Why then did it fly further into enemy territory?"

Stoyanov suspected that perhaps the ship, a B-17, was a specially armed aircraft with extra guns—a purposely-equipped gunship. Flying solo, these ships were supposed to bait enemy fighters and then blast them from the sky with their heavy firepower. Stoyanov decided to lead an attack, regardless of whether or not it was a gunship. At the same time, the American bomber started to reverse its course.

The Bulgarian pilots pushed their throttles full forward and soon drew near the bomber. As they closed, Stoyanov called out that his flight would make the first firing pass. At the same time he sent four of the fighters to a position above him and to the right, kept three of the fighters with him, and ordered the remaining six fighters to a high-cover position on the left. Gradually his flight of four overtook the bomber and moved slightly ahead and to the side while he considered his next move.

"We had in this moment the feeling that we would be the winners, as we were fourteen planes against only one." Stoyanov began his firing pass from about 1,500 feet above and to the right of the American bomber.

The Bulgarian pilot dodged the tracers spewing from the right waist gunner's .50-caliber machine gun and returned fire. He was doing his best to keep the American's head down while he adjusted his speed and maneuvered into a more advantageous firing position. He continued to close with the bomber until he was slightly below and almost directly behind it—very close. He brought his fighter up to a point where he was almost nose-to-nose with the tail gunner. "I saw now the gunner who was in the tail and who until this moment couldn't see me." Stoyanov fired into the gunner's position as he slowly slid to the left. "Seconds later I saw him jump out of the plane and disappear from my sight."

As the Bulgarian pilot continued to move to his left he poured fire into the engines on the left wing until they began to smoke. He broke away and back to the right to direct the attacks of his wingmen. As the second fighter opened fire, Stoyanov could see that his rounds were passing beneath the bomber, so he corrected the pilot's aim. The next fusillade hit home, and the B-17 began to flame. Shortly thereafter six or seven crewmen bailed out of the doomed ship. The third fighter dealt the final blows, and the bomber exploded.

"Someone called out congratulations," Stoyanov recalled, "but our joy lasted only a moment, because suddenly we were surprised by a great danger over our heads." Caught up in the excitement of downing the big bomber, none of the fourteen pilots had noticed the swarm of P-38s screaming down at them.

"In every pilot's experience there are some critical moments when he is exposed to a very close danger to his life. Now, for all of us, it was such a moment," Stoyanov explained. Everywhere Stoyanov looked he saw three or more Lightnings latched onto each Me-109. He caught sight of one his squadron mates diving away from a trio of the American fighters.

Stoyanov turned toward them, spraying a curtain of fire toward the pursuers. In so doing he misjudged the dynamics and geometry of the fight and flew right in front of the Lightnings. Now, he was in the hot seat.

Stoyanov quickly determined that he had no good option but to try and dive out of the fight. He huddled behind the armor plate of his seat and pushed the control stick forward. The negative-g forces he brought on himself were nearly unbearable as they drove blood into his head and eyes and pushed his diaphragm, stomach, and heart toward his throat. But it was the quickest way for him to force his fighter into a life-saving vertical dive. In no time he was leveling out just above the countryside at over 400 miles per hour. He pulled his fighter into turns several times to check that his pursuers had given up the chase. They had.

Warily Stoyanov climbed back up to altitude. The fight was over, so he called his flight together and tallied the missing. Four Me-109s were gone; two had been shot down and two had been forced to land in the valley below where they had been engaged. The pilot of one of the planes that had been shot down outright had been trapped inside his plummeting aircraft. Only when a fuel tank exploded and cracked the cockpit open was he able to fall clear. The pilot of the other was killed. Of the two fighters forced down, one broke up on contact with the ground and was destroyed. The pilot was badly wounded.

The day had taken a deadly turn. Four of the Bulgarian aircraft were gone and two were damaged. For their part, they claimed the destruction of one B-17 and one Lightning. As bad as it had been for the Bulgarian fighters, it would not get any better as the war drew on.

*   *   *

Hauptmann Helmut Lipfert's 6 *Staffel* had seen no action since June 11, when it had suffered three men killed. Now, on June 24, he staged his nine remaining aircraft through Zilistea again, taking just enough time to refuel.[4] At about the time Stoyanov was flying for his life, Lipfert was leading his *staffel* skyward. They were vectored by ground-control radar toward the oncoming American bombers whose presence was confirmed by thick, white contrails.

Lipfert counted three formations of forty aircraft each as he climbed to reach an advantageous position. Large weaving masses of fighters hovered protectively over the bombers. Closing the distance, he wondered at the futility of hurling his half-sized unit against the American ships.

As the German formation overtook and passed the three formations of B-24s, Lipfert outlined his plan to the small band of Me-109s. They would reverse course and execute a head-on attack against the lower, middle group of bombers. He then spun his flight around and—closing at great speed—focused on one of the big, American aircraft. Determined to make the pass count, he warned his men against opening fire too soon.

They began taking fire almost immediately. Tracers from all the formations reached out at them, but they held their formation. Finally it was time. The Me-109s blasted away with their cannon and 7.62mm machine guns with telling effect. Lipfert's careful aim paid off. He could see his rounds hitting the big bomber and only pulled up in time to just narrowly avoid ramming it. Many of the other B-24s were hit, and some lagged out of their protective formation.

After flying out the rear of the bomber formation, Lipfert was able to collect six of his fighters. The rest were missing. He reefed them around again in preparation for an attack from the rear. This time the closing speed was dramatically slower because the Me-109s and the B-24s were traveling in the same direction. It just gave both sides more time to aim.

The German fighters blasted their way to the front of the formation again, then fought their way clear. Lipfert was not satisfied. Once more he wheeled his remaining fighters around for a head-on attack. This time, he caught only the trailing ships, and most of these from the side.

Clear to the rear once again he tried to catch his breath and regroup his fighters. Only his wingman remained. He wondered where the others had gone and realized that he was losing enthusiasm for engaging the Americans further. Still his formation had done some good work. Lipfert counted at least eight stragglers from the bomber formations. He and his wingman singled one out for another attack.

Although the big ship put up a stream of wicked fire, the pair of Me-109s set the bomber aflame. Closing the range, Lipfert slowed his aircraft and filled the fuselage of the B-24 with fire until it exploded. He didn't see any parachutes.

They charged ahead and tore into another damaged Liberator, ignoring the fire from its defensive guns. The bomber was burning and his wingman was out of ammunition when Lipfert planted himself directly behind the stricken ship. He continued to fire until it exploded. This time he counted two parachutes.

Through the entire flight Lipfert had been unmolested by the escorting fighters. Back on the ground he celebrated with his wingman. It was a bitter-sweet moment. Of his nine fighters, five had been shot down, two pilots killed and another had suffered life-threatening burns. Two other Me-109s had to make a belly landing.

Only two fighters of the original nine were still flyable, a loss rate of nearly 80 percent. After only two engagements against the Americans, Lipfert's *Staffel* had been almost completely destroyed. Operations came to a halt and what was left of the unit was transferred to Poland in mid-July.

* * *

Having dropped their payloads, the three groups of American bombers turned for home. Bulgarian fighter pilot Stoyan Stoyanov was once again airborne in his Me-109. Still stinging from the losses his unit had sustained in the morning he was bent on revenge and had the tools to exact it.

The unfortunate victim was another B-17. Stoyanov's flight hacked at it until it was mortally wounded, then followed it until it dropped to earth in Macedonia. After completing their mission and returning to Sofia, their airfields came under attack by strafing American fighters. There was little they could do but run for cover until the marauders left.

* * *

For the Americans the June 24 mission had been a success. Serious damage was inflicted on all the designated targets. Nevertheless, the Romana Americana Refinery would require more attention. And the mission had been costly: 14 of 135 bombers went down. In simple terms this meant that if the loss rates for missions to Ploesti remained this high, a crew couldn't expect to finish ten missions.

Chapter 22

Svengali

AS THE end of June 1944 approached, the Fifteenth Air Force had mounted twelve dedicated attacks against Ploesti since the start of the campaign in early April. But the Axis was able to throw a hundred or more fighters against the Americans each time they came. Many times the bombers were harassed not only over their targets, but also as they made their way into and out of Romania, particularly as they passed over or nearby Sofia. That the enemy was able to do so, despite heavy attrition, was part of the reasoning behind the June 28, 1944 mission plan. This attack called for B-24s to hit not only oil targets in and around Bucharest, but also to directly attack the airfield at Karlovo, east of Sofia. In a focused effort, P-51s from the 31st, 52d, and 325th Fighter groups were written into the plan. Their primary responsibility was to be the destruction of Axis fighters.

The 325th put forty Mustangs into the air from their base at Lesina, Italy. Piloting one of those P-51s was Lt. Arthur C. Fiedler of Maywood, Illinois.[1] A member of the 317th Squadron, Fiedler had already been credited with a probable victory on an earlier mission, but had yet to score a confirmed kill. On this mission—only his eighth—his group was not tied down with escort duties. It was assigned a pure fighter sweep—all the way to the Bucharest-Ploesti sector.

Southwest of Bucharest, his squadron was flying at about 24,000 feet, just below a layered overcast. The other two squadrons, the 318th and the 319th, were flying at 30,000 feet, just above the overcast. Over the radio came a call: "Beaucoup 109s at 30,000 feet!"

The squadron leader wasted no time and called for his pilots to drop their external fuel tanks. Immediately, nearly eighty tanks went tumbling earthward, and the squadron started a climb up through the overcast. Fiedler was caught behind though. His left tank was hung up and because of the extra drag it created, he couldn't stay with the rest of the squadron. Finally, after putting his airplane through some gyrations, he was able to get it to fall clear.

Alone, Fiedler punched up into the clouds hoping to catch sight of the rest of the squadron. He was surprised to find that rather than being composed of a single, solid layer, the overcast was made up of many thin layers—each a couple of hundred feet thick. As he passed through the clear space between two of the layers at about 26,000 feet, he caught a fleeting glimpse of two fighters off to his left, about a half-mile away.

Before he could stop climbing Fiedler was in the next layer of clouds. He immediately started a descending left turn back toward the two aircraft. By now the radio was full of noise and shouts as the rest of the group became engaged with the Me-109s above the clouds. To Fiedler, it was useless information.

As he broke back down into the clear he spotted the two aircraft again. By now Fiedler was close enough to see the oil coolers under each wing and knew that they were Me-109s. He was closing rapidly from behind them and quickly decided to shoot down the leader first and then take on the wingman. But as he approached to about 200 yards the wingman suddenly went into a right skid, and Fiedler knew that the German pilot had seen him.

Without hesitating Fiedler took his nose off of the leader and brought it to bear against the wingman. Still in a left turn he opened fire from about a 30-degree angle off of the other airplane's tail. His bullets found their mark and there were numerous flashes all over the German fighter. Almost immediately the Me-109 snapped over into a split-S and plummeted earthward. Fiedler stayed right on his tail, paying no heed at all to the flight leader.

The wingman and the Mustang plunged straight down. At about 13,000 feet the German pilot started to pull out of his dive. Again Fiedler opened fire from a 30-degree angle off of his tail, above him. Again, there were flashes all over the Me-109, and it began to burn. This time the German did not immediately snap over into a dive, but rather his left wing dropped, his nose followed, and once again he headed straight down with the American behind him.

At about 5,000 feet Fiedler started to pull out of the dive. As he rolled up on a wing to watch, he saw the Me-109 smash into the ground. The explosion sent a plume of smoke and fire skyward.

Because he hadn't been given credit the previous week for an Me-109 that he had set afire but hadn't seen crash, Fiedler decided to take a picture of this burning wreck as proof of his victory. Dropping down, he turned off the guns and took pictures with his gun camera. As he finished and began climbing back to altitude, he was startled by another Me-109 crossing his flight path from right to left. Fiedler quickly turned the gun switch back on and opened fire from a high angle off. He increased the Gs in an attempt to get behind the German and noticed several hits all along the Me-109s fuselage.

It was then that all four of his guns quit firing. They were jammed. This was not uncommon in the early P-51s, but it was extremely frustrating. And dangerous.

Things got worse. Fiedler started to overtake the enemy fighter and found himself slipping into formation with the other pilot, just off of his left wing. There they sat, both of them just looking at each other. Fiedler remembers, "Amazing as it may sound, I noticed nothing about his airplane, but to this day I can describe his helmet and oxygen mask very accurately."

Fiedler was in a dilemma. "We were headed eastbound, toward Russia. I couldn't stay on this heading for long. Too, if any of my fellow P-51 pilots spotted us and identified the lead aircraft as an Me-109, they might shoot us both down." But if Fiedler tried to turn away, he would give the enemy pilot a perfect shot before he could get out of range.

"It seemed like we flew together forever, though I'm sure it was only a matter of seconds. Desperate, I thought that if I took out my .45-caliber pistol and started firing at the other pilot he might turn away. No one likes to sit still while they're being shot at!"

As Fiedler reached to unzip his A-2 jacket to get at his pistol, he was astounded to see the other pilot jettison his canopy and bail out! "I can only surmise that perhaps I had wounded him, or maybe he thought that I was being chivalrous and was gesturing at him to bail out. He would have had no way of knowing that my guns were jammed."

Recovering his wits, Fiedler took time to film the other pilot as he descended in his chute. Of course he was careful to turn off the gun switch.

As he climbed away, Fiedler took a look around and realized that his fight had been only a part of a much larger battle. The countryside for miles around was marked with the wreckage of many downed aircraft. Eventually he found another P-51 and together they made an uneventful return to Italy. "For many days afterward—because of the pilot who had so unexpectedly bailed out—I was known as Svengali around the squadron. Nevertheless, since I failed to hypnotize any other enemy pilots into bailing out, this was a short-lived thing."

*   *   *

In the battles over Romania and Bulgaria that day, American pilots put in claims for the destruction of twenty enemy fighters. The bomber crews put in claims for more. Slowly but surely, the enemy fighter defenses were being ground down.

Ploesti's supporting infrastructure was being destroyed as well. The bombers on the June 28 mission hit oil industry-related targets in and around Bucharest, where much of Ploesti's refined product went before it was distributed. Though Ploesti itself escaped attack, these missions also served to reduce its ability to produce.

*   *   *

Evidence that the Oil Plan was working came from one of the Third Reich's highest-ranking officials. In a letter to Hitler at the end of June 1944, Albert Speer, Germany's minister of armaments wrote: "The enemy has succeeded in increasing our losses of aviation gasoline up to 90 percent by June 22. Only through speedy recovery of damaged plants has it been possible to regain partly some of the terrible losses." There was no doubt that the Oil Plan was succeeding.

Not only were unsustainable fuel losses being inflicted on the Nazi oil infrastructure, but the costs to repair that infrastructure in terms of workers, material and expertise was enormous. These costs were unrecoverable and greatly detracted from operations elsewhere.

Chapter 23

Honor

IN ALL, there were seven Medals of Honor awarded for action over Ploesti. The last of these medals was awarded to a crewman from the 98th Bomb Group's 343d Squadron. This was the group that Col. Killer Kane led on the TIDALWAVE mission—the same mission in which he earned one of the first Medals of Honor awarded for gallantry over Ploesti.

On July 9, 1944, ten bomb groups were tasked with attacking the Xenia and Concordia Vega refineries. The Xenia facility was to be hit by six B-17 groups, and the 98th, based out of Lecce, was one of four B-24 groups directed to strike the Concordia Vega complex.[1]

At twenty-nine years of age, Lt. Donald L. Pucket was a virtual Methuselah among men who typically were in their very early twenties. Still, he was a tiger, and his added maturity was complemented in the air by an aggressive leadership style. Having arrived in Italy in April, he had already been awarded the Distinguished Flying Cross for his bravery. He had slipped out of the larger and better-protected group formation to guard another B-24 that had been badly hit. He took this action even though his own ship had been damaged.[2] Moreover, official policy discouraged heroics of this nature, because the protecting ship was nearly as vulnerable as the straggler.

The official policy didn't matter to Pucket; he saw his actions as part of his duty to his comrades. For this he was well respected.

As was always the case, the flak and fighter defenses were fierce. An estimated 40 to 50 Axis fighters engaged the American formations, although escorting P-51s did a superb job of breaking up several of the enemy flights before they could reach the bombers. But the P-51s could do little about the equally wicked flak that was bursting among the tightly formed Liberators.

Immediately after the bombers dropped their loads Pucket's ship was smashed by antiaircraft shells. The flight engineer was killed instantly and six other crew members were badly injured. The bomber was a mess: the oxygen system was on fire, fuel was leaking into the fuselage from ruptured lines, hydraulic fluid was spraying onto the already slippery fuselage deck, various control cables were broken; and two engines were out.

After stabilizing the airplane, Pucket turned control of the bomber over to his co-pilot, Lt. Robert Jenkins, and went aft to check on the ship's condition and help administer first-aid to the wounded. Stunned by what he saw, he cranked the bomb bay doors open by hand in order to dump the volatile mixture of fuel and hydraulic fluid that threatened to turn the aircraft into a bomb. That done he began to dump everything but his men overboard—seeking to lighten the ship and keep it airborne longer.

It soon became obvious that the crew wasn't going to make it back to Italy. While there was still enough altitude to safely do so, Pucket ordered his men to bail out. The less badly hurt were able to hurl themselves clear, but three of the men were in such a state of shock and hysteria that they couldn't or wouldn't leave the ship. Despite pleas that he save himself Pucket refused to abandon the remaining crew members.

By now the flight deck was unmanned and the big bomber was in a dive. It struck a mountain and exploded. Donald Pucket was gone. His widow was presented his Medal of Honor the following summer.

*   *   *

Lieutenant Arthur Fiedler was flying a P-51 on the same mission that cost Pucket his life. On this day, July 9, 1944, he was one of thirty-seven 325th Group pilots airborne that day.

During several previous missions Fiedler had experienced problems getting his left drop tank to feed. Each time he did the procedurally correct thing and aborted the mission early. Now, again, he was having the same problem. He didn't want to turn back; Fiedler couldn't stand the thought that his squadron mates might start to question his motivation if he turned back early again. He remembers, "Stupidly, I decided to continue on and jettisoned both tanks as soon as the right one was empty."[3]

Approaching Ploesti the three squadrons within the group separated in order to cover more area. No enemy aircraft had been reported up to this point. Then, just west of Ploesti, they caught sight of seven Me-109s making "yo-yo" attacks on a formation of seven B-24s that was lumbering along at about 25,000 feet. The Germans were making diving attacks from about 28,000 feet. After each run they zoomed back up to safety, out of the effective range of the bombers' guns, then set up for another attack. Fiedler's formation quickly turned toward the melee.

As the P-51s closed the distance, the Me-109s turned away and started a climb to the northeast. This was a mistake; the P-51's performance at high altitude was second-to-none. The Mustangs chased them several miles east of Ploesti. The Germans soon realized that the American fighters were drawing into firing range; they broke formation and most of them rolled over and dove for the earth. Nevertheless, the fighter on the right side of their formation turned hard to the right and sharpened his climb even more. With the rest of his squadron giving chase to the diving fighters it became clear to Fiedler that this one climbing ship was going to get away, so he committed the unforgivable sin. He left his flight leader and turned hard to intercept the lone, climbing Me-109.

An approaching African dust storm had turned the sky behind the German fighter a dark, loaming, purplish color. Silhouetted against this background, the brown and green camouflaged Me-109 almost disappeared. Regardless, Fiedler opened fire at a 90-degree deflection angle. As they both continued their turns, the deflection angle decreased to about 60-degrees, and there were so many hits on the German ship that Fiedler felt certain that someone else must have also been shooting. A large rectangular object dropped straight down from underneath the nose of the Me-109—this was most probably the engine cowling. At the same time the propeller began windmilling, the right landing gear dropped, and the airplane trailed smoke. Coming off of the trigger, Fiedler passed slightly above the Me-109 and to its left. The German fighter's canopy was gone, but he couldn't positively determine if the pilot was still in the cockpit. Regardless, the airplane was finished.

Fiedler now checked his fuel supply. The 325th's pilots were under instructions to head home from Ploesti whenever their fuel reached a total of 90 gallons; his gauges showed a grand total of 60 gallons. Fiedler radioed his situation to Maj. Herky Green, his flight leader, and told him that he didn't think he would make it back. Green acknowledged the message and directed Fiedler to head for one of the bomber bases in the Lecce area, as these were closer to Ploesti than their base.

Fiedler had earlier read a report that described how Charles Lindberg recommended extending the range of P-38s in the Pacific Theater by applying full manifold pressure and maintaining minimum RPM. He quickly decided to apply the same technique to his Mustang's Merlin and at the same time set up a rate of descent of approximately 200 feet per minute at 160 miles per hour.

Major Green and another pilot had joined with Fiedler by this time. Fiedler recalls, "With the course to Italy set, I didn't have much to do beyond checking my fuel gauges—which I did about every few seconds. Since the last 135 miles to Italy were over the Adriatic Sea I was certain that I would finish this mission using some variant of the sidestroke." Finally, at about ten miles from the Italian coast and at an altitude of 8,000 feet, the fuel gauges read zero. Major Green stayed with Fiedler while the other pilot raced ahead to find the nearest airfield. A few minutes later the other pilot radioed that there was a base directly ahead if only Fiedler could get over the mountains before running out of fuel. "I immediately cut the fuel to my engine and turned my mighty Mustang into a glider."

Fortunately he made it over the mountains and contacted the airfield with a Mayday call and advised them that he was out of fuel and requesting permission to land immediately. They rejected his request as they were landing their own bombers. "I advised them that unless they had a machine that rolled up runways I was going to land—they could have the bombers take the left side of the runway and I would take the right." Just before landing Fiedler restarted the engine, landed, and taxied clear. About a hundred feet down the taxiway he ran out of fuel.

Fiedler refueled and returned to his base at Lesina about two hours after everyone else. He found Herky and thanked him for getting him safely back. His ground crew was elated at his return, and excited at the new victory claim. The claim was confirmed after reviewing his gun camera film. This was Fiedler's last kill over Ploesti, but it wasn't the end of his success; he finished the war with eight confirmed aerial victories.

*   *   *

German fighter units sent to defend Ploesti often came from the Eastern front. They found a different type of war. First, the conflict had left Romania relatively unscathed relative to the war-torn regions to the east. Also, the Romanian population was, more-or-less, still well fed and clothed, and not entirely unsympathetic to the German fliers. Indeed, there was quite a bit of social interaction between the Germans and Romanians.

Fuel for training was more abundant than it was elsewhere, and the Germans took full advantage of this. They practiced with radar directors, flying in the larger formations that were more effective at cracking through the defending American escort fighters. And because the attacks on the refineries were not a daily occurrence, the Luftwaffe units were able to take time to get their equipment in top condition. One unit's pilots spent part of their time off polishing their aircraft with sandpaper and fuel until they gleamed like mirrors.[4] The exercise wasn't merely a cosmetic effort though; the smoother finish made the aircraft six or seven miles per hour faster. This was an edge that could be crucial in combat.

But if the fight against the Fifteenth Air Force wasn't the same as the wearying constancy of death and dirt and temperature extremes endured against the Soviets in the East, it was just as deadly. Not only were the American pilots better trained and better equipped with increasingly superior equipment, their sheer numbers were absolutely overwhelming. Even though combat came only every week or so, it was too often lethal.

A description of an engagement flown by six aircraft of JG 53's 2 *Staffel*, on July 9, 1944, illustrates the hopelessness of the defending pilots' task. While forward-based out of the airfield at Mizil, six Me-109s led by Maj. Jurgen Harder—the commander of three different *jagdgruppen* around Ploesti—scrambled to intercept an approaching raid. While setting up for an attack on a formation of bombers, the six German machines were set upon by a flight of Mustangs. The American pilots quickly scattered the Me-109s and in short order shot down five of them. Three of the pilots were killed. Only Harder, in a badly damaged machine, escaped. Just two weeks earlier he had had 120 fighters under his command, but now he had only thirty serviceable aircraft. Although Harder had previously had some doubts about the ability of his forces to overcome the Americans, those doubts turned to depression and anguish following this massacre. His distress at the hopelessness of his task can hardly be surprising.[5]

Jurgen Harder understood the futility of the situation, but his Nazi leaders were far from willing to throw in the towel. New fighters were quickly shuttled down to Romania. A week later Harder was in command of 180 aircraft that were immediately thrown into the fight.[6]

Chapter 24

Nightmare

THE JULY 15, 1944 mission would prove to be the largest of the campaign. The field order called for twenty-one bomb groups to field nearly seven hundred bombers. Of the twenty-one groups, ten were scheduled against the Romana Americana Refinery alone and the rest were parceled out against the Creditul Minier, Standard, Unirea Sperantza, and Dacia refineries. Also targeted was the pumping station at Teleajen.[1]

By this point in the campaign, evidence was mounting as to its effectiveness. Exports of gasoline to Germany had dropped by half since April. The intelligence annex to the July 15 field order rightly pointed out that the attack would further cripple the enemy's "tottering oil position."[2] Although the defenders were impressive in their ability to repair the facilities, and while those facilities continued to produce, the strain was telling.

* * *

Louis Eubank was assigned to the 450th Bomb Group, a B-24 unit based at Manduria. He had been in Italy long enough to get six missions under his belt when he got word, at 0430, on July 15, that his seventh was going to take him to Ploesti.

At the airplane, the crew completed their checks together. Each member of the crew had his own specific tasks to complete in order to get the airplane ready. Eubank was the flight engineer and also handled the top turret.

The navigator, Lieutenant Nowell, had been studying to become a missionary before he came into the service. He always asked the men if they would like to say a prayer before they took off. The crew invariably responded with a hearty "Amen."

The takeoff was normal. It took about forty-five minutes to get the formation together, and then they turned east toward Ploesti. They were flying off the right wing of Lt. Col. Colonel William G. Snaith's B-24; he was the squadron commander, a well-liked and respected man.

Their target was the Romana American refinery. The heavy defenses quickly made themselves evident. Eubank remembers, "Just a very short time prior to bomb release I witnessed the most horrible sight I saw during the war. Lieutenant Colonel Snaith's airplane took a direct hit. I'm sure that it must have been hit in one of the wing fuel tanks because the entire airplane just exploded. The 100-octane fuel we used was very inflammable." The ship fell out of the formation in burning pieces.

Bomber crews were briefed to count parachutes when an airplane went down. That day no one saw any parachutes from Snaith's B-24. Eubanks's crew, since they had been on the wing of the lead bomber, took over the lead. They only had a very short time to adjust, but their bombs were laid exactly on target.

All during this time their ship was being hit as well. There was a loud crack, and Eubanks noticed that there were two holes on the starboard side of his turret just a little more than an inch in diameter. On the port side of the turret there were two more much bigger holes. He thought that he'd been hit, but that the extreme cold kept him from feeling it. He called down to Nowell and asked if he saw any blood. As it turned out, the shrapnel had just missed him.

Eubanks wasn't the only one who experienced a close call. Sergeant Nicholas Altemus, the tail gunner, was struck by a piece of flak about the size of a golf ball. It had penetrated the plexiglass, hit one of his twin-.50-caliber machine guns, ricocheted around a bit, and then smacked him in the back of the head. He was fine.

*   *   *

Lieutenant Colonel Snaith survived the fiery crash that Eubank described; he was the only one of his crew who did so. He was knocked unconscious by the explosion, and when he came to, he was alone in the sky, his parachute fully deployed. He managed to return to Italy a few months later to a squadron ecstatic to see him back from the dead.

*   *   *

Also taking part in the mission over Ploesti that day was the 455th crew of Winfield S. Bowers, flying a B-24 named *Squat and Drop*.

Squat and Drop's number-four engine was hit by flak over the Dacia Romana refinery, and Bowers quickly had it feathered. But the other three engines were racing at an extremely high setting, because a wire bundle just forward of the propeller control switches had been hit as well. The higher settings resulted in a very high consumption of fuel, and it did not appear that the ship would make it back to Italy. To make matters worse, Frank Fox, the engineer and fuel systems expert, had been badly wounded while manning the top turret. He was out of action, and was being tended by the navigator.

After putting a reasonable amount of distance between his bomber and the target, Bowers sent his co-pilot back to see if it was possible to transfer fuel from the wingtip tanks into the main tanks. Almost as if on cue the engines began to surge from fuel starvation. Complete loss of power from the engines on one side caused that wing to dip as the engines on the good side overpowered it. This caused a seesaw effect that demanded every bit of airmanship the crew could muster. As the engines on the high-wing side would begin to sputter when the fuel drained away, the engines on the low wing side would roar back to life—gravity fed by new fuel. Subsequently the low wing would become the high wing and the cycle would repeat itself.

As the fuel-starved airplane rocked and gyrated, Bowers called his bombardier up into the co-pilot's seat to help control the big beast. They wrestled with the flight controls—first in one direction, and then in the opposite.

The co-pilot was having a difficult time trying to fix the fuel problem. *Squat and Drop* was a dissimilar model than the crew normally flew, and the fuel transfer system was arranged differently. Nevertheless, he managed to disconnect and reconnect the proper tubes and established a good transfer of fuel into the main tanks—just in time. Bowers had already lined up to crash-land alongside a Yugoslavian stream when the three good engines roared to life and pulled the B-24 skyward again.[4]

After a great deal of calculating, and no small amount of guesswork, the decision was made to continue across Yugoslavia and the Adriatic to their base at Cerignola, Italy. The transit was relatively uneventful and it appeared that—even on three engines—Bowers was going to get the airplane safely on the deck. As they approached the base, the left waist gunner called out that the number-two engine was streaming fuel. This was bad enough in itself, but often when the throttles were reduced for landing, the engine turbo-supercharger would momentarily belch a burst of flame. Bowers feathered the leaking engine.

Bowers still had an operating engine on each wing, and he and the crew were able to put the big bomber safely on deck. Likewise, the taxi back to the revetment was not a problem. An ambulance met them and Fox was carried out and whisked away for medical attention.

Once he saw Fox clear of the aircraft and safely on his way, Bowers settled into his seat and began to debrief—through his window—with one of the squadron's leading maintenance experts. There were obviously quite a few repairs to be made. A moment or two later, Bowers caught a glimpse of another B-24 lumbering across the ground straight at them. He quickly shooed the maintenance man away and went for the escape hatch just above the flight station. The co-pilot was already partway through, but Bowers wasted no time in motivating him the rest of the way and setting a record-breaking exit time himself.

The rogue aircraft collided with *Squat and Drop* just as Bowers was clearing the hatch. He rolled off the wing and hit the ground to find himself completely alone. The other bomber was loaded with fragmentation bombs, so everyone else had scattered. Its crew, too, had jumped clear when the pilot discovered he had no brakes and ordered everyone out. Evidently it hadn't occurred to him to shut the engines down.

The rogue B-24's right wing had smashed into the left wing of *Squat and Drop*. The result was a roaring cacophony of shrieking metal and runaway engines. Propellers were chopping away at whatever they made contact with, and smoke began to cover the scene. No one wanted to risk approaching the twisted, explosives-laden tangle of machinery that the two airplanes had become.

Finally, the group's operations officer arrived in a jeep. After taking the situation in, he calmly walked over to the runaway B-24, climbed up through the bomb bay, made his way to the flight deck, and shut the engines down.

A short time later a truck arrived to take Bowers and his crew to the mission debriefing. He told the men, "Let's get the hell out of here before anything else happens." They climbed into the truck and rode it to where another bomber was parked; its crew was awaiting a ride. The driver parked in front of the bomber. Bowers's head was about a foot below and in front of the twin .50-caliber machine guns mounted in the nose turret.

The armament man must have been new, or poorly trained, or both. As he wrestled with the guns in the turret, he accidentally discharged about ten rounds of ammunition just over the top of Bowers's head. Not only were his ears ringing, Bowers was now so mad he could barely sit still.

When everything finally settled down, the truck driver took them all to the debriefing room. There, Bowers encountered his commanding officer, who had seen everything and had a big grin on his face. Bowers was so angry he could hardly think straight—he punched his fist into the air and shouted "I QUIT!" The CO just laughed him off. As it turned out, Bowers had just completed enough missions to be rotated stateside.[5]

He had seen the last of Ploesti. Two days later he was on his way home.

* * *

No other mission of the Ploesti campaign came close to putting as many bombers over the refinery complexes as did the attack of July 15. In total, more than six hundred B-17s and B-24s from twenty-one groups dropped more than fifteen hundred tons of explosive and incendiary bombs. The damage was significant; the Astra Romana Refinery's throughput of crude oil dropped by two-thirds.[6] Nevertheless, within a short time, the enemy put repairs in place and the facility was increasing output day by day. The campaign would have to grind on.

* * *

Much is made of the courage exhibited by the airmen of both sides while fighting in the skies over Ploesti—and rightly so. But it is possible that the greater courage was exercised while those same men were still on the ground—before the missions. After all, once they were airborne and committed to battle, their courage was borne of the need for self-preservation. One had to fight to survive. Perhaps the full measure of a man was his ability to find the courage to leave behind the relative peace of the airfield—day after day after day—knowing full well that the next mission could very well be his last. After all, at least on the American side, the option existed to refuse to fly—if one could stand the ignominy and the official repercussions. A few took this option; most did not.

Bombardier Lou Hughes of the 459th Bomb Group had this to say after a particularly rough mission Ploesti: "Ploesti again. Fearsome flak and miserable weather at the target. Very confused mission. Groups coming in from all directions and altitudes. Outfit above us dropped bombs through our formation. We lost planes but I don't know how many. I'm getting scared. I never liked mission whiskey but it's getting easier to drink."[7]

Navigator Bob Hill, also of the 459th, recorded his thoughts after the same mission: "I was worried sick all the way to the target but felt better all the way home. It's a feeling I couldn't suppress, and I died a thousand different ways in my mind. Silly!"[8]

It was normal. They all wished the war would go away. But it didn't, and brave men from both sides continued to climb into their airplanes and engage each other in deadly combat. Their bravery is perhaps a partial explanation of why the aerial battles were so gruesome.

Chapter 25

Ingenuity

THE VERY essential roles played by the operations personnel in preparing their units for their assigned missions are not widely known or understood. Typically, the bomb groups received a coded message from their parent wing headquarters on the afternoon prior to a mission. This message directed how many aircraft the group was to contribute to the attack and what the bomb load would be. It did *not* include the target data. The information received was then passed from group operations to the engineering and armament sections. From this point, aircraft were readied and bombs were loaded. Other sections were alerted that there would be a mission the following day.

Just before midnight, sealed orders arrived via courier. These contained all the information required for the mission: target data, timing, route, formation, communications plans, and so forth. In was only then that the operations staff really went to work preparing for the morning briefing.

Especially important was the preparation of pilot "flimsies." These were data sheets that delineated essential and detailed information about the mission. They were generally printed on a single sheet of lightweight paper, and intended for use aboard the bombers.

Also invaluable were the intelligence and weather briefings. These included the latest information about the enemy situation and order of battle, target photos and evasion information in the event that a crew was forced down. Of course, weather played an important role en route and over the target. By the time the bomber crews arrived for their early morning briefings, the supporting echelons had put in a full work schedule.

*   *   *

The July 22, 1944, mission was an all-out attack intended to take the Romana Americana refinery out of commission for the long term. A total of twenty-one bomb groups were committed solely against the one target.[1]

*   *   *

Gerald Mayfield was a B-24 flight engineer assigned to the 461st Bomb Group based out of Torretta, Italy.[2] On July 22, 1944, he needed only one more mission to complete his combat tour. He looked forward to getting it behind him; the reward was a ticket home.

It was with some consternation then that he learned the target for the day was Ploesti. He had been there three times before and was only too familiar with the flak and the fighters and the smoke. For this last mission he was assigned to Col. Frederic E. Glantzberg's crew as a fill-in. Glantzberg, the commanding officer of the 461st, was a sixteen-year veteran with a wealth of experience. He had proved his flying mettle early in his career during 1932, when he was struck on the head by another airplane's antenna. The object, which weighed more than twenty pounds, knocked him unconscious at the controls. When he regained consciousness he was able to shepherd his aircraft back to a safe landing before passing out once more. He had suffered severe head fractures, but he eventually returned to full flight status, even though he was missing four square inches of skull above his right ear.

Glantzberg's toughness, combined with his down-to-earth leadership style, was a good fit for the 461st. Colonel "G" led by example, never asking his men to do something that he wouldn't do himself. As a result he personally led many of the more dangerous missions. Mayfield had this in mind when he began his preparations for the trip to Ploesti.

In making those preparations Mayfield further discovered that not only was he going back to Ploesti but that Glantzberg's ship was going to be the lead ship for the entire Fifteenth Air Force; the 461st was tasked to lead the 49th Bomb Wing, which in turn was the lead wing for the Fifteenth. Their ship that day was a brand new B-24J equipped with H2X radar, which would negate to some degree the effectiveness of the enemy smoke screens.

The takeoff, climb, and rendezvous were normal except for the sight of the *entire* Fifteenth Air Force forming behind their ship. On course to Ploesti, Mayfield managed the fuel system, ensuring that the B-24 burned its gas in a balanced fashion.

The approach from the IP to the Romana Americana Refinery was just as expected. A smoke screen was already in place over the complex, and flak was bursting around the formation. Mayfield moved from the engineer's position to the right waist, where he manned the single .50-caliber machine gun. He was caught by surprise when two flak bursts bracketed the right wing. An instant later someone called out three more flak bursts in front of the nose. At the same time another burst caught the right wing and punched a hole through the top and set the number-four engine on fire. The fuel tank at the end of the wing also caught fire, and as if all that were not enough, the number-three engine also quit.

The big ship started down, out of control. This was absolutely not what Mayfield had in mind for his last combat mission.

*   *   *

Lieutenant George Dickie was the navigator onboard a B-24 just behind Col. Glantzberg's lead ship, and Lt. Lyle Crume was his pilot.[4] Dickie looked up from his navigation table just in time to see Glantzberg's bomber spin out of control. At almost the same instant he felt his own ship rocked by a burst of flak. Both engines on the right side, just as on Glantzberg's ship, were knocked out of commission. And like their leader, Crume and his crew soon found themselves spinning toward earth.

At the same time a ruptured fuel line in the bomb bay began to spray a high-pressure mist of volatile gasoline into the fuselage. Someone called out "fire" and Dickie wasted no time getting down to the nose wheel doors, ready to bail out.

*   *   *

Aboard the lead ship, Colonel Glantzberg activated the bailout bell and ordered everyone out. But almost immediately, the fire on the right wing was snuffed out in the slipstream. From the right waist position, Gerald Mayfield shouted on the interphone that the flames were extinguished. He had no desire to bail out over enemy territory. Passing through about 10,000 feet Glantzberg began to regain control of the big bomber. Soon the ship was upright and the colonel called for a heading to Turkey, the fastest way out of hostile territory. At the same time the crew counted off, one by one. No one had bailed out.

* * *

While Lyle Crume was trying to regain control of his airplane, George Dickie and others in the crew clung to their positions, deathly fearful that spewing fuel from the damaged line would ignite and turn the ship into a fiery coffin. When Crume finally got the ship leveled off they took turns trying to stop the spray. Away from their stations and without their oxygen masks they were only able to wrestle with the line for as long as a breath would last. The fumes from the spray—and the freezing effect on their hands—made the situation that much worse. Finally, someone was able to jam a screwdriver into the line and the immediate danger ended.

* * *

Aboard Glantzberg's bomber, Mayfield was working a fuel problem of his own. The ship was now running on three engines, but it appeared that there wouldn't be enough fuel to return to Italy unless a way was found to get at the fuel remaining in the long-range tanks. Flak damage had made normal transfer from those tanks impossible. Exercising a bit of ingenuity—and his expertise with the system—Mayfield disconnected one fuel line and capped another with a .50-caliber bullet. Fuel soon started to flow from the damaged tanks. When it became apparent that Mayfield's ad hoc repair would hold, Glantzberg turned the ship away from Turkey and took up a heading for Italy.

* * *

Both of the bombers made their separate ways back to Toretta. Like Glantzberg, Crume was able to get a third engine started. And also like Glantzberg, Crume and his crew had to sweat out their fuel situation.

When the two ships finally arrived at Toretta, they found the base bomb dump afire and the runway beset by crosswinds gusting up to 50 knots. None of the aircraft ahead of them had been allowed to land; instead they had been diverted to other airfields. This wasn't an option for either Glantzberg or Crume. Despite the heavy crosswind, both pilots managed to get their ships safely on deck. Glantzberg's bomber, damaged as it was, slid off the side of the runway and sprang another fuel leak. The crew made a hasty evacuation almost before the aircraft stopped. Safely away, they took in the sight of their ship. Before the flight it had been brand new. Now it was a hulk.

Crume's crew's exit from their airplane was a little less speedy. Regardless, all of the men were happy to be back, but probably none of them was more pleased than Gerald Mayfield. His quick thinking and expertise ensured not only the safe return of his crew, but also the completion of his combat tour. He was going home.

*   *   *

Many bomber crews who were hit over the target managed to make it back through enemy territory, across Yugoslavia, and to the eastern shore of the Adriatic. Ahead of them lay one hundred miles or more of forbidding sea. If making it across the Adriatic back to Italy was a doubtful proposition, one option available to them was an emergency landing at the island of Vis. Vis is one of the westernmost Dalmatian islands that hugs the coast of Yugoslavia. A rocky, waterless crag, it was held by the partisans and served as Tito's Headquarters for several months during the spring and summer of 1944. Too prickly for the Germans to take, it was used as a base of operations for several special British military units. From Vis, they made raids on German garrisons in Yugoslavia, and kept various partisan groups armed and supplied.

But most important to the Allied fliers, there was a primitive 3,500-foot gravel runway. For the big bombers it was only adequate for an emergency landing. And once committed, there was virtually no backing out; it was situated such that a crippled bomber had little chance of climbing away from an aborted landing. Once down, a quick assessment was made of the aircraft's condition. If it was salvageable a special effort was made to find room for it on the tiny airfield. If not, it was bulldozed to make room for other aircraft. The crews then waited for transportation back to Italy via a fast torpedo boat or a C-47.

*　*　*

There was some mention by American crews—particularly late in the campaign—of Axis fighter formations that failed to attack or did so half-heartedly. No one questions the bravery or skill of the German and Romanian fighter pilots; when it was appropriate, they were as aggressive as any in the world. But these men were as intelligent as they were brave. By August 1944 it was apparent that Ploesti would not survive the unceasingly regular crush of American bomber streams. It was also obvious that headlong attacks into these same vast assemblies of bombers would sooner rather than later prove to be fatal.

Too, the arrival of replacement aircraft and crews simply did not keep pace with losses. Even had the fire for battle been strong among the defending pilots, the scale of effort—because of these shortages—would have seemed trifling when compared to the earliest part of the campaign.

Chapter 26

Night

THE EFFORT against Ploesti was overwhelmingly American, but other missions were undertaken by smaller formations of Italian-based British night bombers. While commanding the Fifteenth Air Force, Maj. Gen. Nathan Twining also headed the Mediterranean Area Strategic Air Forces (MASAF), the Fifteenth's parent command, and so the three wings of the RAF's 205 Group fell under his purview.

The British group flew four night missions against Ploesti—during the nights of May 5-6, May 26-27, August 9-10, and August 17-18. Like the Americans, they used Liberators, but more often flew Halifaxes and Wellingtons.

Unlike the Americans, who assembled into massive formations for daytime operations, the British crews flew to their targets individually. The field order for the night attack of May 5-6, 1944, was typically British: "Route and time at your own convenience."[1]

The RAF bomber crews relied on pathfinder aircraft, usually specially equipped and crewed Halifax bombers, to find and illuminate the target. The pathfinders used ground-mapping radar, or direction-finding equipment. If the equipment failed they navigated by dead reckoning, using charts, chronometers, and sextants—much like mariners of old.

When the pathfinders located the target they illuminated it with hundreds of brilliant white flares suspended from parachutes. Colored flares were also dumped directly onto the ground to define the target further.

The pathfinder crewmen were under extraordinary pressure. If they were late or had difficulty finding and illuminating the target, the following bombers had to orbit and risk colliding with other bombers or falling prey to enemy fighters. Their only other choice was to drop their bombs blindly in the dark.

*   *   *

The blackness, fire, and terror of the night missions were unlike the horrors of daytime attacks. Searchlights sliced up through the night, trapping British bombers in illuminated cones. Highlighted against the dark sky, the bombers were easy targets for the defending flak crews. Their antiaircraft guns punctuated the blackness with thousands of brilliantly exploding shells that sometimes hit the bombers and turned them into great, fiery, wrecks that cooked their crews alive as they fell burning through darkness to the earth.

German night fighters also nipped in and out of the bomber streams. Torrents of machine gun and cannon fire laced through the dark into the British aircraft. The big ships weren't helpless; they lashed back with their own guns, which were fewer than those carrier aboard USAAF day bombers and, of course, fired by gunners who couldn't necessarily see their assailants and were further hampered by the fact that their tracers pinpointed their position in the night sky.

The bombers made the spectacle even more ghastly. Their exploding bombs sent great boiling masses of oil-fed flames leaping from earth. Before long there was no need for the parachute flares; their light seemed feeble in comparison to the roiling inferno that the targets became.

Then the bombers disappeared toward Italy, the searchlights were extinguished, and the antiaircraft guns went quiet. The flares burned out, and the defending fighters returned to their bases.

The oily fires continued to burn.

*   *   *

The defenses were part of an ingenious system the Germans developed after several years of protecting themselves against British night raids. In fact, the RAF had been bombing Germany at night for four years before it mounted its first night attack against Ploesti. The Germans put this experience to good use. With equipment manned in part by Romanian personnel they inflicted a loss rate against the British bombers that exceeded that which the Americans sustained.

If anything, the night defenses were even more closely coordinated than the daytime defenses. The Germans and Romanians used nine different ground radar stations to control the effort. One tactic borrowed from the night skies over Western Europe was *Himmelbett*. Radar-equipped night fighters were assigned to different sectors to ambush the bombers as they flew into or out of the target area. Using two-way radio communications, a radar station controlling a particular sector guided a particular fighter to a point in trail of a bomber or group of bombers. When the fighter was close enough—typically one to five miles—it could make contact with its own airborne radar, and the pilot continued the attack on his own.

Taking cues from an onboard radar operator who sat behind him, the pilot slowly closed the range. When he could visually make out the bomber's silhouette he powered his aircraft into firing range and dove beneath the bigger ship. When nearing point-blank range he pulled up and triggered a long fusillade of machine gun and cannon fire into the big bird's belly.

This was normally enough to shoot the bomber down, particularly if it was hit in the fuel tanks. Usually caught unaware in the blackness, the bomber crewmen were lucky if they escaped before their ship went down. Bailing out from a crippled bomber in broad daylight was difficult enough; at night it was sometimes impossible. Finding an escape route from a damaged or burning aircraft without getting hung up or hurt depended in part upon training, and sometimes, on luck.

Nevertheless, *Himmelbett* became susceptible to British radar jamming techniques. In its place, the Germans developed a tactic that came to be called *Wild Sau* (Wild Boar). Radar units provided information to searchlight units that used the data to illuminate incoming bombers.

Axis fighters circled above the attacking bombers. If a fighter pilot felt he was in position to shoot down a bomber, he fired a flare of a predetermined color to signal the antiaircraft batteries to stop firing. When the flak bursts cleared, the pilot dove into an attack. This tactic was almost entirely dependant on the human eye, so single-engine day fighters were most often used rather than complicated and expensive two-place radar-equipped aircraft. This tactic allowed the Axis defenders to throw more aircraft into the fight, but the day fighter pilots received little night training and thus sustained a high accident rate during night operations.

*   *   *

Of the 229 RAF bomber sorties dispatched to Ploesti, 17 failed to return. Eleven of these losses occurred on the night mission of August 17-18.[2] The British loss rate over the duration of the campaign—more than seven percent—was more than they could have sustained if their operations over the target had been more frequent and regular.

Chapter 27

Terror

BETWEEN APRIL 5, and July 28, 1944, the refinery complexes at Ploesti had been hit sixteen times. The attacks were anything but routine—the loss rates were still very high and the Axis airmen and gunners always defended in force. The pressure was constant and the damage was becoming increasingly effective. The mission planned for July 28 was intended to knock out two of the major refineries. In particular, it was hoped that the attack would have a significant impact on gasoline production. This was indicated by the intelligence annex to the field order: "This attack should remove Astra and Standard group, including Unirea, for some time. Cracking plants of great importance as they increase greatly the percentage output of gasoline, the primary objective at present."[1]

Gasoline was a primary objective because the Germans were starved for it. The Germans were on the defensive on every front, and everywhere a lack of gasoline was hindering their movements. General Arnold spelled it out in very simple terms a few months later when he said: "It is not out of heedlessness or cowardice that the Germans keep abandoning immense numbers of tanks and armored vehicles by the roadsides of France. Those tanks and trucks are out of gasoline."

* * *

The 459th Bomb Group was tasked to provide four squadrons for the July 28 mission. Piloting one of the B-24s was Capt. Phil McLaughlin, who was charged with flying as the group's deputy mission lead.[2] He had been with the group since it had trained stateside, and had an outstanding reputation as a pilot, and was a well-liked and respected officer who had no problem taking on responsibility and making things happen. At his right side, flying the co-pilot position was Capt. Herbert C. Hawkins, Jr. Like McLaughlin, Hawkins had joined the group in the States. Normally he flew as the pilot of his own crew, but on this day he was backing up McLaughlin. The rest of the crewmen had been drawn from various other crews and were chosen in part because they already had some experience, which could prove to be invaluable if circumstances forced McLaughlin to assume duties as the group's lead ship.

The new team was hard pressed from the beginning. Before taxiing, their assigned ship developed mechanical problems and had to be swapped for another. This was never easy. A great deal of effort went into preparing an airplane for a mission. It wasn't a matter of climbing aboard, starting the engines, and roaring off into the sky; the airmen each had a number of tasks to accomplish before they could man their positions. Once those duties were complete, they set up their personal equipment, charts and paperwork according to their likes and dislikes. It was almost a ritual rather than a hard and fast list of tasks. Once settled in they didn't like to change.

When the situation demanded it, they had no other choice. Once the decision was made they had to extract themselves from their little cocoons, collect their equipment and scramble to the new ship. It was always a rushed affair and there never seemed to be enough time to complete the ritual again. And there was always the nagging thought that something had been forgotten or not done quite right.

McLaughlin and his crew got their newly assigned bomber airborne in time to join the formation and assume position as the deputy lead airplane. But there were more problems. A pressurization defect was siphoning precious fuel overboard. Not one who gave up easily, McLaughlin assessed the situation and determined that they would be able to continue. As the mission progressed the siphoning appeared to stop.

Fighter opposition over Ploesti had been steadily worn down during the previous four months. Accordingly, fewer than fifty German and Romanian aircraft were sent aloft to defend against this strike, and most of them were engaged by escorting P-51s and P-38s before they could reach the bombers. Most of them, but not all.

Prior to approaching the IP the formation came under fighter attack. McLaughlin's crew was savaged. One gunner was shot dead and both of the waist gunners were badly hit. To make matters worse, the ship began to siphon fuel overboard again. The bomber was still flyable and McLaughlin would not be deterred. The safest place to be was still with the rest of the formation.

At the IP, with bomb bay doors open, the formation began its run to the target. Almost immediately it was taken under very heavy fire from the many defending antiaircraft guns. Hawkins, the co-pilot, recalls: "Hardly had we started the run when flak appeared all about us right at our altitude. They were tracking us with extreme accuracy."

The ship took a hit directly in the bomb bay. Immediately the entire inside of the B-24 was engulfed in a raging fuel-fed fire. Hawkins turned around in his seat to look back at a mass of fire that came almost into the cockpit. An instant later another explosion ripped the flight deck. Hawkins was blown halfway through the canopy, upside-down. His legs and much of his torso were flailing in the cascade of air that was tearing over the doomed bomber. Only his head and shoulders protruded into the cockpit. From this gruesome vantage point he could see that McLaughlin and the top turret gunner, TSgt. Donald Sherman, were afire and likely already dead.

Struggling with the plexiglass panels that held him captive, Hawkins broke himself free. It was only barely in time. The ground was fast approaching when he deployed his parachute. Several panels were missing because of the blast aboard the bomber, and the damaged chute failed to slow Hawkins' descent as much as it should have. He suffered a broken ankle and leg when he slammed to earth.

Once down he was quickly united with Adam Wiley, the bombardier. Wiley had lost consciousness when the second explosion blew him clear out of his position in the nose. When he awoke he was in a free fall, passing through about 15,000 feet. Fortunately, he had been scarcely injured and was able to get his parachute open. He and Hawkins were the only crew members who survived.

Romanian militiamen herded Hawkins and Wiley aboard trucks that were already loaded with crewmen from other downed bombers. Several of the men were seriously injured, but were given no medical attention.

Many of the wounded men died during the trip. All of the survivors were taken to the central square at Ploesti.

The Americans were unloaded from the trucks and almost immediately surrounded by a crowd of angry Romanians. There had been civilian casualties. One small and furiously anguished man singled out Hawkins and Wiley and demanded that they be executed because his wife and children had been killed by the bombers. At this point an elderly woman stepped forward and in an extreme act of kindness tore strips from her clothing and began treating some of the injured airmen. Her actions seemed to have a calming effect. No one was executed. Hawkins and Wiley survived, though the experience left a permanent mark on their lives. "It was a terrible day," Hawkins remembered.

*   *   *

The terror over Ploesti that day was especially terrific for the 459th Bomb Group. The group suffered five aircraft lost over the target, and many others put down at emergency strips or other bases along the way. Of the ten 757th Squadron aircraft that took off from the base at Torre Giulia, only three returned directly to the field; three had been shot down over the target and the remainder were scattered elsewhere. And of the three that returned directly to the field, only one ever flew again.[3]

Frank Day was the operations officer on that date and oversaw the launch and recovery of the mission. There wasn't much of a recovery to oversee. Of the three bombers that returned to the field he ordered the crew of the first to bail out overhead because it was too badly damaged to land. The second ship recovered normally. The last of the three bombers broke in two when its nose wheel collapsed and he hurried to the scene. There, ambulance crews were already taking the wounded from the wreckage. He noticed a shoe sitting on the runway near the wreckage and bent over to retrieve it. He was mortified to discover that it still held a foot.[4]

*   *   *

The July 28 mission did not destroy its intended targets. An effective smoke screen obscured the complexes, and accuracy suffered accordingly. Damage was done, but the refineries would have to be visited again. Of the 324 bombers that were sent over the target, nineteen were lost, a loss rate of nearly 6 percent.[5]

*   *   *

Those losses paled in comparison to what the Axis fliers were experiencing. Their losses were especially severe when the Americans returned three days later on July 31. The 306th Fighter Wing was charged with providing a "maximum effort" to defend the bomber formations. They did. Major Jurgen Harder, still leading German fighter units in the defense of Ploesti, lost twenty-three of his thirty-two machines. Nearly half that many pilots were lost or injured. As a leader he felt very nearly helpless; there was little he could do to stem the slaughter of his men. He vowed that regardless of when the American bombers might come next, his units were taking a hiatus from combat operations until they had time to recover.[6]

*   *   *

Only two weeks earlier—after receiving replacement pilots and aircraft—Harder's unit had numbered nearly two hundred. Now it was once again in tatters. The Germans were not going to win the skies over Ploesti.

And now they knew it.

Chapter 28

Straps

QUENTIN R. PETERSEN was a nineteen-year-old bombardier assigned to the 454th Bomb Group at Cerignola. He had left college and reported for duty during March 1943. Eager to earn his pilot's wings, he was severely disappointed when he washed out in the initial stages of primary flight training because of "dangerous flying." He was never even permitted to solo.[1]

While the Army tried to figure out what to do with him he was sent to flexible gunnery school at Kingman Army Airfield in Arizona. The United States was training millions of men for combat, men who would ultimately form the most powerful military on earth. But it wasn't always done efficiently. Petersen, who was quite tall, tells a story that illustrates this point: "As we arrived, we were lined up by height and I, not surprisingly, was at one end of the line. The lieutenant in charge instructed the sergeant to take that side of the line to his left to Martin upper turret training, and those to the right to Sperry lower ball turret training. His left and the sergeant's left were reversed, and I graduated as a lower ball turret gunner even though I was so crammed in that I could reach only one trigger in the turret. Poor Shorty Spires at the other end of the line had to chin himself up on the Martin upper turret until he graduated!" Ultimately, Petersen received training as a bombardier and a navigator.

* * *

The intelligence annex of the field order for the August 17, 1944, mission to Ploesti was heartening: "Recent reports emphasize disastrous effects of attacks on fuel production; some indicating that large scale enemy tank activity is virtually impossible and that air operations will have to be sharply curtailed. It now appears that continuation of attacks will act as counter air effort as well as immobilizing the German Army." The annex further recognized the effects that the repeated attacks were having on the morale of the workers who were trying to keep the various complexes in production. "Workers' morale, already low, is seriously affected, and with each attack repairs become increasingly difficult as replaced equipment is destroyed. Therefore, while even severe damage to vital installations can be repaired, it has been and is possible to keep actual production at a very low figure and in time to stop it entirely by periodic attack."[2]

* * *

Quentin Petersen had only been recently assigned to the 454th Bomb Group when he was awakened in his tent at 0400 on August 17, 1944. He was going to Ploesti. This would be his third trip to the dreaded target, and only his sixth mission overall. At the briefing, the specific complex was identified as the Astra Romana Refinery. It was a critical mission, and the group commander, Col. James A. Gunn, stressed key points for success. At the conclusion of the brief Petersen couldn't help feeling a bit phony—as he always did—when the aircrew removed their side arms so that the chaplain could give his "usual hypocritical" prayer.

The jeep ride to their assigned B-24 followed. "Contrary to what the movies would have you believe," Petersen recalls, "most aircrews did not have their own bomber with their girlfriend's name emblazoned on the nose. Neither did they have a dedicated ground crew, men who were closer than brothers. Rather, the operations officer simply matched a list of functional aircraft with available crews prior to each mission."

Prior to this mission, Petersen had only flown as a substitute with other crews. This morning he was excited; this would be his first combat mission with his original crew. The team was back together, ready to wreak havoc on the enemy. "It is a testament to the effectiveness of the Army Air Forces recruiting propaganda, and the ebullience and ignorance of youth, that I never once envied the guy who woke us up, the guy who cooked our breakfast, the jeep driver, or the chaplain. I actually believed that they envied us!"

As he readied his crew station, Petersen fretted a bit. His normal chest-pack parachute had been damaged by flak over southern France on his previous mission. It still hadn't been repaired, so he was left with no choice but to take what was available—a generic backpack-type parachute. Any flier understands his consternation; airmen are creatures of habit and tend to cultivate an almost fanatical attachment to their personal tried-and-true flying gear. When something varies from the ritual, the effect is often out of proportion to the actual change, and the flier cannot get over the feeling that "something is just not right."

After takeoff, the pilot, John McAuliffe, was unable to find his assigned six-aircraft box. Exercising a little initiative, he joined on a different formation that had only five aircraft. Almost immediately however, a voice on the radio demanded to know what was going on. It was the group commander, Colonel Gunn, at the head of the box. McAuliffe explained what had happened and Gunn begrudgingly permitted him to stay. The crewmen felt a bit like children allowed to sit at the "adult table" on Thanksgiving Day.

As the group winged east and climbed to altitude, Petersen set to work getting strapped to his substitute parachute. Normally it wouldn't have been a particularly difficult task, but the groin straps were too tight, and wrestling with all the buckles and webbing at minus 50 degrees Fahrenheit with oversized, padded gloves proved to be quite a challenge. With help from Cliff Benson, the flight engineer, he finally snapped it into place. "It was still tight though and I felt as if I were walking about a foot off of the deck."

*   *   *

Previous missions to Ploesti had been increasingly confounded by the effectiveness of the defensive smoke screens. For this mission, planners had decided to change tactics somewhat. The mission field order outlined the new plan: "Three attack waves will attack Ploesti targets at 30-minute intervals; each wave to consist of one wing. 30 minutes from the target, the Air Commander of each wing will decide which one of 5 targets will be attacked on the basis of information transmitted to him at that time by a weather reconnaissance a/c over Ploesti."[3] The planners hoped that these attacks at intervals would stretch the defenders' resources, and introduce an element of confusion.

* * *

Petersen was uneasy as his formation neared Ploesti. "As we turned at the Initial Point about a minute or so from the target, I found it ominous that the box barrage of antiaircraft fire that I had come to expect on these raids was missing. The aircraft that had been assigned to precede us and drop chaff to confuse the enemy radar had missed the rendezvous. Those gunners were just tweaking their sights on us!"

The first flak burst directed at Colonel Gunn's formation scored a direct hit on Petersen's airplane and took out two engines. His wasn't the only bomber hit; pieces of airplanes from the front of the formation went flying past. "I realized that some of our bombs had been hit," Petersen recalled, "so I let them go in a salvo." Unknown to him, the rest of the group bombardiers assumed that he was the lead bombardier and—let their bombs go as well. "Our ball turret gunner, Clayton Merrill, pointed out that the group had really blasted the hell out of a wooded area. I spent a little bit of time thinking of what to say at the debriefing when we got back to Cerignola."

As young and inexperienced as Petersen was, he certainly appreciated the costs associated with the bombs that the group had just jettisoned. "Literally tens of thousands of people had been involved in manufacturing, shipping, and loading those bombs." And it wasn't just the bombs. "This didn't include the time and effort spent planning the mission and forecasting the weather. And, of course, all of the crewmen—hundreds of them—that were put into harm's way for naught." Nevertheless, Petersen's decision to salvo the bombs had been an instinctually appropriate response, taken to ensure the safety of the ship and crew.

Even though the B-24 was rid of the bombs, it was in plenty of trouble. With the oxygen and hydraulic systems shot out, and two engines gone, McAuliffe descended to a more breathable altitude and expertly wrestled the big bomber toward friendly territory. Their difficulties continued to compound. Separated from the formation as they were, with a complete undercast below, they became lost. The airplane continued to lose altitude, and it became obvious that the stricken ship was never going to make it back to Italy. The navigator quickly calculated a heading for the island of Vis, just off the coast of Yugoslavia, where the partisans controlled an emergency landing strip.

"The issue was moot though. With only two engines, we were rapidly losing altitude and knew that we were going to have to leave the plane. Survival, evasion and escape became our primary concerns." Petersen had discussed this type of scenario with McAuliffe over "many a beer," and the pair already had a plan. "We agreed that since the bombardier had little to do for most of the mission—particularly in a situation like this—that I would be charged with getting everyone's attention and leading them out of the airplane so that no one would freeze or balk.

Accordingly, Petersen cranked open the bomb bay doors by hand, because the hydraulic system was shot out. Then, he took off his shoes and tucked them into his jacket so they wouldn't be torn off his feet when the parachute snapped open. Finally, he looked into the wide-eyed faces of the rest of the crew, swallowed hard once or twice, and stepped out into empty space. "My dear, sainted mother once asked me if I had prayed before I jumped. I told her 'Why yes, I think I did. I think I said Jesus Christ, I hope to hell this son-of-a-bitch parachute opens!'"

Petersen was startled by the relative silence that enveloped him when he fell clear of the airplane. It was almost eerie, even frightening.

The airplane had been very low when Petersen jumped, but he hesitated before pulling the parachute's ripcord. He could hear gunfire on the ground and didn't want to hang as a helpless target beneath the parachute for too long.

He finally gave the ripcord a yank, but nothing happened. Seized by terror, he grabbed it with both hands and ripped it completely out of its cover. "The last thing I remember was holding the disconnected ripcord in my two hands, reviewing how I might tear open the backpack."

The parachute deployed partially, but the opening shock was still enough to knock Petersen unconscious. The very tight straps around his groin were no doubt a contributing factor. He landed in a tree and was found by Clifford Bennett, the navigator. "Bennett determined that my right hip was dislocated and pulled my leg to relocate it. When I regained consciousness it took some time for me to recall how I had gotten there, on top of a wooded hill. I kept asking 'Where am I? Where am I?' It was like something out of a comic book. Bennett got so annoyed that he finally shouted at me, 'You're on the ground, goddammit!'"

All during this time rifle and machine gun fire ripped through the tress overhead. Bennett gave Petersen a shot of morphine, and together they quickly buried their parachutes and covered themselves with leaves. Thinking that they were in Yugoslavia and were being fired on by pro-Nazi partisans, they remained hidden when one of a group of pro-Allied communist partisans came within only a few feet of their hiding places. "Although I now know that he would have saved us from capture, as his group did for six other members of the crew, I'm glad he didn't see me. I had my gun trained on him and probably would have shot him."

Unknown to Petersen and the rest of the crew, their heading coming out of Romania had been dramatically off course. Instead of coming down over Yugoslavia, they had bailed out over Greece. It was perhaps a good thing that the aircraft had failed. If they had made it out over the sea, they likely would have been forced to ditch, and may have never been rescued.

* * *

By late afternoon, the two men were thirsty enough to creep off the wooded hill and down into a valley. There they found a few huts alongside a dirty stream. With his .45-caliber pistol in hand, Petersen kicked down the doors "just as the *Terry and the Pirates* Sunday comic had taught me to do." The dwellings were all unoccupied.

The two men sat down and looked through Petersen's escape kit—Bennett didn't have his. They pulled out the contents and filled the container with water from the stream. Dubious about its quality, they added a purification tablet and rested. A short time later a group of armed men emerged, single file, from around a bend in a path by the creek. Caught in the open and outgunned, Petersen and Bennett slowly stood up.

"The leader came toward me with his hand outstretched. I went forward, relieved that friends had found us, and shook hands with him. It was then that I noticed the very prominent swastika on his cap!" Petersen stepped back slowly and pointed to his left armpit, where his pistol was holstered. The leader quickly removed the sidearm. Petersen was concerned because the weapon was still cocked, but the other man seemed nonplused. He deftly released the ammunition clip, snapped the pistol's action back, and caught the ejected round in mid-air. "He appeared to be more familiar with it than I was!"

Petersen and Bennett were taken back to an elevated machine gun position where three men were randomly firing into the woods in which had been hiding. It was then that they learned that they were in Greece. Only the leader of the men who had caught them was German; the rest were captured Soviet soldiers who had been pressed into service with the Nazis.

"As dusk approached, we were taken through a marked minefield to a house. At the house a German officer interrogated us, but only very cursorily. For a short time they locked us inside a closet beneath a stairway. While we were in there, Bennett told me that he still had secret orders on his person! We were in no condition to swallow all that paper, so we chewed it up into wads and stuffed it into the cracks and joints of the closet."

"That night my hip really began to hurt badly. I think, for that reason, the interrogating officer let me sleep on his cot."

*   *   *

The August 17 mission was an all-B-24 show with an all-P-51 escort. In total, 245 bombers were put over the target. Particularly noteworthy on this day was the reluctance or inability of the defending fighters to engage.[4] The Germans actually put more than fifty fighters into the air, but none of them made contact with the bombers. One can speculate that with the Red Army advancing ever closer to Ploesti, the defending pilots saw little reason to expose themselves to such risks for a cause that was quite probably lost.

Axis fighters or not, it was a rough mission for the bomber crews. The flak had been unusually intense and accurate, and nineteen B-24s lost. This equated to a loss rate of over 6 percent—one of the highest of the campaign.

*   *   *

Petersen and Bennett were ultimately taken to the POW camp at Sagan, Poland. Stalag Luft III held more than 10,000 American and British prisoners, many shot down over Ploesti. Ultimately they were liberated by General George Patton's Third Army at Moosburg, Stalag VIIA, on April 29, 1945. Quentin R. Petersen returned to the United States in late May 1945.

*   *   *

The Fifteenth Air Force and 205 Group continued to attack Ploesti for two more days. On the evening of August 17 and into the morning of August 18, the 205 Group sent a bomber stream totaling forty-one Wellingtons, five Liberators, and five Halifaxes. They dumped their bombs into the fires that were still burning from the August 17 strike. The pressure was kept up with a medium-size daytime effort on August 18. The mission, composed of 227 B-24s and 146 B-17s, escorted by 176 P-51s, dealt a devastating blow to the remaining operations.[5]

The final attack, on August 19, was mounted by 65 B-17s of the 5th Bombardment Wing and was launched to do little more than stir the ashes. The intelligence annex to the field order began with this sentence: "Final attack to finish off Ploesti and keep the fires burning."[6]

The last heavy bomber over Ploesti was a B-17 piloted by Lt. Milford D. Phillips of the 97th Bomb Group. Phillips's ship lost one engine to flak, and two of the remaining three were damaged.[7] He made it home, but two of the other 65 bombers did not.[8] The campaign was over.

Ploesti was dead.

Chapter 29

Tally

THERE IS no real way to put a price tag on the destruction of Germany's greatest single source of petroleum products, but it is possible to tally some basic figures.

For example, the 24 missions that were officially counted as direct attacks against Ploesti were composed of 5,408 heavy bomber sorties, 229 night-bomber sorties, and 38 fighter-bomber (P-38) sorties. Additionally, these strikes were escorted by 3,498 fighter sorties. If each bomber consumed, on average, 2,500 gallons of fuel per mission, it can be seen that the fuel costs alone were enormous—15,000,000 gallons of gasoline just for the bombers! But the gasoline costs weren't the major bill. Each airplane cost in the neighborhood of $250,000, and the average composition of a daylight raid numbered approximately 270 of the big aircraft. There were 230 American heavy bombers lost on attacks against Ploesti. But even the cost of the aircraft was not the major bill. It is certain that the expenses associated with developing the infrastructure to mount the campaign far surpassed the costs of the aircraft.

But even if a dollar value could be placed on the entire enterprise, there is still no putting a price tag on the most precious of what was lost in the skies over Ploesti: the young men who were killed. There is no precise figure for the number of men who were killed in action during the campaign, but it certainly nears a thousand—or even exceeds it. And no one can put a price on that.

*   *   *

Was it worth it? Germany was denied the lifeblood of her mechanized and air forces at the time it was most needed. The Nazis were squeezed from the West and they were squeezed from the East. They resisted fiercely. Had they the fuel they required, there is some possibility that their stubborn resistance may have ended in something other than defeat—perhaps a negotiated peace. Certainly the war would have lasted longer. If the Nazis had had more time, one can only hazard a guess at the additional death and suffering that would have resulted.

*   *   *

Elements of the Red Army occupied what was left of the oil complexes at Ploesti on August 30, 1944. They were astonished at the destruction. They were also angry they could not turn the wreckage to their own use.

Epilogue

FOLLOWING THE German defeat at Stalingrad in January 1943—well over a year before the ruinous air raids against Romania became a reality—Romanian prime minister Ion Antonescu's hopes of being allied to the winning side began to fade. No longer certain that Germany would win the war, Antonescu entertained and even fostered diplomatic efforts designed to secure Romania's exit from the conflict. To this point Romanian territory had been relatively unscathed. His entreaties were stymied by the insistence of both the Americans and the British that Romania agree to an unconditional surrender. Fearful of falling under Soviet postwar rule should he capitulate to such a demand, Antonescu rejected Allied armistice proposals. Even as late as June 1944, with the outcome of the war nearly certain, Antonescu turned his back on an armistice proposal that he had helped craft himself.

By August 1944, the Red Army was poised at Romania's eastern border and ready to launch a renewed offensive along that portion of the Eastern Front. The operation got underway in the early hours of August 20. Nearly 2,000 Soviet aircraft provided cover for a crushing armored spearhead that swept through Romanian and German defensive positions.[1] Luftwaffe and Romanian aircrews resisted valiantly, but in such small numbers that they made but little difference. The beating they had taken during the Ploesti campaign had left them anemic.

In the face of the Soviet onslaught, Romania's young King Michael—who had been thrust onto the throne in a figurehead role at the same time that the Nazis had entered Romania four years earlier—announced a unilateral cease-fire on August 23. Emboldened by support from opposition parties, the king arrested Antonescu, broke ties with the Axis, and requested an armistice. The move caught the major players off guard. An incensed Hitler directed his forces to capture the traitorous king and his new government. German aircraft split their attacks between the royal palace in Bucharest and the Red Army, to no avail. The new Romanian government declared war on Germany and for the next couple of weeks the military situation inside the country was chaotic and bloody.

The Romanian flyers and their German counterparts adapted to the new politics with some difficulty. After all, they had trained and fought together for years, and they shared some of the same airbases and equipment. For the first few days they generally avoided each other until it could be determined for certain if Romania's new government would hold. But when German aircraft began to bomb Bucharest, any sense of loyalty between the former allies was gone. The armed forces of the two nations turned on one another both in the air and on the ground. By August 26, Romanian fighter crews had claimed fifteen aerial victories against their erstwhile ally. More importantly, they also captured—or took custody of—a large number of Luftwaffe aircraft. Romania put them to good use against their former owners, and unless they were shot down, they planes remained in service against the Nazis until the end of the war.[2]

* * *

The new political situation thrust the American POWs held in Romania into a unique state of affairs. By virtue of their being kept as prisoners in Romania, they were already in a somewhat unusual situation. The country was one of the few Axis satellites that insisted on keeping the downed Allied fliers who fell inside its borders. Allied fliers captured in other countries were typically sent to Germany.

That the downed airmen were kept in Romania was due in no small part to the efforts of Princess Catherine Olympia Caradja. The life story of the ill-fated princess—a tale of kidnapping, betrayal, sickness, death, and brutality of totalitarian governments—stretches credibility. No friend of the Nazis, she took personal charge of several airmen who crashed on her estate during the TIDALWAVE mission.[3] Already the patron and administrator of a large complex of orphanages, she took special care to see that the prisoners—she called them "my boys"—were humanely treated. The Princess exerted considerable influence on the King and his family, as well as on the Nazis, to make certain that the POWs were not shipped to Germany. She also took special care to personally deliver to the POWs as many health and comfort articles as possible. Her personage was a readily recognized and loved one by the many men whose lives she played a part in saving.

Life in the Romanian prison camps, while no means easy, was generally less brutal than in many German prison camps. There were three different prisons, one of which was the King Michael Garrison. An old schoolhouse and a military hospital facility also held prisoners. There was usually more food at the Romanian facilities than offered to prisoners held in German camps, and the Romanian guards were less trigger-happy than their German counterparts. Also, the Romanians did not share the same hatred for the American bomber crews as did the Germans.

*   *   *

The welcome news of the Romanian about-face came quickly to the American POWs. Ken Barmore had been shot down and captured on May 5. He kept a diary that recalled the announcement: "At 2300 we heard the good news that Romania had made peace with the Russians and is now on the side of the Allies. This overshadows the news that our Red Cross packages arrived today. I now have chocolate and cheese, etc."[4]

The Romanian guards abandoned their posts at the POW camps the following day. The unguarded Americans reacted in varying ways. Some struck out boldly and explored Bucharest and the surrounding area. Others were much more tentative and stayed close to their quarters, wary of straying too far from what had become familiar ground. That wariness was not unwarranted. There were widespread skirmishes between German and Romanian forces in the streets of the city, and German aircraft raided the urban center with tons of high explosives.

American POWs suffered several casualties. Barmore recalled the situation on the morning of August 24: "As soon as daylight came, the Germans came over in Heinkels and bombed all around us. They had no opposition except for very little flak. They made bomb runs over

Bucharest at very low levels from all directions. When the all-clear sounded, Me-109s came over and dive bombed and strafed the streets."

Despite the lethal danger lurking in the air, in some respects American forays into the city resembled high-school field trips. Men dined and drank in restaurants and visited with the city's inhabitants. Barmore recalled one of his first encounters: "Of course we whistled and tried to talk to the girls that had walked past our camp for the last few months, and we did meet a couple of them now that we could walk around."

Now that they were free, many of the men were impressed with the hospitality of the Romanians. True, Romanian motivations may have been suspect because of the recent political changes, but for the most part their friendliness seemed genuine and many of the men received gifts of food, clothing, wine and money. In truth, the Romanians held more hate and fear for the advancing Soviets—their new allies—than they did for the American POWs or even the Germans. For their part, the POWs no longer felt any danger from the local population, and as the days passed they began to range farther from their camps. One concern of the senior officer POWs was keeping track of their men as the chaos in and around Bucharest continued.

Working within this chaos was Lieutenant Colonel James A. Gunn III. The senior American POW, he had been shot down only the previous week on August 17. He had been the deputy group commander of the 454th Bomb Group and was lost at the same time as the 454th's Quentin Petersen (whose story was told earlier here). At any rate, Gunn had hardly been in Romania long enough to even lose any weight. Still, Gunn had been in the country for enough time to help put together an audacious plan to return the POWs in Romania to Allied bases in Italy.

Almost immediately after King Michael had made his announcement, Gunn went to work trying to find someone within the new Romanian government with enough authority and power to get the POWs repatriated. It took some doing, as many of the higher-ranking officials were much more concerned with the new order of things. The Germans, for example, were still terrorizing the capitol, and the equally feared Russians were at the outskirts.

Working through the Romanian Minister of War, Gunn was finally able to arrange transport to Fifteenth Air Force headquarters in Italy so that he could help work out an evacuation plan; radio communications within Romania were such that there was no way to generate a plan over the airwaves. Accordingly, on August 27, Gunn climbed aboard an antique twin-engine aircraft that was only airborne for fifteen minutes before its pilot turned back complaining of engine problems. After landing, none other than the leading Romanian fighter ace Capt. Constantin M. Cantacuzino approached Gunn with an unusual proposal. Cantacuzino, a cousin of Princess Caradja, offered to stuff the colonel into the radio compartment of his personal Me-109 and fly him to Italy![5]

Time was of the essence and it seemed that Gunn had few options available to him. He was anxious to get the POWs back into Italy before the situation deteriorated. At this time there was still no guarantee that the Germans would not gain control of Bucharest, or that the Romanians might not change their minds. In addition, few wanted to risk what might happen to them should the Soviets taking control of the POWs. Gunn had little choice but to accept Cantacuzino's offer.

The American colonel drew a detailed map of the southeast coast of Italy and of the approach procedures for his home base at San Giovanni. To help in identifying the Me-109 as friendly (it was perhaps the most universally recognized and hated of all the German aircraft—large American flags were painted on it. The plan was for the unusual mission to depart on the morning of August 28.

There was not time, however. Cantacuzino, a member of the Romanian royal family, approached Gunn and informed him that word of their mission had leaked out and there was a real chance it might be co-opted if they waited until the next morning. Wasting no time, the colonel donned heavy flying gear and pulled himself into the dark and tiny radio compartment of the little fighter's fuselage. At 1720 in the afternoon the Romanian pilot and his American passenger were airborne in their German aircraft.[6]

One can only admire Gunn's bravery. He had to trust his former enemy to run a dangerous gauntlet of German antiaircraft fire and fighters. Then he had to trust that the German machine in which he was trapped would be able to make the two-hour trip that included crossing the Adriatic Sea. Success was not a foregone conclusion. In fact, the Romanian pilot insisted at flying at nearly 20,000 feet so that he would be in a better position to glide to a safe landing in the event the engine gave out—evidently not an unusual occurrence. Gunn had asked Cantacuzino to fly at a low altitude in order to evade radar. At 20,000 feet, he would be chilled to the bone and barely conscious.

In all probability, however, the most perilous part of the adventure would be landing in Italy without getting shot down. Locked in the fuselage as he was, and without a parachute, Gunn would stand no chance in the event they were jumped by fighters or caught by antiaircraft fire. The skies around Italy were alive with Allied aircraft and there was a very real chance they would be intercepted. There was no radio in the plane because it had been removed to make room for Gunn. It likely would have been of no use anyway, because it would not have been set to frequencies any Allied fighters would have used. The pair would have to rely on the hastily painted American flags and lots of good luck.

Despite everything that could go wrong, nothing did. Though the Me-109's engine started to give them some trouble over the Adriatic, Cantacuzino safely landed the German fighter in Italy early in the evening. A very cold and groggy Colonel Gunn was pulled from the fuselage of the tiny fighter. After an enthusiastic greeting from the personnel at his home base he was hurried to Fifteenth Air Force headquarters at Bari.

Planning began that evening. Both to help secure the area and provide some relief to Bucharest, strafing attacks on German airfields around the Romanian capitol were scheduled for the next two days. Meanwhile, Captain Cantacuzino was interrogated in order to gain some idea of the general military situation. By the end of the evening a plan was formulated for the evacuation. Cantacuzino would be given a Fifteenth Air Force P-51—an extremely unusual and unprecedented move. He would pilot the American fighter, escorted by three other P-51s, to Popesti Airdrome, where he would make preparations to receive that day a B-17 carrying advanced personnel. The escorting P-51s were under orders to shoot the Romanian pilot down in the event he deviated from the plan. Once the advance party put down, they would establish communications and arrange for the assembly of the evacuees. The actual evacuation was scheduled to commence on August 31 using B-17s converted for troop transport.[7]

This plan was presented at the highest levels beginning at 0745 the following day, August 28. It was quickly approved and by 2045 that evening the operations order for the initial phase of the evacuation—tagged Operation GUNN—was completed.

The next day, August 29, Captain Cantacuzino took off in a borrowed P-51 named *Sweet Clara II*. Normally flown by Major Robert Barkey of the 325th Fighter Group, the aircraft was escorted by three

American-flown P-51s. The flight to Popesti Airdrome in Bucharest came off without a hitch as Cantacuzino landed his unfamiliar mount in Romania. The escorting fighters circled the field until they received an all-clear signal from the Romanian pilot. Once en route back to Italy, the P-51s relayed the go-ahead to a weather reconnaissance P-38 which, in turn, transmitted the signal back to Italy. At that point the two B-17s carrying the advance party were cleared to Popesti, escorted by another flight of P-51s. After landing and discharging the advance party they took off again and were escorted back to their bases by their P-51 escort. Throughout fighters had circled protectively overhead during the ground operations.

Some concern arose when no radio message was received from the personnel embarked to Popesti. There was no way of knowing what, if anything, had happened or if the plan would proceed as scheduled. The list of things that could go wrong was long and varied, and the staff at Fifteenth Air Force headquarters waited anxiously for news. It arrived in the form of a letter delivered by Cantacuzino. The advance party had been unable to set up communications, and had to rely on the Romanian to fly back to Italy. The message requested that the evacuation begin as soon as possible. Cheered by the good news, the planning staff set to work completing the orders for the evacuation. The plan, dubbed, Operation REUNION, was completed by 2100 that same evening.[8]

*   *   *

Ken Barmore and most of the other POWs had gotten word of the advance party B-17s on August 29—the same day they arrived. The planned evacuation was eagerly anticipated and the POWs did what they could to prepare for it. One very basic task that needed to be accomplished was rounding everyone up. It proved difficult, for many of the men had scattered across the city and surrounding area. Barmore's diary described the situation on the following day, August 30:

> At the formation this morning we had it confirmed that two B-17s were here. They will be coming back tomorrow to take us all back to Italy. Colonel Gunn had gone to Bari in an Me-109 stuffed in the radio compartment and flown by a Romanian captain. He made the arrangements to get us out. McCoy and I got a pass today to go into Bucharest to try and round up as many of the POWs as we can and get them back here. We met a Romanian who had a jeep and he

picked us up. He claimed to be in the ruling family and pretty much a big wheel. We picked up a combat photographer named Woody Mark and he took pictures of the Russians coming in tanks and lots of guns.... We went to the old garrison that was our first POW camp and found it now had a lot of Germans in the same spot we were in. The Romanian that picked us up took us to lunch and rode us all around the town and we saw the damage that was done. AAF wrecked the marshaling yards and several blocks nearby, but the Germans did the real damage in town. The palace was a wreck and surrounded by many buildings that were almost leveled. . . . A Romanian man got down on his knees and pleaded with me to try and get him out of the country with us. He said with gestures that his throat would be cut by the Russians as soon as they arrived. We found that the Romanians were terrified of the Russians.

As it developed, the POWs turned out in force the following morning on August 31, ready and willing to be taken home. By 0830 there was a large crowd in place, including a significant number of curious Romanians. Operation REUNION got under way when three successive waves of twelve B-17s each were launched from Italy. Under protective fighter cover, the waves landed at 1000, 1100, and 1200, respectively. The POWs were loaded in alphabetical order and by the time the last wave was heading back to Italy, a total of 747 downed fliers had been lifted out of Bucharest.

The returning bombers were intercepted by a flight of four Me-109s over Yugoslavia. In the ensuing tangle, one Me-109 and one P-38 went down. There were no casualties sustained among the bomber-cum-transports. When they arrived in Italy the evacuees were met and addressed by General Nathan Twining, the commander of the Fifteenth Air Force. After hearing his words of praise they were sent through a medical clearinghouse, where they received a quick checkup. Barring any health problems, they were sent to a replacement unit and waited for orders back to the United States—and home. These men had helped tear down Ploesti; they had earned it.

The subsequent three days saw 419 more personnel evacuated back to Italy. In all 1,166 American and Allied personnel were evacuated from Romania during the period of August 31 to September 3, 1944. Later missions evacuated another 105 personnel.[9]

Appendix One

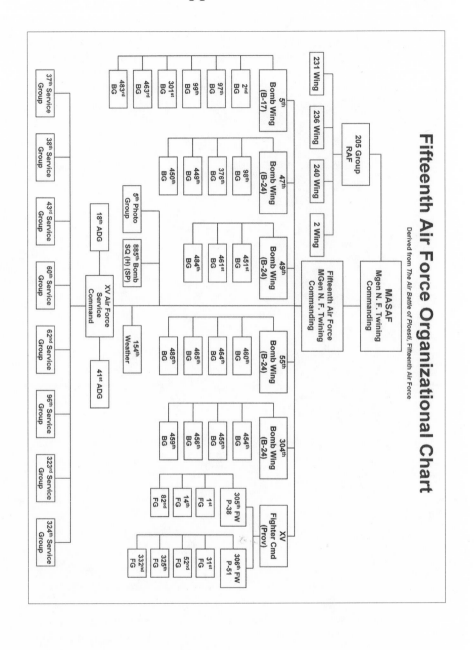

Fifteenth Air Force Organizational Chart

Derived from *The Air Battle of Ploesti; Fifteenth Air Force*

- MASAF — Mgen N. F. Twining Commanding
- Fifteenth Air Force — MGen N. F. Twining Commanding
- 205 Group RAF
  - 231 Wing
  - 236 Wing
  - 240 Wing
  - 2 Wing
- 5th Bomb Wing (B-17)
  - 2nd BG
  - 97th BG
  - 99th BG
  - 301st BG
  - 463rd BG
  - 483rd BG
- 47th Bomb Wing (B-24)
  - 98th BG
  - 376th BG
  - 449th BG
  - 450th BG
- 49th Bomb Wing (B-24)
  - 451st BG
  - 461st BG
  - 484th BG
- 55th Bomb Wing (B-24)
  - 460th BG
  - 464th BG
  - 465th BG
  - 485th BG
- 304th Bomb Wing (B-24)
  - 454th BG
  - 455th BG
  - 456th BG
  - 459th BG
- XV Fighter Cmd (Prov)
  - 305th FW P-38
    - 1st FG
    - 14th FG
    - 82nd FG
  - 306th FW P-51
    - 31st FG
    - 52nd FG
    - 325th FG
    - 332nd FG
- XV Air Force Service Command
  - 18th ADG
    - 41st ADG
  - 5th Photo Group
  - 885th Bomb SQ (H) (SP)
  - 154th Weather
  - 37th Service Group
  - 38th Service Group
  - 43rd Service Group
  - 60th Service Group
  - 62nd Service Group
  - 96th Service Group
  - 323rd Service Group
  - 324th Service Group

Appendix Two

Statistics—1944 Ploesti Campaign
Derived from *The Air Battle of Ploesti*, Fifteenth Air Force

Date	Bomb Wing	Effective Sorties	Target*	Tonnage	Smoke Screen	Aircraft Lost
5 Apr 44	5th (B-17)	94	Marshalling Yards	250.45	Ineffective	3
	47th (B-24)	136	Marshalling Yards	336.9	Ineffective	10
	304th (B-24)	0	Abort—Route Weather	0	-	0
Total		230		587.35		13
15 Apr 44	5th (B-17)	137	Marshalling Yards	316.4	Ineffective	3
Total		137	Marshaling Yards	316.4		3
24 Apr 44	5th (B-17)	154	Marshalling Yards	460.75	Partly Effective	3
	47th (B-24)	136	Marshalling Yards	332.75	Partly Effective	5
Total		290		793.5		8
5 May 44	5th (B-17)	166	Marshalling Yards	469.75	Ineffective	5
	47th (B-24)	75	Marshalling Yards	183.5	Ineffective	4
	49th (B-24)	71	Marshalling Yards	168.5	Ineffective	2
	55th (B-24)	30	Marshalling Yards	59.5	Ineffective	3
	304th (B-24)	143	Marshalling Yards	348.25	Ineffective	4
Total		485		1229.5		18
5 May 44	205 Group	43	Marshalling Yards	34.375	-	0
Total		43		34.375		0
6 May 44	304th (B-24)	135	Marshalling Yards	328.5	Ineffective	6
Total		135		328.5		6
18 May 44	5th (B-17)	33	Romana Americana	99	Effective	6
	55th (B-24)	62	Concordia Vega	124	Effective	1
	304th (B-24)	111	Redeventa	270	Effective	7
Total		206		493		14
26 May 44	205 Group (RAF)	74	Romana Americana	133.75	-	1
Total		74		133.75	-	1
31 May 44	5th (B-17)	53	Xenia	130.62	Effective	0
	47th (B-24)	105	Romana Americana	253.25	Effective	4
	49th (B-24)	105	Concordia Vega	242	Effective	6
	55th (B-24)	95	Redeventa	189	Effective	3
	304th (B-24)	123	Unirea	297.75	Effective	3
Total		481		1112.62		16
6 Jun 44	47th (B-24)	127	Romana Americana	310	Effective	2
	49th (B-24)	68	Xenia	160.5	Effective	1
	55th (B-24)	115	Dacia	227	Effective	11
Total		310		697.5		14
10 Jun 44	82d Fighter Group	38	Romana Americana	18.5	Effective	9
Total		38		18.5		9
23 Jun 44	5th (B-17)	139	Dacia	283.25	Effective	6
	47th (B-24)	0	Abort—Route Weather	0	-	0
Total		139		283.25		6
24 Jun 44	47th (B-24)	135	Romana Americana	229	Effective	14
Total		135		229.0		14
9 Jul 44	5th (B-17)	122	Xenia	361.25	Effective	1
	47th (B-24)	100	Concordia Vega	243.5	Effective	5
Total		222		604.75		6

Date	Bomb Wing	Effective Sorties	Target	Tonnage	Smoke Screen	Aircraft Lost
15 Jul 44	5th (B-17)	153	Romana Americana	458	Effective	2
	47th (B-24)	125	Romana Americana	300.75	Effective	6
	49th (B-24)	93	Creditul	200.75	Effective	1
	55th (B-24)	97	Standard	236	Effective	3
	304th (B-24)	136	Dacia	325	Effective	8
Total		604		1520.5		20
22 Jul 44	5th (B-17)	132	Romana Americana	295	Effective	6
	47th (B-24)	83	Romana Americana	202.75	Effective	6
	49th (B-24)	76	Romana Americana	193	Effective	5
	55th (B-24)	90	Romana Americana	320.5	Effective	4
	304th (B-24)	78	Romana Americana	223.5	Effective	5
Total		459		1234.75		26
28 Jul 44	5th (B-17)	102	Astra Romana	297.75	Effective	2
	49th (B-24)	47	Standard	129	Effective	4
	55th (B-24)	87	Astra Romana	203.25	Effective	3
	304th (B-24)	88	Astra Romana	211.75	Effective	10
Total		324		841.75		19
31 Jul 44	5th (B-17)	154	Xenia	434.75	Effective	2
Total		154		434.75		2
9 Aug 44	205 Grp (RAF)	61	Romana Americana	120.963	-	11
Total		61		120.963		11
10 Aug 44	5th (B-17)	124	Romana Americana	279.625	Effective	2
	47th (B-24)	69	Unirea	167	Effective	9
	49th (B-24)	82	Xenia	170	Effective	0
	55th (B-24)	67	Astra Romana	163.75	Effective	4
	304th (B-24)	72	Steau Romana	171.25	Effective	2
Total		414		951.625		17
17 Aug 44	47th (B-24)	72	Romana Americana	137.5	Operative	6
	49th (B-24)	80	Romana Americana	173.25	Operative	5
	304th (B-24)	93	Astra Romana	223.5	Operative	8
		245		534.25		19
17 Aug 44	205 Grp (RAF)	51	Ploesti	89.125		3
Total		51		89.125		3
18 Aug 44	5th (B-17)	146	Romana American	386.25	Operative	2
	47th (B-24)	42	Dacia	76.75	Operative	5
	55 (B-24	83	Romana Americana	164.5	Operative	0
	304th (B-24)	102	Steau Romana	198	Operative	0
Total		373		825.5		7
19 Aug 44	5th (B-17)	65	Xenia	144.25	Operative	2
Total		65		144.25		2
TOTAL		**5,675**		**13,559**		**254**

*Primary target listed when multiple targets assigned

Chapter Notes

Foreword

1. Fifteenth Air Force, *The Air Battle of Ploesti*. (Bari, Italy, 1944), 104.

2. Howard Mingos, *The Aircraft Yearbook for 1942* (New York: Aeronautical Chamber of Commerce of America, 1943). 35-76.

3. Howard Mingos, *The Aircraft Yearbook for 1946* (New York: Lanciar, 1947), 476-490.

4. Ibid., , 476-478.

5. Mingos, *The Aircraft Yearbook for 1942*, 94.

6. Ray Crandall, Interview with author, 1999.

7. Howard Mingos, *The Aircraft Yearbook for 1946*, 493.

8. Ibid., 492.

9. Ray Crandall, Interview with author, 1999.

10. Enzo Angelucci, *The Rand McNally Encyclopedia of Military Aircraft, 1914-1980* (New York: The Military Press, 1983), 361.

11. Don Whitright, Interview with author, 1999.

Chapter 1

1. John Ellis, *World War II: A Statistical Survey* (New York: Facts on File, 1993), Section 7.

2. Ibid., Section 7.

3. William Brinton, *An Abridged History of Central Asia*, 1998, <http://www.asian-history.com/chap_1.html>

Chapter 2

1. Christer Bergstrom and Andrey Mikhailov, *Black Cross-Red Star, The Air war over the Eastern Front, Vol. I, Operation Barbarossa (*Pacifica, CA: Pacifica Military History, 2000), 98.

2. Ed Cave, Correspondence with author, February 10, 2001. All subsequent references to, or quotes by Cave are derived from this source.

3. Frederick A. Johnsen, *B-24 Liberator: Rugged But Right (*New York: McGraw-Hill, 1999), 51.

4. Harold Wicklund, Letter to author, February 8, 2001.

5. Ibid.

6. Information from translated official Romanian documents provided by a Romanian national requesting anonymity.

7. Translation of Pascu's mission report provided by Romanian national requesting anonymity.

Chapter 3

1. Frederick A. Johnsen, *B-24 Liberator: Rugged But Right (*New York: McGraw-Hill, 1999), 7.

2. Robert Carlin, *History File: The Recollections Of Robert Carlin*, 456th Bomb Group Association, 17 April, 1999, <http://www.456thbomb group.org/carlin.html>

Chapter 4

1. Frank Way and Robert Sternfels, *Burning Hitler's Black Gold!* (Self-published, 2000), 10.

2. Ibid., 73.

3. Ibid., 23.

4. IX Bomber Command, *Field Order No. 58*, 28 July, 1943.

5. John Blundell, e-mail to author, 24 November, 2001.

6. Earl Zimmerman, e-mail to author, 16 December, 2001.

Chapter 5

1. Lyndon Shubert, "Story of the Vagabond King: Raid on Ploesti," *Aviation History*, March 2000. <Http://www.thehistorynet.comAviationHistory /article/2000/0300_text.htm>

2. Way and Sternfels, Addendum, 7-8.

3. Harold Wicklund, e-mail to author, February 2, 2001.

4. Way and Sternfels, Addendum, 8.

5. Ibid., 9.

6. Ibid., 77.

Chapter 6

1. Way and Sternfels, Addendum, 12.

2. Ibid., 13.

3. Ibid., 15.

4. IX Bomber Command, *Field Order No. 58*, 28 July, 1943.

5. Ioan Grigorescu, *Bine ati Venit in Infern* (Bucharest: Nemira, 1995).

6. Ibid.

7. Way and Sternfels, 45.

8. Robert Sternfels, e-mail to author, 8 March, 2003.

9. Ioan Grigorescu.

10. James Dugan and Carroll Stewart, *Ploesti: The Great Ground-Air Battle of 1 August 1943* (New York: Random House, 1962), 151-155.

11. Ibid., 129-130.

12. Earl Zimmerman, e-mail to author, 16 December, 2001.

Chapter 7

1. James Dugan and Carroll Stewart, 193.

2. Ibid., 201-202.

3. Vesselin Stoyanov, Letter to author, 2001.

4. James Dugan and Carroll Stewart, 203.

5. Ibid., 209-212.

6. Lyndon Shubert.

7. Ibid.

Chapter 8

1. Way and Sternfels, Addendum, 18.

Chapter 9

1. Steven M. Rinaldi, "Complexity Theory and Airpower," in *Complexity, Global Politics and National Security*, ed. David S. Alberts and Thomas J. Czerwinski (Washington D.C., National Defense University, 1996), Chapter 10.

2. Scott E. Weusthoff, "The Utility of Targeting the Petroleum-Based Sector of a Nation's Economic Infrastructure," (Air University Press: Maxwell Air Force Base, Alabama, 1994). Chap. 2, 4.

3. Robert J. Modrovsky, "1 August, 1943—Today's Target is Ploesti: A Departure from Doctrine," (Air University: Maxwell Air Force Base, Alabama, 1999), 9.

4. Ibid.

5. Ibid. 7.

6. Ibid.

Chapter 10

1. Lyle McCarty, *Coffee Tower* (Paducah: Turner Publishing Company, 1997). 22-36.

2. Alfred Asch, Hugh R. Graff and Thomas A. Ramey, *The Story of the Four Hundred and Fifty-fifth Bombardment Group (H) WW II—Flight of the Vulgar Vultures* (Appleton: Graphic Communications Center, 1991), 57.

Chapter 11

1. Fifteenth Air Force, 9.

2. William H. Harvey, e-mail to author, May 3, 2001.

3. Ibid., May 2, 2001.

4. Ibid.

5. Ibid.

6. Fifteenth Air Force, 10.

7. Ibid.

8. Ibid.

9. Damon A. Turner, *"War Diary: 449th Bombardment Group."* <http://www.norfield-publishing.com/449th/wardiary.html>

10. Richard G. Davis, "Gen Carl Spaatz and D-Day." *Aerospace Power Journal*, Winter (1997): 26.

Chapter 12

1. Fifteenth Air Force, 15.

2. R. K. Barmore, Letter to author, 28 January, 2002. All subsequent references to, or quotes by Barmore are derived from this source.

3. Alfred Asch, Hugh R. Graff and Thomas A. Ramey, 107-108.

4. Richard E. Drain, *The Diamond Backs: The History of the 99th Bomb Group (H)*. ed. Bill Schiller (Paducah: Turner Publishing Company, 1998), 64-66.

5. Fifteenth Air Force, 16.

6. Sam Marie, e-mail to author, May 2, 2001.

7. Fifteenth Air Force, 18.

Chapter 13

1. Fifteenth Air Force, 83.

2. Ibid.

3. Ibid. 87.

4. Ibid.

5. Ibid.

6. Ibid. 86.

7. Ibid. 97.

Chapter 14

1. Fifteenth Air Force, 23.

2. Bill Correll, "Ball Turret Gunner," *Southern Oregon Warbirds.* All subsequent references to, or quotes by Correll are derived from this source. <http://www.southernoregonwarbirds.org/b24b.html#corel>

3. Winfield Bowers, "John Lutz—Fifty Years Ago." *Cerignola Connection*, Winter (1995).

Chapter 15

1. Norval R. Seeley, *A Front Row Seat: The True Story of a Bombardier in a B-17 in WW II* (Self published, 1999), Sec. 2.
2. Ibid. Sec. 2.
3. Alfred Asch, Hugh R. Graff and Thomas A. Ramey, 53.

Chapter 16

1. Russell Christesen, e-mail to author, December 21, 2001. All subsequent references to, or quotes by Christesen are derived from this source.
2. Fifteenth Air Force, 27.
3. Fifteenth Air Force, 27.
4. Ibid. 104.
5. Ibid. 28.

Chapter 17

1. Eric Hammel, *Air War Europa* (Pacifica: Pacifica Press, 1994), 314.
2. Fifteenth Air Force, 30.
3. Ibid. 31.
4. Ion Dobran, "Junalul locotenentului Dobran," (Bucharest: Editura Modelism, 1998). Translation of Ion Dobran's diary provided to author by Romanian national requesting anonymity. All subsequent references to, or quotes by, Dobran are derived from this source.

Chapter 18

1. Headquarters, 306th Wing, *Proposed Third Citation of 82nd Fighter Group, Army Air Forces* (undated), 1.
2. Ibid.
3. Ibid. 2.

4. Ibid.

5. Ibid.

6. Ibid.

7. Ben Mason, Interview with author, 11 February, 2001. All subsequent references to, or quotes by Mason are derived from this source.

8. Headquarters 82nd Fighter Group, Mission No. 702, Narrative Report (10 June 1944), 1.

9. John D. Mullins, *An Escort of P-38s: The 1st Fighter Group in World War II,* ed. John W. Lambert (St. Paul: Phalanx Publishing Company, Inc., 1997), 117.

10. Steve Blake and John Stanaway, *Adorimini (Up and at Em): History of the 82nd Fighter Group in WW II* (Idaho: 82nd Fighter Group, 1992), 169.

11. Mullins, 116.

12. Bruce Gordon, *A Mission to Remember: The 1st and 82nd Fighter Groups over Ploesti* (Unpublished paper, October 21, 1999), 4. All subsequent references to, or quotes by Vizante are derived from this source.

13. 71st Fighter Squadron, Mission Report, June 10, 1944, 2.

14. Ibid.

15. Gordon, 4.

16. 71st Fighter Squadron, 3.

17. Headquarters 82nd Fighter Group, 6.

18. Ibid. 2.

19. Jochen Prien, *JG 53 Pik As, Vol. 3* (Atglen: Schiffer Military History, 1998) 821.

20. Headquarters 82nd Fighter Group, 3-4.

21. Steve Blake and John Stanaway, 172.

22. 71st Fighter Squadron, 4.

23. Mullins, 120-121.

Chapter 19

1. Werner Girbig and Helmut Lipfert, *The War Diary of Hauptmann Helmut Lipfert,* trans. David Johnston (Atglen: Schiffer Publishing Ltd., 1993), 117-118. All subsequent references to, or quotes by Lipfert in this chapter are derived from this source.

Chapter 20

1. Hammel, 317-324.
2. Fifteenth Air Force, 36.
3. Ibid., 37.
4. Ibid.
5. Thomas Gulley, *Venit Hora, The Hour Has Come: The 97th Bomb Group in World War II* (Dallas: Taylor Publishing Co., 1993).
6. Ibid.
7. Ibid.
8. Ibid.

Chapter 21

1. Fifteenth Air Force, 39.
2. Ibid.
3. Vesselin Stoyanov, e-mail to author, February, 2001. Mr. Vesselin Stoyanov—son of Stoyan Stoyanov—provided translations of his father's book, *We Defended You, Sofia.* All subsequent references to, or quotes by Stoyan Stoyanov are derived from these translations.
4. Werner Girbig and Helmut Lipfert, *The War Diary of Hauptmann Helmut Lipfert*, trans. David Johnston (Atglen: schiffer Publishing Ltd., 1993), 119-121. All subsequent references to, or quotes by Lipfert are derived from this source.

Chapter 22

1. Arthur C. Fiedler, e-mail to author, September 26, 2001. All subsequent references to, or quotes by Fiedler in this chapter are derived from this source.

Chapter 23

1. Fifteenth Air Force, 41.
2. John L. Frisbee, "Of Tradition and Valor," *Air Force Magazine*, Vol. 74. No. 7 (July 1991).
3. Arthur C. Fiedler, e-mail to author, October 11, 2001. All subsequent references to, or quotes by Fiedler are derived from this source.

4. Prien, 819.

5. Ibid., 823.

6. Ibid., 824.

Chapter 24

1. Fifteenth Air Force, 44.

2. Ibid.

3. Louis Eubank, E-mail to author, May 4, 2001. All subsequent references to, or quotes by Eubank in this chapter are derived from this source.

4. Alfred Asch, Hugh R. Graff and Thomas A. Ramey, 118-119.

5. Winfield S. Bowers, Correspondence with author, 2001.

6. Fifteenth Air Force, 76.

7. McCarty, 72.

8. Ibid.

Chapter 25

1. Fifteenth Air Force, 47.

2. Gerald Mayfield, *Mission #50, The 461st Liberaider*, Vol. 6, No. 2 (May 1989) 12. Previously published in *The Torretta Flyer*, edited by Bud Markel.

3. Ibid., 13-14.

4. Ibid., 14-15

Chapter 26

1. Fifteenth Air Force, 18.

2. Ibid., 63

Chapter 27

1. Fifteenth Air Force, 50.

2. McCarty, 78. All subsequent references to McLaughlin and his crew, and quotes by Hawkins are derived from this source.

3. Ibid., 79

4. Ibid.

5. Fifteenth Air Force, 59.

6. Prien, 826.

Chapter 28

1. Quentin Richard Petersen, *Selected Recollections Chosen from a Fortunate Life: The War Years—4th Edition* (Michigan: Self published),18-31. All subsequent references to, or quotes by Petersen are derived from this source.

2. Fifteenth Air Force, 60.

3. Ibid.

4. Ibid., 61.

5. Ibid., 63-65.

6. Ibid., 67.

7. Gulley.

8. Fifteenth Air Force, 68.

Chapter 29

1. Fifteenth Air Force, 1-104.

Epilogue

1. Denes Bernad, *Rumanian Air Force, The Prime Decade, 1938-1947* (Carrollton: Squadron/Signal Publications, Inc., 1999), 28-29.

2. Ibid., 30-44.

3. James Dugan and Carroll Stewart, 189-192.

4. Robert Ken Barmore Diary. All subsequent references to, or quotes by Barmore are derived from this source.

5. John L. Frisbee, "Operation Gunn," *Air Force Magazine*, Vol. 78. No. 1 (January 1995).

6. Ibid.

7. Fifteenth Air Force, 100.

8. Ibid.

9. Ibid.

Bibliography

71st Fighter Squadron, Mission Report, 10 June, 1944.

484th Bomb Group Association. "Torretta Flyer."

Ardery, Philip. *Bomber Pilot: A Memoir of World War II.* Kentucky: The University Press of Kentucky, 1978.

Angelucci, Enzo, Paoloa Matricardi, Pierluigi Pinto. *Complete Book of World War II Combat Aircraft.* ed. Maria Luisa Ficarra, trans. Ruth Taylor. Italy: White Star S.r.l., 2000.

Angelucci, Enzo. *The Rand McNally Encyclopedia of Military Aircraft 1914-1980.* trans. Arnoldo Mondadori Editore. New York: The Military Press, 1983.

Antoniu, Dan and Gheorghe Cico. *Vanotorul IAR-80, Istoria Unui Erou Necunoscut.* Modelism, 2000.

Asch, Alfred, Hugh R. Graff, and Thomas A. Ramey. *The Story of the Four Hundred and Fifty-fifth Bombardment Group (H) WWII: Flight of the Vulgar Vultures.* Appleton: Graphic Communications Center, Inc., 1991.

Barmore, Ken. "A POW in Romania." *15th Air Force-451st Bomb Group-725thSquadron-49th Bomb Wing-Castellucia, Italy.* 13-19, Spring 2001.

Bergstrom, Christer and Mikhailov, Andrey, *Black Cross Red Star, The Air War over the Eastern Front, Vol. I, Operation Barbarossa.* Pacifica: Pacifica Military History, 2002.

Bernad, Denes. *Rumanian Air Force: The Prime Decade, 1938 1947.* Carrollton: Squadron/Signal Publications, Inc., 1999.

Birdsall, Steve, and Roger A. Freeman. *Claims to Fame, the B-17 Flying Fortress.* London: Arms and Armour, 1994.

Birdsall, Steve. *The B-24-Famous Aircraft Series.* Arco Publishing Company, Inc., 1968.

Blake, Steve and Stanaway, John. *Adorimini (Up and at Em): History of the 82nd Fighter Group in WW II.* Idaho: 82nd Fighter Group, 1992.

Brinton, William, *An Abridged History of Central Asia,* 1998. <http://www.asianhistory.com/chap-1.html>

Carlin, Robert, "The Recollections of Robert Carlin," *456th Bomb Group Association,* April 17, 1999. <Http://www.456thbombgroup.org/carlin.html>

Correll, Bill. *Ball Turret Gunner, Southern Oregon Warbirds.* <http://www.southernoregonwarbirds.org/b24b.html#corel>

Davis, Richard G. *General Carl Spaatz and D-Day, AerospacePower Journal,* Winter, 1997.

Dear, I.C.B., ed. *The Oxford Companion to World War II.* Oxford: Oxford University Press, 1995.

Donald, David and Robert F. Dorr. *Fighters of the United States Air Force From World War I Pursuits to the F-117.* New York: Military Press, 1990.

Drain, Richard E. *The Diamond Backs: The History of the 99th Bomb Group (H).* ed. Bill Schiller. Paducah: Turner Publishing Company, 1998.

Dugan, James and Carroll Stewart. *Ploesti: The Great Ground-Air Battle of 1 August 1943.* New York: Random House, 1962.

Ellis, John, *World War II: A Statistical Survey,* New York: Facts on File, 1993.

Frisbee, John L. "Of Tradition and Valor." *Air Force Magazine.* Vol. 74, No. 7, July, 1991.

Frisbee, John, L. "Operation Gunn." *Air Force Magazine.* Vol. 78, No. 1, January, 1995.

Girbig, Werner and Helmut Lipfert. *The War Diary of Hauptmann Helnut Lipfert.* trans. David Johnston. Atglen: Schiffer Publishing Ltd., 1993.

Giurescu, Dinu, C. *Romania in al Doilea Razboi Mondial.* All Educational, 1999.

Gordon, Bruce. *A Mission to Remember: The 1st & 82nd Fighter Groups over Ploesti.* Unpublished paper, October 21, 1999.

Grigorescu, Ioan. *Bine ati venit in infern.* Bucharest:Nemira, 1995.

Gulley Thomas. *The Hour Has Come: The 97th Bomb Group in World War II.* Dallas: Taylor Publishing Co., 1993.

Gunston, Bill. *The Illustrated Directory of Fighting Aircraft of World War II.* ed. Ray Bonds. London: Salamander Books Ltd., 1988.

Hammel, Eric. *Air War Europa: America's Air War Against Germany, Europe and North Africa 1942-1945 Chronology*. Pacifica: Pacifica Press, 1994.

Headquarters 306th Wing. *Proposed Third Citation of 82nd Fighter Group, Army Air Forces*. Undated.

Headquarters 82nd Fighter Group. *Mission No. 702, NarrativeReport*. 10 June, 1944.

Johnsen, Frederick A. *B-24 Liberator: Rugged But Right: Walter J. Boyne Military Aircraft Series*. New York: McGraw-Hill, 1999.

Keegan, John, ed. *Atlas of the Second World War*. London: Harper Collins, 1997.

Mayfield, Gerald. *Mission #50, The 461st Liberaider*, Vol. 6, No. 2, May 1989.

McCarty, Lyle. *Coffee Tower: A History of the 459th Bombardment Group in World War II*. Paducah: Turner Publishing Company, 1997.

Mingos, Howard, *The Aircraft Yearbook for 1942*, New York: Aeronautical Chamber of Commerce of America, 1943.

Mingos, Howard, *The Aircraft Yearbook for 1946*, New York: Lanciar, 1947.

Modrovsky, Robert J. "1 August 1943-Today's Target is Ploesti: A Departure from Doctrine." Maxwell Air Force Base, Alabama, April 1999.

Mullins, John D. *An Escort of P-38's: The 1st Fighter Group in World War II*. ed. John W. Lambert. St. Paul:Phalanx Publishing Company, Inc., 1997.

Office of the Assistant Chief of Air Staff, Intelligence. *Operations of Heavy Bombardment Units against Rumanian Oil Refineries in Ploesti Area 1 Aug 1943*. Washington, 1943.

Peterson, Richard Quentin. *Selected Recollections Chosen From a Fortunate Life: The War Years*. 4th ed. Michigan.

Prien, Jochen. *JG 53 Pik As*. Vol. 3. Atglen: Schiffer Military History, 1998.

Rinaldi, Steven M. *Complexity Theory and Airpower*, in *Complexity Global Politics and National Security*, edited by David S. Alberts and Thomas J. Czerwinski. Washington D.C.: National Defense University, 1996.

Russell, Edward T. "Leaping the Atlantic Wall: Army Air Forces Campaigns in Western Europe, 1942-1945." *Air Force History and Museums Program*, 1999.

Schneider, Sammy, ed. *Missions by the Number*.

Seeley, Norval R. *A Front Row Seat: The True Story of a Bombardier in a B-17 In WW II*. Bettyhill House Publishing, 1999.

Shubert, Lyndon. "Story of the Vagabond King: Raid on Ploesti: A pilot's detailed firsthand account describes the mission to bomb Romania's oil

refineries   in   August   1943." *Aviation   History.*   March   2000.
<http://www.thehistorynet.com/AvaitionHistory/article /2000/0300_text.htm>

Somers, F. William. *Fortress Fighters: An autobiography of a B-17 engineer/gunner with a collection of men of the 15th Air Force who flew the heavies from North Africa and Italy to smash the formidable German underbelly during World War II.* Tempe: Somers Printing, 2000.

Turner,   Damon   A.   *War   Diary—449th   Bombardment   Group.*
<http//www.norfield-publishing.com/449th/wardiary.html>

Fifteenth Air Force. *The Air Battle of Ploesti.* 1944.

Way, Frank and Robert W. Sternfels. *Burning Hitler's Black Gold!: Ploesti "Low Level" Bombing Mission, 1 Aug. 1943.* 3rd edition, 2000.

Wuesthoff, Scott E. "The Utility of Targeting the Petroleum-Based Sector of a Nation's Economic Infrastructure." Air University Press: Maxwell Air Force Base, Alabama, 1994.

INDEX

DATE DUE